ALFIE

ALFIE

My Story

Alfie Boe

**SIMON &
SCHUSTER**

London · New York · Sydney · Toronto · New Delhi

A CBS COMPANY

First published in Great Britain by Simon & Schuster, 2012
A division of Simon & Schuster UK Ltd
A CBS company

1 3 5 7 9 10 8 6 4 2

Simon & Schuster UK Ltd
1st Floor
222 Gray's Inn Road
London WC1X 8HB

www.simonandschuster.co.uk

Simon & Schuster Australia,
Sydney

Simon & Schuster India,
New Delhi

A CIP catalogue record for this book is available from the British Library

ISBN: 978-1-84983-975-4 (Hardback)
ISBN: 978-1-47111-059-7 (Trade paperback)

Typeset by Hewer Text UK Ltd, Edinburgh
Printed in the UK by CPI Group (UK) Ltd, Croydon, CR0 4YY

Thank you for reading this book. I hope you enjoy 'My Story'.

CONTENTS

Chapter One

INTO THE ABYSS

Bizet nearly killed me. I don't blame him, it's not his fault. How was he to know, when he wrote *The Pearl Fishers* in 1862, that it would be responsible for giving me chlorine poisoning? How was he to know the hell his opera would unleash upon my eyeballs?

I was in a somewhat fragile state of mind anyway – exhausted, dispirited and disillusioned. Record deals had come and gone; my career was in flux. I had opera work, but my solo hopes were fading away, and I'd considered abandoning it all to become a personal trainer for the Salt Lake City Police Department in Utah. I was 36 and it was time to stop chasing my dreams, to settle down, get a regular wage and provide a stable life for my family. May 2010, desperate times. Still, I wasn't prepared for the blindness and the drowning.

I was rehearsing for my stint as the fisherman Nadir in *The Pearl Fishers*, at The Coliseum in London. The director wanted to film me swimming in a water tank for a minute-and-a-half's worth of sequences that would be projected during the production. The tank must have been 10 metres deep, and each time, to get to the bottom, I had to dive down and blow all the air out of my body, to sink low enough to get in front of the camera. I'd been borrowing valves from the divers to breathe in compressed air when I was under for extended periods; if you did that and came up too quickly you could get the bends. Is this what Bizet would have wanted from his leading men? I'm not sure.

We filmed for seven hours, and I was sitting in wet chlorinated clothes all day. The hot water bottles and blankets they were using to try to keep me warm were no match for that soaking costume. And down I went again, this time for too long. I pushed myself up from the bottom of the tank, panicking, swimming frantically to get to the top, but I just wasn't getting there. I put my thumbs up for the divers, to signify I needed them to bring me up, which they did, but really slowly, and I swallowed a lot of water, a *lot*. When I finally reached the surface – gagging, spitting, coughing my guts out and absolutely exhausted, the director said, 'Do you think we can do it again, Alf? We didn't quite get the right angle and focus.'

Yeah, OK. I'll do it. For your show. For the sake of the art. For the sake of my bills. And I went down again, bust myself silly again. I finally finished the shoot, got showered and changed, and my eyes started to burn. They were on *fire*. I needed to get to Stansted Airport to fly to Glasgow for a Scottish Opera audition, and when I came out of the studio and the sun hit my eyes, it felt like somebody had jabbed needles into them. I stumbled into a cab, got to the airport, and everything went cloudy. The whole place. It hurt to even have my eyes open. And all I could see were tall black shadows moving past me, people. I couldn't see the board for my flight details. I'd gone blind.

I was frightened to death. I asked someone for assistance.

'Can you help me? I'm having trouble with my eyes and I need to get through to security to get on my flight.'

He said, 'Are you alright? I think you need someone to have a look at you.'

'No, no, I'll be fine,' I said.

But my eyes were on fire, the pain was outrageous. My nose was running, my skin was peeling, I was itching like mad. I got through security and after some protest from the staff I waited while they sent for a paramedic to look at me. He asked me if I'd been diving or swimming and I told him the story. He asked if I'd used any compressed air. And he said, 'Right, you can't fly. You could have air bubbles in your blood.' They took me off to a room and checked my blood pressure, which was rocketing. My heart was thumping, my skin was red raw, I had a huge blood-red rash all over my body. I was shivering and shaking, and my eyes were killing me. They were syringing them with saline to get the chlorine out, and feeding me painkillers, rinsing my eyes constantly, washing my face, wiping my arms and my legs. I was in a wheelchair. I thought I was dying, man. I thought I was dying. Certainly felt like I was. I guess I'd missed the module on how to cope with chlorine poisoning while I was studying at the Royal College of Music.

I went to Moorfields Eye Hospital, who had major concerns. They said the chlorine had burnt my retinas, and they gave me antibiotics. I was on so many pills, painkillers, saline sprays. Washing my eyes every half-hour. I was living on my own at my friend's flat, he was out of town, and my wife and two-year-old daughter were at home in Salt Lake. It was miserable. I had to lie at night with pads on my eyes, and sometimes during the day, to stop light getting in. I caught pneumonia, was in bed shivering and shaking, coughing and sneezing. And all the English National Opera seemed concerned about was me getting back into the show. I managed to get myself together for the first and second performances, but by the third, the stress from everything was just killing my voice, it was really rough. And eventually it went. I was still recovering, sore throat, head full of cold, and I pulled out of five performances. They asked me to come in and mime the role while my understudy sang in the wings. They said, 'We don't have any other option, Alf.' I had an option. I said no. I could barely get out of bed, let alone get on stage. I'd get out of bed and fall over. I was virtually dragging myself to the loo. So no. And my understudy went on, except he had a throat infection and had to abandon his voice halfway through, and he did indeed mime the remainder of the show while someone else sang for him from the wings. What a circus.

I remember sitting in the living room on my own one evening after a rehearsal day and I just didn't get out of the chair. TV wasn't on, nothing. I just sat there, numb, practically comatose, and I didn't get out of that chair to get to bed till 3am. That was me in May 2010. I was so depressed, so down, fed-up and sick. I just felt rotten. I was doing various opera gigs, some great, some awful, but my situation with record companies was . . . well I didn't have a situation with record companies, that was dead in the water. Three labels had come and gone, three deals, and there were no more doors left to bang on. I'd had enough, and was so jaded, so tired, running out of steam, seriously considering other options, other careers that would enable me to settle down in Utah with my family, like the personal training. The only glimmer of hope, the last crack at big success, was this *Les Misérables* gig I'd signed up to do five months later, playing Jean Valjean for the show's 25th anniversary concert. But it was an unknown quantity and a risk – I hadn't really done musical theatre before, I wasn't certain it was right for me, it had the potential to destroy my opera career, I didn't know how big it was going to be, what it would bring. Over the past few weeks I'd started to build up my confidence again, I'd gained a lot of optimism, things were starting to look up, but *The Pearl Fishers* brought it all crashing back down. I was as low as I'd felt in a long time, I was having counselling, I felt adrift. And I sat there in that flat thinking, 'What if this *Les Mis* thing is not everything I hope it can be? What then?' Yet it would turn out to be so much more. It was the best thing I ever did. It saved me, and not a moment too soon.

1862, when Bizet began work on *The Pearl Fishers*, was the same year Victor Hugo's *Les Misérables* was published. How odd that that year was to be so instrumental in the life of some bloke from Fleetwood, Lancashire, almost 150 years later. I love the parts that these great French artists have played in my life, unwittingly determining my fate from beyond the grave. Little did Georges Bizet know that he'd be responsible for my temporary blindness. And thanks to Victor Hugo, I never did join the Salt Lake City Police Department.

Chapter Two

LITTLE DRUMMER BOY

As a kid in Fleetwood I spent a lot of time going up to the beach on my bike. Riding and riding along the promenade. I rode up to Blackpool, that was the furthest I ever got, but as a kid that was a long way, a good eight miles. And I always used to stop and look out to sea. I'd have my Walkman on, I used to listen to a lot of 1950s and '60s rock and roll – The Beach Boys, Buddy Holly, Elvis. I'd dream of getting away, doing something different, without realising how all that music was having a more specific influence on me. I'd look out to sea and wish I was in 1950s America. And a lot of the stuff I would dream about has happened. When I first went to work in America, to perform in *La Bohème* in San Francisco, it was just as I'd always imagined it, it *was* a dream. I met my wife Sarah there, I told her being in America felt like candy. That was the feeling I got, the same feeling you get eating candy when you're a kid. Sensory overload. Excuse me for calling it candy. That's what happens when you marry an American.

It took me a long time to realise I could sing my way out of Fleetwood. For years I wanted to be a drummer. I *was* a drummer. I don't know why I got into it so quickly, it was just instinctive – the beat, the rhythm, it got me. I'm rarely not drumming. I have sticks with me whenever I'm on tour, my dressing rooms have taken a bit of a beating. Every night of the *Bring Him Home* tour we'd finish the gigs with 'Jacob's Ladder', the fantastic old gospel song. I discovered it via the Bruce Springsteen *Seeger Sessions* version. And halfway through the song I'd leg it round to the drums at the back and finish the set with my sticks, so exhilarating, every time. When I was doing *Les Misérables* in the West End, Matt Lucas, who played Thénardier, bought me a drum machine because all he ever heard through his dressing-room wall was my incessant table-drumming. I took it home and my daughter Gracie, three years old at the time, claimed it as her own, smashing all hell out of it. Maybe she'll be a drummer. At the moment her style is similar to Animal from The Muppets, which is no bad thing. Bit of Keith Moon going on. Sometimes I'd be in the spare room on my kit while she'd be in the living room on the drum machine, that flat was a racket. My poor wife.

I could say I was born with it, drum fever, but I was drumming before that. As my mum tells it, one time while she was pregnant with me, her and Dad were watching a band on *The Royal Variety Performance*, on the telly, and when a drum solo came on I kicked a cup of tea off her knee. I was dancing, she says, her stomach was moving to the music. I reckon I was drumming. Rocking in the womb. That's a good name for a band, Womb Rocker. I was in a few bands growing up, we were always trying to think of good names. On the whole I think we failed in that regard. Edison's Eye. Roadhouse. Whisky Train. You decide.

Mum taught me how to drum pretty quickly, with a wooden spoon and a biscuit tin, she taught us all that. Nine of us. I remember belting the heck out of this tin, I could only have been about three, and I pretty much buckled it because I hit it at every angle I possibly could to get different sounds out of it. After the biscuit tin I graduated to a Quality Street one, then one Christmas she and Dad bought me a tiny little plastic kit, with really thin cellophane skins and an old tin cymbal. Big time. I was gradually working my way up to a proper man-sized drum kit.

The first time I ever got on a proper kit was in Blackburn when I was 12. My brother Michael was living there, and I found our visits pretty dreary, but one afternoon we went to this music shop called Reidy's and I very quickly located the drum department. Well they called it a department; it consisted of one drum kit. I got on this kit, picked up some sticks and just went crazy on it, was all a bit *Wayne's World*. But that was the first time I ever properly drummed, and it just came to me. And Mum and Dad's faces when they saw me on there, it was a wonderful moment, really cool to feel that from them. So every time I went to Blackburn I'd run into that store and jump on the kit; Michael would poke around in the music department looking at the classical scores, and I would bound upstairs to the so-called drum department. Then one week that kit got sold, and they never got any more in, I was gutted. The next one I found was in a shop in Cleveleys. I was there with Dad one day and saw this great little white kit in the window.

I said, 'That's a nice kit, innit, Dad?'

He said, 'Yeah, it's nice son, you like the drums don't you?'

I said, 'Yeah Dad, I like the drums.'

That was the dream, that kit.

I managed to save up some money and buy a pair of sticks from a shop in Blackpool called The Sound Centre, which was very exciting, and in the absence of a kit I'd sit in my room drumming on my pillows. One night Dad shouted at me from downstairs: 'Alf, come down, you're making far too much noise, you're thumping on the floor and it's driving us crazy.' Sorry Dad. 'Go in the front room, there's something in there that I want you to take up to your room.' I went downstairs and opened the door and there it was, accompanied in my mind by heavenly lights and angels, this white drum kit I'd seen in the shop a few weeks earlier. Dad had gone out and bought it for me.

I never stopped playing it. I didn't have lessons, I just watched other drummers. I used to go to The Royal Hotel in Cleveleys; they had a session band on every Friday and Saturday. The house drummer Ronnie Brambles was a bit of a legend, used to drum in The Glitter Band, did a bit for Rainbow, he was in Whitesnake at some point, I think. Now he runs a fish and chip shop in Fleetwood. Bloody good drummer. I watched him a lot. And I got together with a couple of guitarists from school, a Mike and a Michael. Michael Gawne, wicked guitarist, he's still in bands now, he plays locally. He could have made it, that guy. Maybe he didn't want to. He was into Stevie Ray Vaughan and got me into him, that's when I fell in love with blues. There was a blues club in Fleetwood on a Friday night, we'd go every week and soak it up, and we eventually set up a blues band of our own. We could never find a bass player, because everybody wanted to be a lead guitarist or a singer, so our band consisted of rhythm guitar, lead guitar and drums. A guy called Grant played with us on keys sometimes as well. We didn't have a name.

Edison's Eye was the next band I was in. The logo was a light bulb. My cousin Derek was the guitarist, and the bass player was an Italian fella called Tom, they both lived up the road, Tom lived above the chip shop. Derek was a big Beatles fan, and then he became a big Cure fan, so we got into a bit of indie music and goth music. Not that I ever became a goth, but I happily drummed along to Cure songs. We were a good little three-piece, we had a nice sound. Derek played rhythm and lead pretty well, Tom was a solid bass player, and my drumming was good, we were tight-knit, it was cool. We rehearsed in my mum and dad's garage and made a good old noise, and something about the acoustics outside made it hard to hear exactly where the sound was coming from. Mum was washing the dishes in the sink one day and saw two policemen running through the garden, they ran right past the garage, they thought it was coming from the school next door. We had a lot of fun with that band, until Derek brought in this fella who completely messed it all up. I wasn't singing at that point, Derek could sing a bit but he didn't want to, and he decided to get this singer in without asking us, he played guitar too, and he was bloody awful. He belted out his guitar, out of tune, didn't play the right chords, clashed with us all the time, couldn't sing for toffee, and I got sick of it. We were just making noise, it wasn't music. I knew what we should have sounded like, what we could have sounded like if we'd done it properly, and this wasn't it. So I told Derek, in confidence, that I didn't think the guy was any good and that if he stayed on I'd quit the band. And Derek went off and told him. Next minute this lad came round to my house and said, 'Why did you say I'm no good?'

I said, 'Well you're not. You're rubbish. You can't play, you can't sing, and I don't wanna be part of the band. What's the problem?'

He said, 'Well your Derek thinks I'm alright.'

I said, 'Well Derek's an idiot.'

So I left, and they pretty much disbanded, they didn't get another drummer. Derek became a police officer.

I then auditioned for a band in Preston, The English Roses. I saw an advertisement saying they were going on tour and needed a drummer. So I turned up to this town hall and met this two-piece band, a guitarist and bass player, another drummer was already there trying out for them, and I really liked their sound, that sort of late '80s British indie music. I set up my little white kit and they started up a song and I seemed to fit right in. We improvised constantly for about an hour and it really worked – I knew where they were going, they knew where I was going. And they offered me the job, but it was a big tour, a proper tour; they were supporting The Mission. I was only 15, I was in school, these guys were 19, 20. They didn't know I was 15 – I looked older. So I couldn't do it, and I stuck to playing in local Fleetwood bands. I joined one called Roadhouse, with two brothers, Peter and Jon McLoughlin. They were a couple of likely lads, real funny fellas. I'd known Peter, the singer, from a coach firm I worked at when I was 11. At my first rehearsal with them I was drumming away and Jon was going, 'Hit yer drums harder, I can't hear ya!' And I was really bashing them. He said, 'What sticks have you got?' They were good sticks, regular sticks. I told him he needed to turn his amp down. That's why he couldn't hear me, he was standing in front of this amp, turned right up, blasting out. He said, 'Get bigger sticks!' So I got these big sticks, they were practically baseball bats, and I really gave it some. Bashed the hell out of the drums, and he was still going, 'I can't bloody hear ya!' He just wouldn't turn that amp down. Peter was your archetypal '70s rocker, and he hasn't changed one bit, still got the long curly hair and the skinny jeans. Their bassist had a motorbike accident and lost some digits, played the bass with two fingers. They're still doing it, they have a band now called Hooker. Their logo's a naked woman. Oh yes. They shafted me anyway. I got this awful glandular fever, my throat felt like it had two tennis balls in it. I was flat out, and while I was ill the bastards got a new drummer.

I sold my first kit to a lad for £150, and Mum and Dad bought me new cymbals and a proper five-piece kit, really great. I was around 17 by this point, working in a car garage, and I joined a band called Whisky Train. We were just a cheesy covers band, but we were pretty good. We did 'Live and Let Die', the Guns N' Roses version, 'Paradise City', 'Hard to Handle', all that stuff – 1990, you get the picture. The lead singer fancied himself, wanted to be a bit like an Axl Rose, had the bandanna on his head and the tight jeans, real show-off. And we got into Battle of the Bands, I think it was in the ICI club in Thornton. There was a good vibe for us because we were playing songs that everybody knew and wanted to hear. Roadhouse were on the bill as well, and some band called Dr Bone, both playing original material, so the only time the crowd got up and danced was when we played – we really got them going. I think we came second or third. Roadhouse were playing after us, and their new drummer Alan Smith tried to take my cymbals. As I was packing my kit away he asked to borrow them for his set, then later as he was packing his stuff away he stuck my cymbals in his case.

I said, 'Hang on a minute, man.'

He said, 'No, you said I could borrow them.'

I said, 'Yeah, just for the set.'

He said, 'I've got a gig tomorrow night and I want to use them.'

I took them back. That's what that little group were like. And they're still Fleetwoodites, still hanging around. They play a pub called Deaduns. Well it's called The Royal Oak, but everyone calls it Deaduns, because back in the day, fishermen used to go in there and drink till they died. Literally died. Get carried out.

There was a band there that night at Battle of the Bands, I can't remember their name, but later they asked me to play with them for a bit, and I went along to a session and they got weirdly technical about it all. They were just kids sat in a room drinking Coke, and they said, 'So, Alfie, what we want you to do is to really connect with John, our bass player here, really get the rhythm together, get it tight . . .' I thought, 'This is really, really weird,' telling a teenage kid to connect with the bass player so the rhythm was right, it didn't feel very rock and roll. And when they started playing they were crap. I stopped playing in bands at that point, more or less. I did a few more gigs with Whisky Train, and then I started drumming in the clubs in Blackpool, the cabaret circuit, getting paid to do the backup for whatever woman was singing dodgy Tina Turner covers that night. And by that point, I'd started singing as well.

Kits come and kits go. You always keep your cymbals and your hardware, you never sell them. The older the cymbals are, the better they sound. I own some earth-toned cymbals, they've been buried in sand, which gives them a darker, warmer quality; they're beautiful. You shouldn't even dust them properly. Drums are a different matter, they're replaceable. But I really wish I'd kept hold of that first kit Dad got me. I wish I still had it. It was a lovely little kit, but it's sentimental more than anything, because Dad had bought it for me. I can't find it. I can't find it anywhere. At one point I knew where it was, in St

Nicholas Owen church at the top of our road in Fleetwood. The guy I'd sold it to had sold it on to a vicar, and I went in there and saw it once, but then they sold it on somewhere else. And I haven't been able to find it since. I'm sure it's broken and battered and bruised and discarded now.

Chapter Three

MADE IN FLEETWOOD

Dad was a dancer. Not by trade. He'd whip the bread board out after a drink and clog-dance on it. I used to copy him, there's cine film somewhere of me in my little clogs doing a jig on the patio. Singing and dancing, always after attention. I used to imitate sounds I heard, used to do a Tommy gun. When I was four, 'Mull of Kintyre' was played on the radio 29 times a day and I used to walk around strumming along with my sister's tennis racket. Mum would say, 'Sing "Mull of Kintyre" for me, Alf, while I'm cooking the dinner,' and I'd say, 'Mum, I'm tuning my tikar.' Couldn't say guitar. I sang 'Mull of Kintyre' in a concert in Devon once, and it went down really well, except with the other singers who thought it was stupid. But that was my song.

Dad did like a dance, that's how he met my mum, quickstepping at the Marine Hall in Fleetwood. Doctors practically prescribed it, to keep him on his toes, because he had flat feet, fallen arches, after suffering a pretty horrific accident when he was a kid. He'd been playing football with his mates, or so-called mates, climbed over a fence to get the ball, got stuck going over the top and got both his ankles caught in the wire mesh. He was bent over the top of the fence, hanging upside down from his ankles, his feet twisted in the wire, and they left him there screaming for help. Someone eventually got him down, and he was operated on a couple of times, doctors broke his legs to try to straighten him out, he was in a wheelchair for a bit. He went out with some friends in that wheelchair, to the top of The Mount, this hill that overlooks the beach, and they let him roll down. He jumped off at the last minute as the wheelchair crashed into a wall and smashed to pieces. So the legend goes.

He was born and bred in Fleetwood, and a good kid. Alf Boe, hence my name. He wasn't the eldest son but pretty much brought up his family on his wage, worked at the Co-op delivering groceries, and brought most of the money in because his dad was away with the Navy most of the time. His brothers and sisters used to call him "Our daft Alf" which would really upset him, because he was working damn hard to make sure they were all clothed and fed, yet they treated him so disrespectfully sometimes. Out of order.

Chris, his father, wasn't a particularly likeable guy, so I'm told. Nobody really spoke about him much to me, possibly for good reason. I figured a few things out: he was a big drinker, a bit abusive. His own father was Norwegian, which is where the name Boe comes from. He sailed into Fleetwood and settled, we think. Chris married Evelyn Jones, the only grandparent that was alive when I was a kid. She was a darling, my dad's mum, always smiling, always laughing, always singing, lots of fun. At Christmas she'd come over and empty a massive sack full of toys onto the floor. Her grandfather, Alfred Jones, there's a man I would have liked to have met. When Buffalo Bill's Wild West circus came to Manchester to perform for Queen Victoria in 1887, Alfred joined the circus as stage crew, then travelled to Canada with them as a rider, re-enacting Cowboy and Indian fights. He got kicked in the face by a horse and grew an enormous handlebar moustache to disguise the scar. Another of the circus horses became blind, and he stopped them from shooting it; he wanted it. As the story goes, some months later they were all riding on a mountain trail and got lost in the fog, couldn't find their way back. Alfred took charge and his blind horse led the way, sensing its way back down the trail. There's not a lot of performer blood in my family, but Alfred Jones seemed pretty cool.

My mum grew up in Fleetwood, as well as my dad. All the local kids used to play on Arden Green, where she lived, and Dad insisted they used to play together, but she doesn't remember meeting him. It sounds like he'd had a crush on her forever.

Mum's parents were Irish, and although they were both gone by the time I turned up, I felt like I knew them, because she always talked to me about them, made me feel like I'd actually spent time with them. Her mum, Annie Mulligan, was a beautiful woman, generous, kind, and by all accounts a very good singer, a soprano. She sang all day while cleaning the house, washing up with her dolly tub and posser, in those pre-washing machine days. When my mum was a baby, Annie stuck her in the tub to keep her safe, away from the kitchen boiler, and sang away. The neighbours would come in and say, 'Give us a song, Annie,' and she'd regale them with a bit of 'Danny Boy'. Mum said she could have gone professional. I love that; it's great to think that that's maybe where I get my voice from.

Mum's dad, Samuel Dutton, was born in Irlams o' th' Height, Salford, from farming stock. He ran away from home as a teenager, went to sea as a cabin boy, and became a stoker on the

ships. He ended up in Fleetwood and met Annie, who refused
to marry him unless he stopped going to sea because so many
of those trawlermen lost their lives out there. So he became a
stoker at the gasworks in Fleetwood, a foreman eventually. They
both got tuberculosis, but while he recovered, poor Annie died
when she was just 45. Mum was 12. He re-married, a lady called
Jane, who didn't see eye to eye with my mum at all, just didn't
seem to like her. Doesn't sound like she liked anyone much, was
prone to throwing tantrums, generally very abusive. One afternoon Sam asked Jane to go to the cinema with him, and she
didn't because she said she wanted to get on with the ironing.
He said, 'OK, I'll bring Pat,' and he went to get his hat and coat.
And Jane leant over to Mum, held the hot iron right close to her
face – she could feel the heat – and said, 'You get your coat and
I'll brand you for life.' That was the type of person she was.
Mum still says, 'God rest her soul.' But I look at photos of her
and wonder why on earth my granddad married her.

My mum, Patricia Dutton, was born in 1932. The priest who
baptised her, Canon McKenna, was a local legend, he'd saved a
lot of lives when Fleetwood was swallowed by an enormous
flood in 1927. A freak tidal wave came over at midnight and the
whole town went under. And Canon McKenna got an upturned
table, rowed it about and whisked a lot of people to safety before
getting hold of a boat and saving more lives. That story was so
vivid to me when I was a kid, visions of this priest in a long
black gown, on a table, paddling up Fleetwood High Road. Very
biblical.

Fleetwood was booming when Mum was a kid. The Marine
Hall, where everything that was anything used to go on, was
built in 1935. Back then, before everyone could sod off to
Majorca, Fleetwood was a pretty attractive tourist spot, compet-
ing with Blackpool to some extent. It was a big fishing port in

those days, and remained that way up until the 1970s. There was even an old slogan, 'Fleetwood: Recommended by the medical board,' because the sea air was good for your lungs. Get some good solid fresh air in you, go to Fleetwood. It's not like that now. My parents had the best of it.

Saying that, Mum was a really sick kid, she spent most of her teenage years in and out of hospital. Pneumonia was rampant, she had it three times. She stayed at home a lot, had to leave secondary school after just a few months because she was ill, they didn't want her infecting the rest of the kids. She was happy though, despite growing up ill and during the war. Then when her mum died, she had those problems with her step-mum, and was never really happy again until she met my dad. She felt very unstable at home, told the parish priest she wanted to be a nun, went to a nursing home in Blackpool to look after the sick for a bit, then went off to be a postulant in a convent in Romsey, near Southampton. She was just craving stability really; she hadn't thought of being a nun before. And she speaks very fondly of her time there; she's still in touch with one of the girls, who did make the grade. Mum scrubbed floors and washed dishes, learnt dressmaking and knitting, cooked. She says it was God's way of training her for the job she had to do – i.e. raising nine kids – which is a cool way of looking at it.

But she was only there for eight months because she too got tuberculosis, and was sent to a sanatorium in Surrey, where she basically spent a year in bed being given injections and tablets, painting and reading Agatha Christie books. Her brother Joe visited her once, the only visitor she had the entire year she was there, because she was so far away from everyone. After that she was moved to a sanatorium near Fleetwood, and was discharged just before her 21st birthday, desperate to get home to see her dad, who was ill. He was never the same after my nan died. He married Jane because he wanted Mum to have a mother again. He later died of a heart attack – his heart had been weakened by bronchitis, most probably from the decades of stoker work, but his death certificate did indeed state that he died of a broken heart. It actually said that.

Shortly after that was the time my dad, still an errand boy cycling around Fleetwood for the Co-op, saw Mum walking down the street and fell off his bike, hurtling everyone's vegetables all over the road. Maybe it was the surprise of seeing her again after she'd been away so long. Poor Alf, with his crush on my mum, yet to properly meet her. She didn't even see him fall off that bike, carried on walking, oblivious, while he scrambled around on the ground. Apparently he said to one of his friends, 'I'm gonna ask that Patsy Dutton to marry me,' and they told him he'd better stay away or her brothers would get him. But he wasn't frightened of anything, or anybody, Dad.

They finally met a few months later, ballroom dancing at the Marine Hall. The big bands used to play there, Joe Loss, Edmundo Ros, Mum used to go with her brothers. And Dad impressed her with his dance moves. He'd taken the doctor's advice and had been to dance school. He won medals for his dancing; I've got them. He cut in while she was dancing a quick-step with someone else. 'I heard this "Excuse me," he tapped this other kid on the shoulder, and we've been dancing ever since,' says Mum.

Her dad met him at the garden gate. Alf had come along to ask her for another dance the next Saturday, and he ruffled his hair, gave him a slap, and said to her, 'He's a good lad you've got there. Don't make a fool of him.' And she said, 'Alright, Dad.' And she married him, three months later, 31 March, 1954. They had a ball. Fleetwood was thriving, great butchers and bakers, fresh fish, no trouble, lots of fun, lots of dancing. Mum was working as a housekeeper for a pretty wealthy family called the Prestons, and wanted to leave to start raising kids. Mum and Dad always wanted a big family. But she didn't know how to tell Mrs Preston she was leaving, so Dad went and told this woman, 'You don't pay her enough and you don't treat her well enough and this is the last time that she'll ever work for you.' And that was that.

Dad got a job at the back of the docks building two enormous cooling towers, since demolished, that everyone in Fleetwood called Gert and Daisy, after a comedy duo who were big radio stars at the time. When Mum was in hospital having Joseph – my eldest brother, their first baby – someone shouted up to Dad, who was sitting on top of one of the towers, legs dangling over, eating his sandwiches. He shouted, 'Alf, you've got a son,' and Dad threw his sandwiches in the air and slid down the ladder, feet either side, and bombed it down to the hospital. He was such an Action Man, my dad. He never used to open the garden gate, he just used to jump over it. He'd grab the top of the fence and jump over, like he was Starsky and Hutch. And he always cleared it. I never saw him fall once.

They finished building Gert and Daisy, and Dad's mum told him to get a job at the ICI factory, to get a better wage, and he did. Mum wasn't overjoyed to have her husband working at a chemical plant. And he did get gassed a few times there. We nearly lost him a couple of times. He was working with chlorine gas, and sometimes there'd be an explosion and the gas would escape and he'd inhale it. He said it was like an elephant standing on your chest, he couldn't catch his breath. He was hospitalised a number of times. And there was no compensation back then, just, 'Get back to work.' He once saw this fella stealing mercury from the factory and shoving it in his bicycle frame. What the hell he was doing with mercury, who he was selling it to, I don't know. Making a lot of thermometers? They found him out because as he was cycling through the factory gates, the bike was so heavy he fell over, and couldn't pick it up again. And the staff went over to help him and they found this mercury.

Dad's legs were always really rough because he used to work with powder that burnt his skin if it came into contact with sweat or moisture which, naturally, it did all the time. At least his bad feet got considerably better, those dislocated ankles of his, because Mum insisted he had an inside piece put on his heels to support the inner foot. And all the dancing was help-ing. One night every week they'd get a babysitter and go to the Catholic Club in Thornton for a dance with another couple. And he was a bit of a flirt, my dad, but a harmless one. It was just in his nature, he was a chatty guy. He loved people, he loved everybody. He'd say, 'I'm just going down town,' and would return with stories of all the people he met. The wife of this other couple they were out with one night saw him talking to a friend of theirs and said to Mum, 'Look at Alf, he's flirting with that Alice over there.' Mum said, 'Yeah but he's taking me home tonight.' As she puts it, he made ladies feel like ladies. And all my sisters were his princesses.

They went through a couple of houses while the family expanded, before settling for good in the one I was raised in, the same four-bedroom house Mum still lives in. I was the last of nine, and a few had grown up and left by the time I was born in September 1973. She wanted one last boy, to name after Dad, got the rest of the family to pray for one every night. And she says as soon as she fell pregnant she knew I would be a boy. Nothing can stop my mum when she wants something, even nature. She was so sure, she got my sisters Theresa and Anne to go and find a cardboard box and write 'Alfred the Great' on it and draw soldiers on it, so I'd have my first toy box ready and waiting for me when I was born. Theresa dutifully went and found a box, outside the off licence, brought it home complete with a rogue bottle of whisky inside, and was promptly ordered to take that whisky back.

Mum was 41. 'Don't worry, we'll have this baby here today by the grace of God,' the doctor told her in hospital, which she thought was wonderful, and they did, but not before another doctor marched into the room brandishing a pen and a form. He said, 'Mrs Boe. Sign this. We want to sterilise you, you shouldn't be having all these babies.' Mum said, 'On your bike,' leaving him fuming. When she was younger, doctors had told her she shouldn't have any children because of her tuberculosis. When she finally got rid of it for good, at 36, the doctor who discharged her said all the babies had lifted her lungs up, rested them, and cured her.

Chapter Four

BUSTER BOE COMES TO TOWN

There was another big flood in Fleetwood, in 1977. The sequel. This time, it's personal. And it was in a way, purely because of the sheer amount of houses that had been built in the 50 years since the first. So while it wasn't quite as biblical as its predecessor, it did wreak a lot of damage, striking down upon our town with great vengeance and furious anger.

I was four and don't quite remember the initial havoc but I remember everybody freaking out. And a lot of rain. Most of the flood was down in Chatsworth and we weren't allowed to go to the beach. We could see in the distance the sea had come over the wall. Everyone was doing what they could. Nana Boe, Dad's mum, piggy-backed an old lady across the road. 'Get on me back, Em,' she said. sixty-eight years old too. Mum and my sister Anne helped out a lot, drying out people's carpets in the youth club they used to run. Jim Lynch, the youth leader, who did a lot for Fleetwood, wonderful guy, came a cropper when a tent covering a sizeable roadworks hole had floated away. Poor

Jim parked his car, stepped out and fell down the hole. Carry On Fleetwood.

I used to get called Buster a lot in those days, because that's what the midwife had called me. I was born Alfred Giovanni Roncalli Boe, named after Pope John the 23rd, who died 10 years before I arrived. Giovanni, Italian for John, even though his actual English name was Joseph; he was born Giuseppe Roncalli, but as Pope he chose John. Buster's certainly less of a mouthful. 'Buster Boe's got the biggest head in the ward and he popped out like a pea in a pod,' this midwife said – she was enamoured with me. 'Nobody else is to touch this fella. I carry him through the ward every time.' Some of my family came to see me at an album signing I was doing in HMV Blackpool last year, and Anne called out 'Hiya, Buster!' while I was meeting and greeting. Thanks, Anne.

We always had a dog. Mum's gone through five of them. When she was a kid, her mum gave her a collie called Flash, and they were inseparable, best pals. Because Mum was too ill for school, she spent most mornings on the beach with him. One afternoon he caught a rabbit, killed it, and laid it at her feet. She didn't want to touch it, funnily enough, so he carried it home in his mouth. Her brother skinned it, cleaned it, and they ate it for dinner. Good dog. And since then she always got collies, cross-collies, as thoroughbreds are happier with the sheep, whereas the crosses like to be at home with the humans.

When I was growing up we had Chess – Dad got him from a neighbour whose dog had a load of pups, he was the runt of the litter; he'd been kept out of the way, in a shed in the back of the garden. The stories I'd hear about that dog, the things he did before my time. Saving lives every five minutes. Near mythical. He'd lie under the babies' prams until the prams rocked, and then he'd bark to tell Mum and Dad they were awake. He barked

for Mum once and she came into the living room to find little
Maria's nappy on fire on the carpet. It had been put over the
top of the fireguard to warm up, and Maria pulled it off while
Mum was in the kitchen. Life saved. One weekend my brother
John, 10 at the time, was playing football in the road and Mum
went outside to find all hell breaking loose. John had bent down
to pick up his ball and this Alsatian had jumped on his collar,
was on his back biting his neck. 'Get Chess!' Mum told Anne,
and Chess raced up the street, jumped up, dragged this Alsatian
off John's back. Mum says she's never seen anything so beautiful in all her life. She tells the story like Chess was some sort of
superhero dog. 'He bounded out the house and in one move he
cleared the fence . . .' you can almost hear the *Superman* theme
as she tells this story. 'In mid-air he grabbed this dog and pulled
it off John . . .' Some woman in the street told her husband to
get a broom to break up the ensuing scrap and Mum said, 'You
leave those dogs alone.' And she looked at Chess and said,
'That'll do,' and Chess let go and came over to sit by her. And
they walked home. And the Alsatian died. And they gave Chess
an entire chicken for dinner.

I've got to say though, that dog was something special. When
I was little I'd walk down the street with him, and every time I
got too close to the road, he'd nudge me back to the pavement
with his nose. Before I was born, my brothers used to camp on
the beach in a tent, and Mum would insist Chess went with
them. A policeman poked his head inside the tent once and
Chess bit his hand. Joe apologised and the policeman said,
'Don't worry, son, he's only doing his job.' Chess was above the
law. After Chess we had a little cattle dog named Gandalf, which
we then shortened to Dandy. Every morning we'd come down
for coffee and would be greeted by him nipping the back of our
ankles, just like he would have been doing with the cattle. He

died of a heart attack, I buried him in the back garden in a
Co-op box, and then we got Boscoe, another dog with higher
than average canine IQ. He was around when Dad retired, they
were especially close. And now Mum's got Sully, a rescue dog,
good little dude.

I had a blast in that house and in Fleetwood, despite the
town's declining fortunes. It's funny when people talk to you
about how good the place you live in used to be. I'd think, well
why do I get the rotten end of the stick living in it now! But it
was a fun place to grow up in, a lot seemed to be happening all
the time, everybody seemed to be partying. Chatsworth was
dodgy, Mum and Dad lived down there some time before I was
around. There were a few dodgy areas in that part. I remember
going down there once as a kid and seeing a fight in the street,
this fella just smacking an old guy's head against the ground. It
really shocked me. That image sticks in my head today. This
fella was on top of this older guy, smacking his head on the
ground, relentlessly, and he was limp. It was horrible to see
fighting like that. But on the whole Fleetwood was always cool
to hang out in. We'd have our veg delivered by this Polish fella
called Walter. Mum told us how he was tortured during the
war. He had this veg stall on Fleetwood market, and we'd go
there on Friday to order cabbages and carrots, and he'd bring
them to us in the evening. Those carrots were seriously enormous. Cabbages the size of fruit-bowls. And every single week
Mum would get a sack of potatoes, and we'd go through the lot.
Full of soil as well. I've picked that up, I can't go food shopping
without getting a load of potatoes. We'd be virtually at the end
of the sack and Mum would say, 'Go and get a couple of spuds
out of the sack. Big enough for baking.' You'd have to go fishing
around in the soil to get a spud out. But you'd always guarantee
there'd be a few in there that would be perfect. They were big

old spuds. I can exaggerate, but they were the size of rugby balls.

Our Sunday dinners were amazing, Mum would put the meat in the oven before we went to church and ah, we'd come back and the house would smell of incredible cooking. She used to bake pies, rice puddings, bread puddings. Somewhat leathery beef, you'd chew on a piece for what seemed like days, but it tasted good. And the fish . . . we'd have bags of fresh fish delivered every Friday by Chas Wilson, a friend of the family and one of the biggest fish merchants around. Uncle Chas. Again, massive bags, big pieces of cod and haddock, and he'd sometimes surprise us with some skate. To add to that, me and my friends would chase the fish lorry through the back of the docks and catch the fish that fell off the back, shove it in a bag, bring it home. Very enterprising!

There was a strong DIY mentality in our house. Mum and Dad had me wearing clogs on the ice-rink in Blackpool when I was five, I think we got kicked off. Dad had DIY in his genes. When he was a kid he used to make himself fireworks, a bowl of powder, cardboard cartons, open fire in the living room. Don't try this at home. Decades later, when we were kids, Grandma Boe came over and told us about the time he nearly set fire to that room with his shenanigans. 'Did I clatter you for that?' she asked him.

'No, Mum.'

And she whacked him there and then.

Mum would make us ice-lollies, these really sickly sweet orange things, they were fantastic – we'd sit in the back garden and eat them. We never wanted for anything, we never struggled. Always had enough food and clothes, and great toys. Christmases were wonderful. Dad would build toys for us and Mum would paint them. Christmas smelt of paint. And there was always some surprise. I came down one Christmas morning and the curtains were drawn, and Dad said, 'Look at the snow outside.' And I threw open the curtains and it was a beautiful sunny day. Snow? What snow? And I looked down and there was a bike for me. Birthdays were the same. Mum always made me a cake. On my 10th birthday she made me this big galleon ship out of chocolate. Massive big galleon ship, big sails, sponge and chocolate, it said 'Happy 10th Birthday' on the sails and had little pirate figures on it. I've still got them. I put them on my daughter Grace's birthday cake a couple of years ago, and I'd like to put them on my son Alfie's 10th birthday cake.

Halloween in Fleetwood was something to experience. You couldn't get pumpkins in Fleetwood in the '70s, so we'd carve out turnips and put candles in them. It was always really hard to hollow out a turnip. And you'd hold these lanterns and your hands and arms would stink of burnt turnip. For days. It was horrible. You'd see all these dead waxy turnips all over the road that kids had abandoned. If Christmas smelt of paint, Halloween stunk of smouldering soggy turnips.

I liked my train sets. I had pictures of trains on my walls, I wanted to be a train driver, driving a big steam train. And Dad built me a train! From scratch. The size of a sofa. It was *amazing*. It was a train! It had two compartments, chimneys, a carriage on the back . . . we'd sit in it and he'd pull us down the road, it had big old-fashioned pram wheels off the old Silver Cross prams that he'd no doubt found in a skip. He was always poking around in skips, looking for scraps of wood, seeing what he could make out of this and that. So many times I'd be walking down the road with my mates and they'd say, 'Oh there's your dad,' and I'd just see these legs sticking out of a skip. I'd say 'Just keep walking, keep walking . . .' Dad made wine too.

One Christmas, all of my brothers had come home for the holiday and took Dad to the pub, and there was a lot of wine in the barrels, he'd been working on it. I wasn't old enough to go to the pub, I was upstairs on my drums, and I heard all this raucous laughing and shouting. I went downstairs and Mum and my sisters were plastered, dancing, all over the place. They'd got hammered on the wine; they didn't know at the time, but it hadn't finished fermenting yet and was really strong. They said, 'Why should the boys be having all the fun in the pub?' Dad and my brothers came home and were not nearly as smashed as the girls. Christmas dinner was ruined. We had such a laugh, that was an amazing Christmas.

The Boe DIY ethos didn't always work for me. There's a carnival every year in Fleetwood. Mum and Anne used to help paint the floats; it all came past our house, everyone in fancy dress. When I was nine I was part of my school float, and they made a Paddington Bear outfit for me. Nine years old, a fur head on, big duffel coat, big hat, wellington boots and woollen trousers, in the middle of the blistering hot summer of 1982. Dressed for the Antarctic. And that head was massive, and a bit dodgy. It looked like Paddington Bear had been a bit mangled.

I hated school, and I mean properly hated it. My first year at St Wulstan's Primary was particularly horrible, and I think that tainted the whole thing for me. I had this teacher who just didn't like me at all, she didn't like any of the family – we all went to St Wulstan's. She only took a shine to the pupils whose families she knew were rich and popular. It was really hard, always a fight, always a battle. She didn't give me the time of day, and I got overlooked, so I couldn't do maths, couldn't add, couldn't subtract. The only thing I was ever good at was sports day. I was put in the sprint race once and came first even though

I set off last because I hadn't heard the gun go off. Legged it and overtook everybody.

My second year was much better, I had a fantastic teacher called Mrs Atkinson, really sweet, she taught me baking, helped me a lot, a lovely lady. But she was a glitch in the system. The third year brought me a teacher who used to go around the class and ask everybody to read a page of the book we were all reading, and she'd always leave me till last. And by the time it got to me the bell would go and she'd say, 'Right, we'll start with Alfie tomorrow,' and she never did, I never got to read. That's why I don't feel I'm a good reader even now. I didn't really learn to read for a long time, until I went to juniors. She was part of a big family in Fleetwood, and again, they didn't like the Boes. There were always issues with people. We didn't go with the flow as a family, we made our own journey, our own path, we created things ourselves. Quite a strong force in Fleetwood, the Boe family. The church was a big deal for our family. Mum and my sisters did – and still do – a lot of work for the church, fundraising events, jumble sales, things like that, and I think some people felt intimidated by us.

So my confidence was knocked at school, I didn't think I was very intelligent. There was a teacher in my junior school called Maria O'Halloran who smacked me across the head for sticking a picture in a book a week early. *BAM*, right across the head, I nearly fell over. But I didn't say anything, never told Mum until I was about 16. And she said, 'I would have gone in, I would have gone in.' Mum had been through worse herself, she never liked school either. She got her knuckles smacked every morning for being a left-hander. We'd get the cane a lot at junior school. Bamboo on your hand or on your backside, or the back of your legs. They used to say, 'Put your hands on the table,' and they'd smack your knuckles with a wooden ruler, bruise your fingers. I'd had it in infant school as well, which was obviously terrifying. I was frightened of teachers, of what they would do and how they would turn on me. They really scared me, until I met some that were nice. Miss Hogborn was wonderful, played piano, and taught the class personably, a really beautiful lady. Mr Sumner and Mr Osmand were smashing fellas, but the good ones were few and far between. Most of them were horrible, really cruel to us. I hated it, absolutely hated it. The amount of times I wanted to burn that school down. Secondary school wasn't much better. I couldn't even take music as a subject, because I couldn't play piano or violin, so they wouldn't let me. Some of the teachers there were just odd. One insisted on calling me Albert, and not for any comedic value. She said, 'Who cares what your name is. Albert.' Mrs Lamb was bizarre, she came in one day and told us all that from that point on we had to call her Mrs Austin because she said she'd married Steve Austin, the Six Million Dollar Man. OK.

All of those teachers really helped to shape my personality, just not quite in the way teachers are supposed to. I think one of the reasons I hate injustice – which is why Jean Valjean appeals to me so much – is because I suffered it so much at school. I don't take crap from people any more. I can be pretty confrontational. I had to learn to stick up for myself. That certainly happened after I left home and came down to London, and had problems with people at music college. I have awful aggression sometimes, and I've had struggles with it. I get incredibly frustrated and angry and I flare up, I can lose my temper badly. It doesn't take much if I think someone's out of line. My wife Sarah's seen me get angry with people a lot and she says it's frightening, which I don't like, and I try to control that, contain it. I think it comes from Mum's side of the family. She doesn't stand for any nonsense. She gave a lad a black eye once when she was 15. She was coming home through an alleyway and saw a boy being bullied, and told this other kid to leave him alone. The kid turned on her and she punched him in the eye. She's always been a feisty one, my mum. And her dad was like that. When my uncle was a little boy, he fell off his bike, and their dad, old Sam Dutton, picked up the bike, took it into the backyard, bent it double and hurled it over the fence. He was angry that the bike had hurt his son.

Chapter Five

FINDING MY VOICE

As a young kid, before I went to bed, Mum used to read from Foxe's *Book of Martyrs* as bedtime stories. If you're not aware of that grisly tome, it's 500 years old and tells incredibly graphic stories of British Protestants who sacrificed their lives for their faith. Some of them were crushed with blocks of stones. Some were hung, drawn, quartered. Eyes prodded out, fingernails removed and chopped up into tiny little pieces. Strapped to a rock until the tide came in. Frightening stories. And then I'd have to go to sleep. And I'd have nightmares, and for ages we couldn't understand why, until finally Mum said, 'Maybe I should stop reading the *Book of Martyrs* to you.' Ya think? I don't think she'd read it to my brothers and sisters. But she thought they were good lessons for me to learn, because these people had given their lives for something important.

We were a strong Catholic family, I had a pretty religious upbringing. We used to say the Rosary at night before we went to bed, and then we'd do a novena, a set prayer with a reading to a certain saint. In a way it was a real time to meditate, to connect with each other and be together. And I love my faith, I would never turn against it because it's helped me through so much of my life. But, man was I afraid of our parish priest, Father Cochrane. He was a force to contend with. His sermons could be pretty damn hard. 'If you believe in Heaven you have to believe in Hell, and that's where you'll go if you don't do this.' Proper fire and brimstone sermons, terrifying. He was at church for years and years and it was always, 'Canon Cochrane rules with a rod of iron, and you will go to Hell if you don't do this.' It was horrible. He made me wet myself one day when I was serving on the altar, because I was that scared of him. He was cruel, he was aggressive, and he didn't give a damn about shouting at you, putting you in your place. I was terrified of him, a lot of us were. I eventually stood up to him, years later. Just after my dad died, I was 25, it was only me and him in the church, and when I walked across the altar he accused me of not treating it with respect. In the moment I was shell-shocked, but afterwards in the church coffee shop I went up to him and said, 'Do not accuse me of not having respect for that altar. I've served on that altar for many years, for you and other priests, and I've never lost respect. Do not accuse me of that.' He said, 'Sorry, sorry.' I'd had enough of that sort of thing from him as a kid, I wasn't going to take it as an adult.

There was pressure to do the church thing, and the prayers. Mum could make us feel guilty on a Friday night, we'd have to go and serve Mass at church, half an hour. And I'd serve on a Sunday. And then Sunday afternoon when you've been to Mass and you've had dinner and you're just chilling out watching telly, Mum would walk in and say, 'Right, I'm off to benediction. Does anybody want to come with me?' You couldn't say no. You could try. She'd say, 'I think you should go. I'm going,' and if you didn't she'd give you the guilt trip. But Mum was having a hard time I think, she'd had 20 years of pushing prams, pregnant year in year out. So my sister Anne became a mother to us all. She got some stick from our elder brothers, Joseph and John, because they thought she was a fuddy-duddy. 'Matron's here.' But someone had to do it, and she was the one. She was only in her mid-20s. She's a beauty our Annie, she's a saint, she's a stronghold. She's the gentlest soul on Earth, she puts up with a lot. And I love her to pieces, she's my godmother, and she's like my second mum. She also introduced me to Guinness, when I was 11, gave me a quarter pint topped up with lemonade at her wedding. Good girl.

Catholic guilt is something you always have. It still hits me now, it's ingrained. That thing of there always being something bigger than you, watching over you, and you have to always be conscious of doing the right thing. Church taught me a lot of that. I remember just after finishing my *Les Misérables* run at the end of 2011, I went to church to give thanks for what I'd achieved in the show. I was feeling pretty emotional because it was the morning after my last night, and that show meant a lot to me and took a lot out of me. But I just wanted to go there to give thanks for getting me through those five months. And it was nice, it just felt like I connected. I was really grateful, because I felt like I got through that stint with a lot of faith, with support. That was the first time I'd been to church in a while. I just don't feel that you *have* to. I think you can be as spiritual or as close to God by being with your kids, or just by being on a mountainside or on a beach. And I like the ritual of the Mass, it's special. I went to a beautiful one last Christmas on Soho Square, St Patrick's. It was lovely to go in there and hear the choir. It can be so meditative and peaceful. You can't beat a good church choir, especially the Gregorian ones. Beautiful music.

There was always music at home. Certainly more than the TV. It brought us together. A lot of music was played around the table, and it kept us in the room, kept us entertained and having a laugh, singing along and chatting, and really, in a way, getting to know each other as a family. That might be a tradition that's been lost these days. Music really links families, it unites them. It's a real warm sociable outlet for everybody to share each other's company and share each other's emotions.

We had classic tunes that would always come out, like Karl Denver's 'Mexicali Rose'. He had this amazing voice which switched from a wonderful baritonal quality to a high falsetto, wailing country sound. Dad loved music, he loved good singers, and he had pretty eclectic tastes. He wasn't particularly into opera – he liked Caruso and Richard Tauber and Gigli, but he loved Paul Robeson, Val Doonican, Elvis. A mixture. We used to listen to this Ivan Rebroff record, this German nutcase with a crazy, crazy voice. He had a five octave range. I think all that was where I got my philosophy for music, that there are no boundaries in terms of what you can be into, and indeed what you can sing.

Dad *never* stopped singing. He was good, he could flip from being a baritone to a falsetto, because he loved Karl Denver. Dad used to sing 'Mexicali Rose' all the time, all the time. He was a big fan of Slim Whitman as well. 'Indian Love Call'. The one where all the Martians' heads explode in that movie *Mars Attacks!*. Mum's taste in music was not as varied as Dad's, although they both loved Slim Whitman. She liked a lot of big band music, the Glenn Millers, and the Val Doonican types. She liked a good singer, I think the classical side of my music came from Mum; she liked Kathleen Ferrier, Maria Callas, that lot.

We had a proper turntable for the records, and little wooden box radios, and later we had a huge thick industrial metal radio with a tape player. That was shifted around the house. It was a kitchen radio, then somebody would steal it for their bedroom while they were getting ready to go out. I was big on Pink Floyd, still am – nobody in my family was into that sort of thing but I used to hear a lot of it on Radio 1. I'd tape songs from the radio, finger poised on the pause button so you wouldn't get any of the talking, you'd stop when the DJ came in. I liked Sinatra a lot. Sinatra loved classical singers, he liked opera. And I got into Elvis. My brother Joe was a big Elvis fan, so I grew up listening to a lot of his records. Elvis liked his classical stuff too. Obviously 'It's Now or Never' is 'O Sole Mio', same tune, same song. In my live shows at the moment I play a medley of both of them to pay tribute, to blur the lines between styles and genres, we start it off all classical and Neapolitan then midway through we switch to boogie-woogie, it's a carnival. Elvis did 'Surrender' too, an English-language version of 'Torna a Surriento'. Dean Martin did all those songs, the Neapolitan stuff.

It's funny how the influences in your early life really do pave the path for you as an artist. And all the singers we listened to as I was growing up, Slim Whitman, Gigli, Caruso, Frankie Laine, Don Williams, the country music, through Dad – they all had an influence on the way I sing now. I mean Elvis had an incredible baritone quality. And then people like Karl Denver and Slim Whitman, who used to sing way, way high, influenced the tenor side of my voice. You can definitely get a sense of that on the likes of 'Bring Him Home'. Without those influences I really don't think I'd have the same interest in music that I have, and I probably wouldn't have the same style of singing either.

I used to sing around the house all the time, but it wasn't something I considered pursuing professionally, not till my late teens really. My first public performance was an unofficial cameo in a play at a youth club day Anne put on. *Alice in Wulstanland.* I was two. A local actor, George Kennedy, was playing the executioner, and I shouted out, 'I'm not scared of you.' I wasn't. He said, 'Come up here and sing us a song then,' and I got up on stage with him and sang 'Humpty Dumpty', a classic jam from my youth. I can just about remember being up there singing that, or at least I think I can. I followed that up two years later with an appearance in my school's nativity play. I was Joseph, I had a couple of carols to sing and one line on my own, 'Yes, I said he would be born in a stable,' which I was really nervous about. Joseph being a carpenter, I had to kneel on a chair and pretend to saw through the back of it, and I got lost in the moment, so focused on what I was doing, the chair was getting closer and closer to the edge of the stage. Finally I went flying off into the first row with the saw in my hand, which must have been a little disconcerting for the audience. Although I guess if you're the type to get to the front of a gig you're up for a bit of excitement.

The next thing that happened was something I was practically pushed into doing, yet in its own ramshackle little way it started everything off for me. I was 14, vegetating on the sofa watching telly, just home from school, and my sister Maria was getting ready to go to her amateur operatics evening, a weekly night in an old spiritualist church called Lottie Dawson's Choir. Lottie Dawson was this nice little old lady who gave singing lessons and put on music shows in the Marine Hall. She did a lot for the kids in Fleetwood, and she was pretty funny. Everybody called her Auntie Lottie. And once a week she'd have a group who'd sing songs from the shows. That evening, Mum said, 'Why don't you go with Maria tonight, you'll enjoy it,' because I was always singing at home.

I said, 'Nah, I don't really think it's me, Mum.'

And she said, 'Go Alf, it'll do you good, you can sing, have a go.'

'Alright Mum.'

She can be quite persuasive, my mother. So I walked down there with Maria, got to the door, peeked in, and that was as far as I got. 'Forget this, I'm off home.' I just saw all this prancing around, these guys pretending to be pirates, and I thought, 'What the hell?' It just wasn't me. And then as I was leaving this girl walked in. Lynn Wright. I knew her from town, I fancied her rotten – she was really beautiful. She was sporty, she had this very 1987 haircut, curly but all shaven up at the back, a lot of boys fancied her. And I was 14, my hormones were kicking in, and I thought I'd go back the next week to see if she was there again.

So the next week I went back, made more of an effort, but not much more. I tried to just hide away in the corner, sat down, but eventually I got dragged over to join in the men's rendition of *Pirates of Penzance*. So after watching them all prance around like pirates and scoffing the week before, I ended up having to do it myself, to some extent. I went over to the piano, they gave me the music, and I started singing, and at the end of the song I blasted out the big top note. It came naturally to me, I wasn't trying to prove a point. My voice had broken by then. I went through a lot with my voice, I had tonsillitis, often had a bad throat. My tonsils are ingrown now, it's a little weird. I've never had them taken out, but when you look down my throat you can't see them.

So I belted out that note, and Lottie Dawson was gobsmacked. I remember the expressions on people's faces, it was something else, and I really got a buzz from it. Most of the lads were chuffed, although there were a couple whose noses were put out of joint, wanted to be the stars of the show and got a bit jealous and all that. You get that all the time really, that doesn't change. And Lynn Wright was obviously impressed too, because she started talking to me, I got to know her a bit and, mainly because I fancied her, kept going there every week. We did have a little snog a couple of times, outside the school next to our house. She wore thick, thick lipstick – I came home with it all over my face. Teenagers kissing, not a pleasant sight.

I hadn't told my schoolmates I was going there, because I'd started drumming in rock bands by this point and I didn't want anybody to know that I was prancing around in tights and a tunic. And after a few weeks I did my first public performance, *Songs from the Shows*. We did scenes from *Cats* and *Phantom*, and I had to sing one line from *Les Misérables*, from 'Do You Hear the People Sing?' I was so nervous about singing it, I threw up round the back of the stage before I had to go on, but it was fun. Then we did a scene from *Brigadoon* and I had to wear a kilt, and because I couldn't dance I felt I had to make a fool of myself to make it work, to win over the audience. It was a comic song anyway. So I wore a pair of Bermuda shorts under the kilt, Dad's hobnail work boots, massive hiking socks rolled down to my ankles, a string vest, and this huge Tam o' Shanter Scottish hat on my head that kept falling over my eyes whenever I danced. I came on half-way through the scene and the audience fell about, they found it hilarious, although Lottie Dawson's assistant was a bit annoyed – she found it a little disruptive. Regardless, the next show we did, I thought I'd do a similar thing, because it got such a good response and I wanted to get one again. It was an amateur production, I didn't see why we couldn't have a laugh, bit of comic relief. But I was about to go on, all these guys in kilts were dancing at the front of the stage, and Lottie Dawson's assistant said, 'This is *not* musical comedy!'

I said, 'Is it not? Oh I'm sorry, I thought that was the title of your company, Lottie Dawson's Musical Comedy Society.'

Mr Facetious. And she said, 'This is *not* pantomime. You take that hat off and go and do it seriously.'

And I never went on, and they said, 'Don't you ever turn up here again!' So I didn't.

Chapter Six

BACKSTAGE IN BLACKPOOL

Around that time I had my first real kiss, just before my success with Lynn Wright. Don't remember who she was but I do remember that it was like sucking a drainpipe. I thought I was gonna fall in at one point. It wasn't pleasant. It was like falling down a black hole. Sucked into a void. I was on holiday in Keswick in the Lake District, we used to go there for our summer holiday every year. We did everything as a family. Fleetwood was great in the summer too, we'd have day trips, go blackberry picking, Mum would make blackberry pie or blackberry crumble. We'd have blackberries coming out of our ears. You never wanted to see another blackberry again. We spent a lot of time on the beach and the fells, till eight or nine at night. I know it all sounds a bit *Darling Buds of May*, but it was really fun. The beach was clean and warm, and the sea was fantastic to swim in. The ice cream van would come down and you'd get sand on your ice cream but you'd still eat it. And that van used to play 'O Sole Mio', that might have been my first exposure to

Neapolitan music, of sorts. I did that song on my *Passione* album in 2007, took me back to those summers on the beach. Mum would always do these great big barm cakes, like big flat bread rolls, and she'd halve them and put ham or chicken inside with lettuce, cucumber, juicy tomatoes, and lashings of salad cream which would pour out when you took a bite. I've yet to find a better sandwich.

We went to Keswick a lot, camping, climbing, hiking for miles. We used to go to a place called Castlerigg Manor, a huge youth club with some sort of connection to the church. My brother John's girlfriend came camping with us once, in high heel shoes. Classy. But they laughed at Anne because she was in fell-walking boots. What? Our Annie was like a Swiss Army Knife. If you were hungry or something broke she'd always have what you'd need in her rucksack. 'Oh you've snapped a shoe-lace Mum? I think I have some spares here . . .' So I've always been a fan of the great outdoors. I love hiking, I love to camp. It's one of the reasons Sarah and I moved to Salt Lake a few years ago, the incredible mountain view. I spent some time riding around there on my Harley last Christmas, just before our son Alfie was born. Can't beat that. Me and Sarah have trekked in America a lot. We love Moab, in Grand County, especially Canyonlands, where they made *127 Hours*, the film about Aron Ralston cutting his arm off. That's where it actually happened. John Ford and John Wayne made a lot of their films in Moab, including *The Searchers*. I love John Wayne, I always have, and Moab's Apache Motel has a John Wayne Suite, which I insisted we stayed in once – it was fractionally larger than the regular rooms and not, to be honest, a suite. You can buy John Wayne toilet roll there, it says it's just like John Wayne: 'It's rough, it's tough, and it doesn't take crap off anyone.' I grew up watching westerns and couldn't believe it when I went to these places for the first time. It's all real! I just fell in love with it all. We've hiked in Fisher Towers down in the Colorado River, there are these amazing, delicate looking fins of rock, skyscraper high, carved out by water and wind, and the acoustics are incredible. Amphitheatres of rock. At one point I was standing a quarter of a mile from Sarah and she could hear me singing. We even went camping for part of our honeymoon in Zion, an utterly beautiful national park in southern Utah. We started in Capitol Reef, went through Monument Valley, and one night, when all the motels were booked, we found an open space on the side of a road and stopped there for the night. The next morning we realised we were on the edge of Grafton, this ghost town from the 1800s. The church is still there, with a graveyard with wooden crosses saying things like 'KILLED BY INDIANS' on the stones.

We went to Castlerigg Manor with school sometimes, for treks and activities. Things like that made my education just about bearable. When I was 16, a teacher, Mr McAvoy, sponsored me to go on a three-week Outward Bound programme in Eskdale, also in the Lake District. It was good fun, lots of hiking, mountain climbing, canoeing, abseiling, and we had great challenges to do, group expeditions. My solo expedition was a proper fiasco though. We all had to get through the night without shelter and just a lump of cheese, some porridge oats and a teabag to make use of. Unfortunately the instructor who took us out there had only just been employed and didn't quite get what he was supposed to be doing. He was supposed to drop five of us off, all within a mile, the first person at the beginning of the mile, last person at the end. He dropped everybody off a mile between each other and I was the last, dropped off after hiking five miles since 6.30am. I built my shelter, this sort of tarp thing, on a rock face and went off to catch some fish, failed.

So I built a fire, soaked my porridge oats in water I'd filtered from the river and made flatbread, melting the cheese on it, that was lunch. Then I took a nap. I woke up hours later when I heard some voices coming over the ridge, and it was a couple of the other guys, who'd found each other. So the three of us hiked down the valley, and at the bottom, literally a 45-minute walk away, was a youth hostel with a bloody tuck-shop. Nirvana. We laid in, cans of Coke, crisps, sandwiches, and went back to our little camps for the evening.

We were due to get picked up at seven the next morning, not aware at that point that we were miles off course. I woke up, crawled out of the bivouac and stood on this mountainside, on the edge of this cliff, in the fog and the rain wearing nothing but my underpants, just as a family of Norwegian hikers, a guy and his wife and daughter appeared. 'Morning!' they said. I asked them the time and they said it was 3pm. I'd slept for about 20 hours, and, it transpired, a rescue team had been sent out for us with our locations, but the map coordinates they'd been given didn't match up to where we were because this clueless instructor had dropped us off a mile between each other, so they'd only found the first two people. They found me eventually. And then I got sick, caught an abominable bug. I was in a right mess. The instructors didn't do anything for me, they said, 'Either get up and do the tasks or go home.' So compassionate. But I did, I dragged myself out of bed and threw myself into a canoe and started paddling, feeling really ropey, but gradually worked through it. It's impressive, what your body can do when it's not given a choice.

Soon after that I got some semi-regular work as part of the stage crew for the Blackpool Opera House, where I met a guy called John Ginley, who'd recently started working there, and we hit it off straight away. I wasn't on the payroll, it was a part-time job. I'd be brought in if they needed a hand. The first gig I did was on *Swan Lake* for the Moscow Classical Ballet, carrying dry ice, putting it in the machines, turning the machines on at the right time, watching this dry ice fill the stage, shifting sets and scenery, packing up. The get in and get out – get the show in, then get it out of the theatre after it's finished. The get out, you could be working from 10.30pm when the show came down to 4 or 5 in the morning. But it was good money, £200 cash in hand. And sometimes if it was a concert gig John would call me in to do backstage dressing-room security, get my tie and shirt on. First floor, dressing room number one. Most of the time I'd turn up without knowing who I'd be doing security for.

The first security I did was the Pet Shop Boys. I was sitting outside Neil Tennant's dressing room and their personal assistant, Peter Andreas, had an apoplectic fit in the dressing room when the band were on stage and I had to go in and help him out, it was really frightening. Next was Don McLean, the 'American Pie' guy. He was a really sweet fella, really nice guy, no airs or graces, sat in the corner of the stage with his guitar waiting to go on, did the job and left. But the one I was really thrilled by was The Everly Brothers. That was one of the times I didn't even know who I was doing the security for. I was sitting outside the dressing room and some fella came up to me, combat trousers, army boots, army jacket, greased-back hair with a plaited rat's tail down his back. He started talking to me in this crazy American accent, I presumed he was their manager. He asked me what my favourite food was, I told him I loved Italian, and he said, 'Pizza, you like pizza? You know, son, to make a really good pizza you need the best ingredients in the world. In my house in California I have a huge brick pizza oven, it really does the job.' And then Phil Everly appeared and this guy followed him into the room. Some time later Phil came out, on his own, all done up in his black suit and tie, and went down to the stage. And John radioed me and said, 'Alf, you've got a minute break, you can come down if you want, go get a brew.' Someone came to take over from me and I went downstairs and there rehearsing onstage with Phil Everly was the pizza guy – it was Don Everly. And I'd been talking to him about pizzas. So cool. John told me to go back up because the support act had arrived, and there was this huge Texan fella with an enormous Stetson on, rhinestones, and a mother of pearl guitar. Duane Eddy. I could tell who it was this time because it said Duane Eddy on the neck of his guitar, bit of a giveaway. And he came and sat next to me outside the room and started chatting as well, it was wicked. What a job.

Tom Jones played one night. I just remember loads of knickers being thrown at him. They all went in a bin-bag afterwards. You don't wanna be taking those Blackpool knickers back to LA with you. Shirley Bassey played, it was like royalty had arrived in Blackpool. Big artists like that coming into town were few and far between, so when the likes of her and Tom Jones and The Everly Brothers played it was a big deal, the whole area knew about it. After Shirley Bassey's gig I was peeling some tape off the stage floor, crawling along the stage, backed into her by accident and her security guards stepped in front of me, blocked me. I'll be on stage with her one day, I thought. A few years later she sang at a Prince's Trust concert at the Royal Albert Hall, I was there singing that night as well and I was on stage next to her at the end, so I was just about right, but I was more excited to meet Eric Clapton. I went up to him at the after-show party, I really wanted to pay tribute, to shake his hand, and I introduced myself. I couldn't believe I was shaking the hand that had played 'Layla'.

I nodded off one night while I was working at the Opera House, and that was the end of that. We were doing a production of *42nd Street*, the fit-ups took a long time, and you'd lose sleep with one thing or another. I was due to work on the whole run, doing cues throughout the show, and in the rehearsal for one of the early ones, I nodded off for a minute, missed the cue. And I wasn't asked back again. Duncan, the guy who ran the place, wasn't particularly endearing. His dad had been stage manager before him – we knew him when he was crew. And he became stage manager and quite liked to push us around. I think it must have been that my face didn't fit, because I worked really hard, worked round the clock quite a few times with John. But there you go. At least I got a great friendship out of it. He's like a brother to me, John. I sang at his wedding a few years ago while he and his wife signed the register, it was lovely. He's a project manager now at a big lighting company, works with loads of massive bands, Coldplay, Chemical Brothers, Kings of Leon. Incredible stuff he does. I want to get him involved with my next tour. I've always been so proud of him – he got out of Fleetwood and has done great work. He worked on the animatronics in the *Doctor Dolittle* show in London in 1998. I went to a preview. I was sat next to Phillip Schofield's parents – I didn't know it at first. I leant over to this lady towards the end of the show while Phillip Schofield was flying over our heads in the car, and I said, 'You see that horse down there? My mate's operating that horse.'

And she said, 'Oh, very good. My son's in the show too.'

I went, 'Oh is he? Who is he?' She said, 'He's flying the car.' Ah.

One night while I was still working at the Opera House, John phoned me at home and said, 'Put a shirt and tie on, Alf, you're needed for security.' So I smartened up, turned up to work and

he said, 'Right, we're off out.' What? I thought we were working? 'Nah, that was a ploy. Let's go out.' And me, John and a
friend of ours called Darren Williams went off to this nightclub
called Rumours and got wholeheartedly plastered. Before
moving on to what undoubtedly would have been some other
awful cesspit we went to a cash point, except as we were crossing
the road John did a vanishing act, jumped into a cab and disappeared into the night before we even knew he'd gone. I got a cab
to his house to see if he was there and alright, knocked on his
front door, one in the morning, and his mum, thankfully still
up, came out. I said, 'Hello Mrs Ginley, is John in? We lost him.'

And she said, 'Yeah he came back, but he's in a bit of a state,
Alf. He's never usually like this.'

I said, 'I don't know why, I'm sorry, we all had a few drinks,
I'm pretty sober myself.'

And my trousers fell down. In front of John Ginley's mum.
John says she delights in telling people that story whenever she
sees me on TV, which is nice.

I never used to go out much in Blackpool, mostly Fleetwood.
I hated going out in Blackpool really, it was always a bit of a
production. It was expensive, drinks were twice as much,
watered-down lager, and then getting home consisted of a
kebab on the town hall steps, stumbling around trying to find a
taxi which would cost you ten quid, and you wouldn't get back
until three or four in the morning. There was one place we went
to a lot in Blackpool called Your Father's Moustache, otherwise
known as The Tache, fantastic rock club. They had some really
wicked bands there, cool venue. Dingy old dive, sticky floor,
sweaty roof. They closed it down last year – the council bought
it. They ordered its closure for safety reasons, said the building
was in an appalling state, that the carpet was "encrusted with
filth". Erm yes, rock clubs generally are. What did they expect?

But they didn't like some of what had gone on in there, people got glassed a few times. That was just the sort of place it was. Some guy did apparently get his ear bitten off in there one time. To be fair.

Chapter Seven

HARD GRAFT AND HEARTACHE

I rarely got into any trouble, but I did a bit of karate and used to go kickboxing once a week, because my brother was into it. John, black belt in karate, third dan. I didn't stick at it, I only went a few times, wasn't any good, but I worked out a bit. And when certain people hear about that sort of thing they want a fight, see what you're made of, and I did get into a couple of scraps in Blackpool. There was one guy, Billy Mullan, who had a bit of a reputation. I was in the Broadway pub and he started coming on to my sister Maria, who didn't really want to be bothered by him, so I just stepped in and said to her, 'Let's go, let's leave.'

But she'd said, 'I'm alright Alf, leave it be.'

So I said, 'Please mate, leave her alone.'

Next minute, he grabbed hold of me and pulled me back off the chair, I crashed onto the floor. And he jumped on top of me and put his hands around my neck. The weird thing was that although he had his hands around my neck he wasn't squeezing. I thought, 'That was a waste of time, wasn't it?' So I got my leg underneath him, put my foot on his chest and kicked him off, he went flying into the table, and as he got up I smacked him in the face. The bouncers stepped in, kicked us both out and he disappeared. And Maria came out and I said, 'Don't piss around any more.' Because she was really upset that it happened, we could have just left. But he really was the cock of Fleetwood, Billy Mullan, big fighter. Somebody said to me, 'You got in a fight with Billy Mullan. He'll come after you again.' I said, 'Well if he does he does.' And I saw him a few months after that when I was working in a pub. I went up to him and said, 'Alright mate, how you doing, remember me?' I just didn't want to ignore the fact that he was there. And we had a chat, I bought him a beer and he bought me one.

There were a couple of good pubs John Ginley and I would go to where there was never trouble. The Queens was alright for a good beer. Some nice little bars here and there, but I was never exactly blown away by Blackpool. It was a bit of a dive. Fleetwood had its fair share of trouble spots too. There was a particularly rough club called Planters where there would be a fight every single night. Without fail. It had a pretty grisly reputation, a real last resort, all the parents would worry about their kids if they'd gone to Planters that night. Big scraps, gangs of lads just beating all hell out of each other, inside and outside. If you were on the dance floor you'd invariably get dragged away into the crowd while the bouncers sorted out some trouble. And when it closed you stood a good chance of being followed home by someone who wanted to have a go. If we ended up there we'd usually hang out in the back bar doing shots and tequila slammers, having a good time but trying to keep our heads down. And every six months or so the police would shut it down because it was full of kids under 18. They'd wait a bit until it was buzzing and happening, and then raid it again, and someone would take over the licence and rename it and reopen it a fortnight later. I think they knocked that one down too. No great loss to mankind.

One night in a bar I convinced a couple of girls that John was the stuntman who did the bungee jump in *GoldenEye*, the James Bond film, because one of his mates had worked on that film and had given him a crew jacket with the logo on it. Why John thought it was a good idea to go out for the night wearing a *GoldenEye* jacket I do not know. We did have a laugh, we used to go out in Fleetwood quite a bit, but later on, once I started to get known for my singing, especially after I'd done a couple of shows at the Marine Hall, I started to feel self-conscious around people. Because, certainly in places like The Queens or The Broadway or Planters, a small minority would take the piss. 'Give us a song!' Someone would do some opera impersonation, assuming that I was big-headed. Most people I've known in Fleetwood have always been really supportive, but there are some like that who have a pop, and it put me off going out around there really.

I was always trying to find a way out of Fleetwood, some sort of exit. Working at the Opera House inspired me to do something musical with my life. I'd watch all those people perform on stage, wishing I was there, wishing I could do it, I got a real buzz simply for being that close to live performance. I thought my drumming could have done something for me, could have maybe helped with my escape, but it didn't. Everything around there seemed so insular. There were three things you could have done – become a fisherman, got a job in a local industry, or joined the Army. A lot of my friends joined the Army, went in the forces to get away. I went to sixth-form college after I left school, when I was 16, but I lasted less than a year because I hardly went. I used to stay on the bus instead of going to college and do stage crew at the Grand Theatre. I'd started working there too. Same sort of thing I'd been doing at the Opera House, on a smaller scale. It was a smaller venue, I'd be working on theatre shows, pantomimes, comedy gigs, local drama things, just the odd little job to keep some money coming in, and it was a better alternative to college. Eventually I got a letter sent home because I wasn't turning up. So I re-sat my GCSEs, and that was it. Didn't pass them, other than art and graphics. I wanted to work, I wanted a job. I thought you learnt better by throwing yourself in at the deep end, getting stuck into something. I'd always had that work mentality. Mum and Dad told me I could get a Saturday job as soon as I was 11, and I couldn't wait. The day I turned 11 I went looking for work. I walked around town, went in to practically every shop, asking if they were taking anybody on for a Saturday job, and got lucky in this garage, C & H Coaches, who were looking for an MOT assistant. It was child labour basically – they were getting away with an extra pair of hands. But it was great for me because I learnt a lot about cars, about chassis and suspensions and exhausts and tyre treads. Dad used to tinker around with cars on the drive, do his own maintenance, so I'd already learnt quite a lot from him.

I loved the MOT job. I worked with a great fella called Terry Fleming. He always used to give me an extra bit of cash from the till. I couldn't believe it. I was only on £7 a week, and he'd always give me a tenner. A tenner! And I'd go to Kwik Save over the road and get these fantastic Cornish pasties for my lunch. I drove one of the coaches, backed it out onto Dock Street, 11-year-old coach driver, watch your backs. Peter McLoughlin worked there too, who was in that band Roadhouse I joined a few years later. He used to get up to all sorts of pranks. He was always getting fired but would turn up to work regardless the following day. He just refused to get fired, and the boss, Roy

Coupland, would let him carry on working. It was a sitcom. One Saturday morning Roy was pushing Peter's P45 under his flat door and Peter was there on the other side pushing it back saying, 'I'll be in on Monday, Roy!'

I eventually left and when I was 14 got a glass-collecting job at the pub in the North Euston Hotel, which was a lot more money but pretty grotty. Lots of dodgy fishermen in there, proper undesirables who I don't want to dredge up in any detail here. So I switched to the portering side, which was better, bit of catering. I worked at the Marine Hall for Fleetwood Council, as a caretaker and stage crew, waiter, silver service, bit of every- thing. I just liked working. Even on the summer holidays in Keswick when I was 15 I got a part-time job in the kitchens, as a commis chef for a fella called Donald Turnbull. I peeled spuds, chopped onions, all of that. He taught me how to do a wicked roast ham, I still do it the same way. And after my short stint at sixth-form college I started looking for something serious, a career. I traipsed around Blackpool asking businesses if they were taking on any apprentices, and finally landed a job at the TVR sports car factory in Bispham, just on the edge of town. It was an apprenticeship scheme, to learn the process of body mechanics. I think Dad would have loved to have been a mechanic, tinkering around with engines, rather than working in that chemical factory. I used to watch him fiddling with carburettors, tuning them up, and that was what I thought I could get into doing by way of this job. I wanted to be an engine mechanic, but I never really got the opportunity. They were sending me to college once a week to get a body mechanic qual- ification, so I was learning how to weld, how to use jigs, how to straighten cars that had been in accidents, panel-beats, paint- ing, spraying. I started off as a matte blacker, which was one of the lowest jobs in the factory, spraying the undersides of bonnets and boots and insides of doors, protecting the paint, then polishing. The work wasn't much fun at all. I was laid under cars all the time, spraying and spraying and spraying, but we had a laugh, as you have to do to stave off the insanity. Insanity from inanity. There was a guy called Gerbil, because his name was Kevin, like Roland Rat's mate. Another fella called Abdul, Absey. Cabbage, who looked like a Cabbage Patch Doll. And then there was Limper Jeff, who had a bad leg and hobbled around the place, nice guy. He was my boss to some extent, working with me in my corner.

It was a pretty safe working environment except for the time I nearly got blown to pieces. There was an engine room where they tested out engines. They'd mount an engine on a plinth, and the exhaust would fire into this steel box. There was a brick box around the steel box, and a huge chimney with an Xpelair fan to take the fumes out of the building, and we always used to know when they were testing these engines because it made an unholy racket. They used to *scream*, those engines. One day they fired one up when I was right next to the box. I was masking up a door, and they hadn't turned the Xpelair fan on, and within seconds of my brain registering that something sounded odd, the engine backfired and there was an almighty explosion. I was a foot away from this steel box, which burst like a balloon, bricks flew everywhere, and I got hit, thrown about 20ft. I grabbed the door I'd been working on to shield myself and bricks were smashing into it, one smacked my leg. The door was practically destroyed. One brick whacked a guy on the side of the face. There was a huge ball of fire, flames everywhere, incredible. And the foreman, Mike Penny, said, 'Come on, get back to work, don't piss around. Things like this happen, get off the floor.' Didn't seem to give a damn about anything except turning the cars out. Now you'd get sued. I'm sure I damaged my eyes, because I had to wear glasses for a bit after that. Nice work if you can get it.

Turning those cars out was clearly a big deal to Mike Penny, because when I started we were turning out 16 a week, and then they doubled it to 32 a week, but didn't increase the manpower. So inevitably the quality of the cars went down. They were powerful cars, 5-litre engines, 5000cc engines, proper racing cars. People would come from Manchester and London to buy them, because they looked beautiful, truly stunning. But ridiculously fast. Scarily fast. And it *was* scary, because I'd finish a car, and we'd see it get driven out of the factory by some 25-year-old kid whose parents had bought it for him. We'd think, 'That's gonna be back in here within a week, all smashed up,' and it was. The front end would have gone, and you could tell if he'd survived or not by the state of the driver's seat, if that was smashed up too – it was horrible.

I went out with a girl who worked in the offices there, my first serious girlfriend. Sally Sanders. She was a gorgeous girl, tall, blonde, blue eyes. She used to come round showing customers the factory floor and all that, and I would chat to her a little bit, and I asked her out to see me play in the Battle of the Bands I was doing with Whisky Train. Beautiful girl. But what a witch. Evil. Spoilt as anything; her parents really doted on her. *I* really doted on her. Whatever I did for her, she'd just take it and she'd want more. I bought her jewellery, spent all my wages on her. A year of that. And I didn't get anything in return.

She treated me so badly, she'd shout at me so much, she was so cruel. The last straw was when she started complaining about our Annie. I was singing in a competition at a cabaret club called Talk of the Coast, in a hotel in Blackpool, which I'll talk about in a bit, and she said, 'I really don't like your Annie, she's horrible.' Our Annie's salt of the earth, but she says what she wants and what she means – she doesn't hold back. She won't say anything to intentionally upset anybody, but she speaks her mind, which I think is really admirable. She's lovely like that. I can't remember what conversations she'd had with Sally, but when she said that, that was it. And I finally got over my infatuation with her.

She was the first torment in my life. It was awful – I couldn't cope with it all. When I finally finished with her she wrote me an 18-page letter, which I didn't even read, because Mum said, 'Don't read it, don't read it, because you'll just screw yourself over. You'll go round and round in circles, you'll be back to where you were, and she'll keep tormenting you.' And she was right. I started reading it. 'Dear Alf, I think it's really unfair that . . .' and I couldn't handle it. I threw it in the fire.

Chapter Eight

GETTING THE BUZZ

Regardless of my Lottie Dawson débâcle, it had at least given me a buzz, given me the bug. I wanted to sing, I wanted to get on stage again, I wanted to pull more girls. I looked around, found and joined a company called Thornton Cleveleys Operatic Society, just outside Fleetwood. We did *Oklahoma*, and the only move I had to do through the whole show – the dancing thing has been the bane of my existence, I could never dance – the only move I had to do was cartwheel over a haystack. And I tried, and I failed, landed flat on my face, in the middle of the show. Complete wipe-out, it was pathetic. But while I was with that lot the conductor, Frank Salter, asked me if I'd go down to the opera company he ran, Preston Opera, with a view to performing in their next production. So I sang to him round the piano and he said, 'You're a tenor. I want you to join the tenors' chorus.' That was the first time I'd really sung any opera, and certainly the first time I'd been told I was a tenor.

Preston Opera was an amateur company and I was only in the chorus, but it was my first real opera work and I really loved it. It was music I'd not sung before and it was a release, really fulfilling to realise I could sing like that. I did a couple of operas for them, *Il Trovatore* and *Carmen* in the Charter Theatre, and they were simple productions – you basically walked on stage, stood there and sang, walked off. But it was interesting to develop that side of my singing, because I did start to push myself a bit with it, the singing and the acting. Frank was giving me half-hour singing lessons every week, helping me out vocally. I was gonna do *Nabucco* for them too but I had to skip out on it because by then I'd started working on my apprenticeship at TVR. I was about 18, 19, wanted to work, wanted a career, and I thought I'd better stop with all the singing because it was taking up too much of my time and I wasn't really considering doing anything with it, it was just for kicks. So I packed it all in, the singing lessons, the opera company, and just worked in the garage, on my trade, to try to make a success of it, thinking that that was all I had in my life.

But something wasn't right. To a certain degree I'd really thrown myself into my work at TVR, but I quickly got sick of riding there on my bike every day, sick of the same trudging, sick of painting cars black. I was always singing around the factory, along to the radio and all that stuff, and they loved it. Sometimes, obviously, Mike Penny would hear me singing and he'd say, 'Stop fookin' larkin' around, Alfie. Get on with your fookin' work! Stop your fookin' yackin' and polish a few cars!'

'Sorry, Mike . . .'

And one morning I was cycling to work and I got this thing in my head where I felt, 'I need to do another show.' Something inside me had just ignited. I just needed to sing again, to perform. Anything. And the only person I knew who I could talk to about it was an old friend from the Thornton Cleveleys Operatic Society who I'd been in a show with. I spent the entire day thinking about it, and I sped round to her house on the way home and asked if she knew of any companies that were looking for people to join a show. She said, 'Yeah there's a company in Preston who are going to do a production of *West Side Story*. Why don't you come along next Friday night?' So I went along, borrowed my sister's Mini, and immediately joined the company as one of the Jets, I don't think they even heard me sing. All the lads there were complaining because they hadn't been given the opportunity to audition for the principal role, Tony, because, amazingly, it had already been given to this 40, 50-year-old fella who was the local star of amateur operatics. He was always the lead role of the company, so nobody else really had a look-in. But they were making such a noise about it, the musical director Philip Wooley said, 'OK, alright. Stop all your bickering, stop all your arguing, we're gonna hear you sing. Everyone, all the lads get in the back room now, let's sing "Maria". You all know it; bring your scores.' So we all went into this back room and started singing. I'd grown up listening to the Johnny Mathis version, seeing my sister Maria getting so elated by this beautiful song really irritated me. It haunts me now when I sing it live. She fancied herself as Stevie Nicks, Maria. She sang that song to death, that and 'The Power of Love' by Jennifer Rush: unbearable. So I knew 'Maria' all too well and started singing it with the rest of the lads.

There are two ways you can do the bit towards the end of that song. You can either keep repeating the name Maria over and over again, or just sing it once on a huge high note which takes you over the whole phrase. And that was the only version I knew, to hold that top note. So all the other lads were repeating the name Maria, Maria, Maria, over and over again, and I hit this note and held it. And when I came off the end of the note, everyone else had stopped singing. I didn't realise because I was so into the song, I'd just carried on. And when I stopped, the musical director asked everyone else to leave, and he asked me to stay and sing some more. And he offered me the role of Tony. The other guy had never even turned up to rehearsals, assuming the part was his. So I did it. We did a full week, seven shows, again in the Charter Theatre. It was wonderful, it gave me an amazing buzz, and that was really the performance that told me I could do something with this, despite my dismal attempt at an American accent. I was getting a lot of advice from members of the cast, people telling me I should audition for things, to go and study at the Royal Northern College of Music. That was the first time I started to seriously consider singing as a career.

At the same time I started drumming for the backup bands in the Blackpool working men's clubs. I wasn't drumming in rock bands any more, I'd had my fill of Whisky Train, but I lived over the road from a keyboard player who worked the club circuit, and I hooked up with him, had a go drumming with him in the Blackpool Central Working Men's Club. And it was hilarious, drumming for these 70-year-old women who thought they were Tina Turner. A lot less melodrama on that scene, none of the ridiculous teen-rock politics, and you got paid, £20, £30 a night – it was good money. In the big clubs you could get £40 for a session. Every night there'd be a singer, a keyboardist and someone like me on the drums. They'd give me the music but I couldn't read dots, so I'd ask them what the songs were and learnt them pretty quickly. Got them all locked in my memory. The amount of times I drummed along to 'Simply the Best' by Tina Turner. So many times. 'Please, not "Simply the Best" again.' Tom Jones's 'Delilah' was wheeled out the wrong side of regularly too.

And I started mixing it up, I wanted to try singing to those crowds too. So I entered a competition in Talk of the Coast – the night I had my upset with Sally Sanders about my sister – I sang some stuff from *West Side Story*, and Buddy Holly's 'True Love Ways', and I came second. It was a pretty major thing for me to perform in front of an audience like that. I'd never really played a Blackpool crowd, or even a club crowd. And it felt like I was doing something productive with my singing, taking it to another level, or somewhere at least, somewhere that might lead to something exciting. Talk of the Coast is a weekly cabaret night in the Viking Hotel, which back then was compèred by a fella called Georgie King, who ran a little agency with Stu Francis from *Crackerjack*, the kids' TV show from the '80s. Stu was a really nice guy, very funny. I couldn't believe I was hanging out with Stu Francis from *Crackerjack*. Crush a grape. 'I could rip a tissue. Wrestle with an Action Man.' Georgie was a dodgy bloke though, bit of a shark; you never knew if you could really trust him. But they put some good nights on, and they wanted to be my agents, not that they could do a heck of a lot. They did get me involved with a local folk band called The Houghton Weavers, who started in the 1970s and are still going. They were a good band, played some really cool songs, back in the '80s they had their own regional BBC TV series called *Sit Thi Deawn*. I'd go and see them every year at the Marine Hall with my family. They used to put on charity celebrity golf tournaments, which were fantastic, and also involved good piss-ups. Georgie and Stu got me a spot singing at their cabaret nights in the evenings. I did that a few times throughout the summer season, lots of fun.

Those Blackpool clubs could be pretty miserable. Backstage would be a little room with a mirror and a single 25-watt bulb swinging from the ceiling. Dodgy curtains that had been there

for decades, smoke-stained walls. Beer-splattered carpets.
Always smelt of beer. Stale beer. And you'd walk out onto the
stage and be engulfed by a cloud of cigarette smoke. Lights right
there in front of your face, really close to your head, so hot,
practically burning your face off, and the same old colours
every time, reds, blues, greens, tangerine-orange. Those clubs
had aspirations to be like Las Vegas, which was ambitious. It
was hardly Sinatra at The Sands. Old geezers with their dyed
comb-overs, satin shirts unbuttoned down to their belly
buttons, big fat beer-guts, medallions and sovereign rings, gold
chain bracelets. Little grannies with no teeth sitting in front of
you, smoking their cigarettes, just staring up at you, people
talking throughout. But I got good responses from those
crowds, and it was bloody good training for me because you
never knew what was going to happen while you were singing.
Fights breaking out, something landing on the stage, a glass
swinging past your head, drunks coming up to you on stage. I
did a bit of musical theatre, and because it was that sort of audience I did a lot of '60s ballads, Buddy Holly, couple of Elvis
songs, some Sinatra. And I was really enjoying that scene. I got
to meet loads of the old comedians and celebs. One night when
I was singing at Talk of the Coast, Little and Large were on the
bill, coming on after me. I finished singing and the audience
were going crazy, and those two were backstage, about to go on,
and as I walked off Eddie Large leant over to me and went,
'Alright, we fookin' heard ya. We fookin heard ya.' Nice.

I loved hanging out with the comics though. Billy Pearce was
around a lot. I met Frank Carson at a charity gig in Blackpool
– he lived around there. Great comedian and a sound fella,
really nice guy. He gave me probably the best bit of advice I've
ever been given in my career. He said, 'Alf, the only bit of advice
I can give you, son, is when you're not working, rehearse.

Whenever you're not working, practise, train, study, rehearse.' And I've always stuck to that, from that day on that's what I did. I found songs, I learnt the songs, I found the lyrics and I practised performing, practised my stagecraft. How to handle an audience, how to work the crowd. It was an incredible bit of advice and I respect him and thank him for that. I remembered that moment when he died a few months ago. Thanks, Frank.

These were old-school comedians – they'd done it all, the whole business. They'd done the shitty dives, played *The Royal Variety*, the lot. They'd been up there at the top and way down there at the bottom. They'd been cheered and booed. They knew every side of it, every bit of that world. And when you meet somebody like that all you can do is try to get as much information out of them as you can, or as much advice as you can. Frank was a comedian, not a singer, which is a completely different ball game, unless you find my singing hilarious, but it's still performing, you're still up there on stage working with an audience. And that's there in the way I handle myself on stage today, the way I involve the crowd, the jokes, the inclusion. I always try to have fun with it all. You know, you can take the man out of Blackpool ... So that was something I really respected him for, that little bit of advice. And that cabaret scene was a big deal to me. You could be up with a comedian who was on telly the night before in London, big names. I was in the factory spraying cars all day in my overalls, then putting on a shirt and trousers and getting up on stage and singing my heart out – it was a real escape. It gave me a taste of what I could turn my life into. Every time I sang I just got more and more thrilled and overwhelmed by the response I was getting from the audiences, and I wanted it more and more.

Chapter Nine

OFF TO THE OPERA

People in the TVR factory would talk to me about my singing, because I was always belting something out while I was working, much to Mike Penny's annoyance. Customers who'd seen me in *West Side Story* would ask if I was going to be in more shows. Workmates who'd gone to see it told me to stop wasting time spraying cars and go and take up the singing somehow. One customer, who had some involvement in the record industry, was very emphatic about it. He heard me singing as I was polishing his car, and we started talking. I told him what I'd been up to. He told me to get down to London and audition for a company called D'Oyly Carte, which didn't mean a lot to me. D'Oyly what? Who the hell's a D'Oyly Carte? 'If you want it to happen you've got to get out of here. That's where it's gonna work for you,' he said. I'd been looking out for local opportunities in the ad section of *The Stage and Television Today*, this trade paper that came out every Thursday, and as I was going through the job sections that week – cruises, auditions, male dancers for *Cats* – I saw this advertisement: 'D'Oyly Carte Opera Company,' as the customer had mentioned. They were holding open auditions in London for their next UK tour chorus members, and I went to the factory with it playing on my mind all day, spurred on to do something about it. I had a lot of time to think when I was working on that job. Your mind tends to wander when you're just squeezing a trigger and pointing paint for eight hours.

I was seeing a singing teacher in Chorley at the time, Laurence Newnes – had a few lessons over a few weeks to get a bit of help with my voice. I mentioned it to him and he'd seen the D'Oyly Carte ad too and said I should go for it, so it was like I was being pushed towards this thing from all angles. I mentioned it to my parents and they encouraged me. Dad said I had nothing to lose, the factory would still be there when I got back from London. So I went to the library to investigate the company. Richard D'Oyly Carte, a theatrical agent, started it in the late 19th century, producing Gilbert and Sullivan's operas. They all had some sort of falling out, over cash and contracts, which led to Gilbert and Sullivan splitting up at one point, but the company carried on producing their operas along with other productions, Strauss, Lehár, operetta really, and still do. What a world to get into! So I took the day off work to go down and give it a shot. It was my first time in London, other than a school trip for a couple of hours once, and walking out of Euston Station was overwhelming enough, let alone going through the door of this theatre as a 19-year-old kid. I walked through the foyer, peeked into the auditorium and heard all these singers warming up. I was wearing a lumberjack shirt, T-shirt, jeans, boots, and I looked around at all these suits and ball gowns, pristine singers, Crystal Kens and opera Barbies, and I thought, 'I don't fit in here. This is completely wrong.'

They called my name and I walked into this abyss, total darkness, other than the stage, which was lit up with one guy sitting at the piano looking utterly bored. I walked up onto the stage and they said, 'OK, what have you brought to sing?'

I said, '"You Are My Heart's Delight" by Franz Lehár.'

And they said, 'OK, that's great, please carry on,' and I tentatively handed my music to the pianist. I'd chosen that because I thought I'd better sing something other than *West Side Story*, what with it being a fancy opera company, and that was the only classical song I'd really worked on. It was one of Dad's favourites. I listened to it so many times growing up, and my brother Michael had the music so I'd learnt the words.

I was so nervous. But the pianist started playing, and the minute I started singing that song a fire started inside of me. I felt like my whole body had lit up. I thought, 'This is it. I've got this.' Confidence filled me, and I blasted it out just the way I always had in our living room in Fleetwood. When I finished there were a couple of seconds of awful silence, and then they clapped. They came down to me for a chat, asked me how old I was. I met John Owen Edwards, who was the Musical Director for the company and a great guy. Years later he introduced me to Neil, my manager, and conducted my first EMI album. And they said, 'We'll be in touch, see you very soon.' I danced out of that theatre, I was so happy. I knew I'd done a really good job. I felt great. I ran down the road, jumped on the train back, and it all went quiet for a bit after that. I went back to my job at the garage, and waited. And I had a phone call asking me to come back for a second audition, and I did the song again, along with some *West Side Story*. It was much less formal, but it was in a church and they were all sat in pews so I could actually see them this time, which made it a little more nerve-racking. They played through scales to see how high I could sing, I went up to a top C. They asked me if I was a member of Equity. I said, 'No I'm a mechanic, I work in a car factory.' They asked if I was willing to give up my job to go with them on tour. I said I'd love to and they said they could wangle an Equity membership for me, and two days later they called: 'We'd like to offer you a position in the chorus for the D'Oyly Carte's next UK tour.' I nearly fainted. It was the most wonderful feeling. I'd be on £300 a week, which tripled my car factory wages, and the chance to be on the road for a year, performing every night on stage . . . I couldn't believe it. I came off the phone, walked into the living room, and Mum and Dad said, 'Well? What was it?' And I said, 'They've, um . . . I'm in! I'm in! They've offered me a job!' Mum was thrilled, and Dad's face . . . well I'd never seen him so happy – he was so elated. Best I ever saw him. He just cried and cried and they gave me a big old hug.

The excitement of going in to work the following day was electric. 'Mike – there's my week's notice. I'm leaving. I'm going off to be an opera singer.'

He said, 'An opera singer! You're crazy. What do you wanna do that for, you fookin' idiot. You're on a good wage, you could go far here.'

I said, 'I don't wanna do it Mike, I wanna be a singer.'

And he said, 'I think you're daft. But good luck anyway, all the best.'

I went back there for an album promotion a few years ago, and he said, 'Still as ugly as ever, you fooker!'

I went, 'Cheers man, you haven't changed have you, ya bastard!'

When I finished my job I had a little time to kill, and I went back to do some stage crew work at the Grand Theatre in Blackpool, a few shows, and really enjoyed it because I was buzzing so much, knowing that I was going to be joining this opera company in September to hit the road, to perform in *Die Fledermaus* and *HMS Pinafore*. I spent the whole summer doing the pantomimes, working on the shows that were coming in and out of the theatre, rigging up the sets, taking them down, bringing on the scenery, taking it off. I worked with Steve Williams, lovely fella – he's the house manager there now. We had to carry this revolving carousel onto the stage during the pantomime and had to dress accordingly, red and yellow dungarees. We had to walk on, put it down and walk off, in a particularly sprightly manner. But the part got bigger and bigger and bigger, and before we knew it we were waltzing on and off with this thing, grabbing props – it was wicked, we became part of the show. I was having a laugh and I was so happy about D'Oyly Carte, but sweating it over what I had to do. I was nervous about this adventure I was going on, and whenever I had a night off I'd play the music I was supposed to be learning for the shows, study, learn, rehearse. Just like Frank Carson said. I was getting each show in my head as much as I could, picking out the tenor line, which I couldn't find very well because I couldn't read music. A lot of the tenor stuff is predominantly around the melody anyway. You end up singing a lot of that, I figured it out.

Mum and Dad drove me down to Birmingham, where we'd be doing five weeks rehearsal before going on tour. My B&B was run by an old and very theatrical lady called Marlene Mountain, who ploughed on the make-up like crazy, bright blue mascara, ginger-blonde hair she dyed herself, all of that. She had this photo of herself dressed as a 1950s dancer with a leotard on, feathers, the works, although she was never actually a performer; she'd just wanted to be one. She was a lovely lady, very sweet, but so nosy. She'd walk into your room when you were getting changed, coming out of the shower, didn't give you any privacy at all – she'd just appear. Incredibly intrusive. There were half a dozen of us staying at that place, all D'Oyly Carte people; we'd pretty much booked up the whole house, and she appointed herself as a mother to us all. She wanted to take care of us just as much as she wanted to make sure we weren't up to any funny business, you couldn't bring girls back there; you had to be more creative. I soon had enough of old Marlene's nosiness, so moved in to a house with a couple of fellas from the chorus.

Rehearsals were a lot of fun – it was great working with the dance choreographer, Lindsay Dolan, who'd done a lot of big opera work, Royal Opera, ENO. I still couldn't dance at all, and getting through that was tricky. I had to learn these tap routines because I was doing a sailor's dance with a mop at the beginning of the show and I had it driven into me, tap tap tap. Every single night I was back at my digs practising these bloody tap steps, frustrating myself, trying my best to do it properly, to get it in me.

The first show was a bit of a disaster, and it was all my fault. *HMS Pinafore* at the Alexandra Theatre, Birmingham. We were sailors and all had kitbags over our shoulders and had to throw them into the wings, get our mops, and come back on stage for a tap dance routine. There was a cable on the floor which had a control box at the end of it that brought this enormous curtain down. I threw my bag, it caught the cable, the control box fell off the side and hit the floor, triggered the button and the curtain came in. I reached for my mop and it belted me, landed right on top of me, knocked me for six, knocked me over. Another of the sailors got caught on the wrong side of the curtain too, and poor Carl Donohue was left on his own in front of the curtain with his mop, doing a solo tap dance, looking around sheepishly for the rest of us. I was laid flat on my back underneath the curtain. That was the start of my opera career.

Chapter Ten

LEARNING THE RULES, BREAKING THE RULES

We somehow managed to get the show back on track that night and it was a minor triumph. And D'Oyly Carte was really exciting, I loved every minute. Eight shows a week, different towns each week, lots of B&Bs. It was a new world for me, being on the road, meeting lots of girlies, getting to see a lot of the country. It was a lot of fun, I went to Scotland for the first time, played Edinburgh, sung in a proper Irish bar in Belfast, and I had my 21st birthday on the road in Darlington, late night in the pub. Mum and Dad came up to see me, it was the first professional show they'd seen me in – it was fantastic to share that with them.

I got really close with the French horn player, Bob, who unfortunately had a bit of a drinking problem. Sometimes he'd turn up to the show completely plastered. The great thing about D'Oyly Carte though is they really give people a chance, give them understanding, and they rode that out with him. Me and Bob used to get up to all sorts of nonsense – we swam in the sea in the middle of the night in Llandudno, carried some of the girls in, your bog standard horseplay. I remember one moment in the show where all the sailors had to do press-ups, and I looked up and Bob was doing press-ups in the stalls – had me in stitches. We hung out a lot; he used to come over and stop at my house; we partied out in Blackpool. I lost him late one night; he disappeared with this girl, and when I got back home he was knelt at my front door with his hands through the letterbox, letting the dog lick his hands to keep them warm – he didn't want to disturb anybody. Mum came down, 'Come on in, Bob.' The next Christmas, he got hit by a car in Glasgow, and died. I got a phone call one night from his girlfriend – she told me. Hell of a shock.

The first time something like that had happened to me was when I was at school. I was seven. Dominic Taft, who was one of my cousins actually, always joking around, got knocked off his bike going home from school. I was sat at the back field with him that day – it was a beautiful hot summer's day, we were having our lessons outside. And I came to school the following morning and we were all told he'd been knocked off his bike on his way home from school and was killed. Then there was a guy at school called John; it was the first time I'd really heard of cancer. He had to have his legs amputated. He went onto crutches, and he became really angry, and he died not long afterwards. And there was Steve Gillespie. I got really friendly with Steve when I was on that Outward Bound course, lovely Welsh fella, we stayed in touch after. He got involved with the Army, and they sent people on Outward Bound courses, as retreats. He was on his way back to his camp one day and got hit by a car and died. All these kids getting hit by cars. Those experiences hardened me up a bit I think, certainly gave me new perspectives. Things like that prepare you for the rest of your life, in their own way. So later when Dad died, as much as it hurt, I think I was more equipped to deal with it than I might have been.

And Bob was a great guy – the drinking was such a shame. The thing about the D'Oyly Carte giving him a chance, that was pretty special I think. I was fairly confident on that tour because I'd done a lot of rehearsal, but I did feel a bit like I was kidding myself that I was an opera singer, deluding myself that I could do it, because I hadn't trained, I didn't have the qualifications, I didn't feel legitimate. But if you had the ability to sing, the D'Oyly Carte gave you the opportunity regardless, and that's priceless. They did a lot for me. My first ever recording was with them, the D'Oyly Carte recording of *Die Fledermaus* – we did it in Abbey Road. I had one line to sing, but it's there, on CD. I fell in love with recording there and then. I loved the process of making a record – it made me want to make my own ones, absolutely. And, indirectly, the D'Oyly Carte led me to the Royal College of Music, where I would spend my next three years. For better or worse.

The lead singer in *Die Fledermaus*, David Fielding, playing Eisenstein, was a bit of a local celebrity in Norwich, and he put on a master class when we played the Theatre Royal there, got some local singers in and trained them through a song. One of them pulled out and David asked me if I wanted to step in, and again I sang Lehár's 'You Are My Heart's Delight', still the only song I could properly do as a solo. There were three other singers on stage, and an audience, and each time one of us did our bit David would talk us through the song, give us some tips, coach us through it, and he'd sing it through. It was really my first time standing on a stage on my own with an audience and I'd never really done a master class, so I was pretty nervous. It's quite a thing to stand on a stage in front of people and get picked apart by someone else on what you're doing wrong. Not that he was aggressive about it – it was all very constructive. I've certainly been involved in some ugly master classes. Royal College of Music and the Royal Opera House, they take no prisoners. I've seen young singers ripped into at those places, no mercy. But it's part of the training, part of the classical training. You've got to be told what you're doing wrong for it to be right.

Bear with me while I introduce the enormous number of people I was passed along to get a place at the Royal College of Music. Sitting in the audience at the master class that night in Norwich was a fella called Donnie Sanderson. Well his name's Gordon, but everyone called him Donnie. Great baritone, worked at the Royal Opera House a lot. He came up to me afterwards, said he saw potential in my voice and offered to help out, and we met up one afternoon and he gave me some coaching. He suggested I go to sing for a friend of his in London, Paul Griffiths, who was one of the head coaches at the Royal Opera House, and Gordon took me through 'Che Gelida Manina' from *La Bohème* – it was the first aria I ever really studied. I went down to London to meet Paul Griffiths, and I couldn't believe I was in the Royal Opera House, absolutely stunning building. I'd been spraying cars in Bispham a few months earlier. Paul Griffiths took me over the road to the rehearsal studios, the coaching rooms, and I sang the aria for him. He told me to wait a minute and he went and brought over a chap called Richard Van Allan, who ran the National Opera Studio, and after Richard heard me sing he said I should study, to go through the training I didn't have, and asked me to come back a week later to sing for James Lockhart, who was running the opera school at the Royal College of Music. I sang for him, and he said, 'I think there's a place for you here at the Royal College of Music, and I think you should consider it. But you'll have to have a singing teacher.' To study on the vocal course, you needed to have a personal teacher. And James introduced me to Neil Mackie, who was Head of Vocals, Head of Vocal Studies as well – James said he would be the best person for me.

I then had an official audition in front of Neil Mackie and all the heads of music, the director, the head of the opera department. I sang my socks off, and then one of them said, 'Could you show me your musicality? Could you clap this rhythm?' and he handed me a piece of paper with notes on, obviously in a rhythmical pattern, and he said, 'Try and clap that.'

I said, 'I'm sorry mate, I really don't know where to begin, I can't.'

He said, 'Well just have a look at it and try.'

And I just clapped anything. It was completely wrong. I didn't know what I was doing. I couldn't read rhythms, I couldn't read music, couldn't do any of that. I can now! But I didn't then, and I felt like a right idiot, because there I was standing in the Royal College of Music with all these teachers, not being able to read music. But they obviously liked my singing enough to get through the rest of it, because I was offered a place. Later, studying there, I learnt how to read scores, I learnt how to read music, to know the note values, the rhythms, to clap rhythms, play the melody on the piano, all of that. That's what you go to college for in a sense, but a lot of people turn up knowing that already, and I just hadn't had that education. And that frustrated me, because I would have loved the opportunity to have learnt music earlier. I wish I'd had it.

At that point I learnt everything by ear. I still do that now, I really do, despite knowing how to do the rest. Classical music is a bit trickier, because you can easily mishear something and make a mistake musically. You can slightly misread a rhythm or a note value, or . . . not so much the pitch of a note because you should be able to hear that already, but you can be mistaken on rhythm if you're just learning it by ear. Whereas if you learn pop music by ear you learn the basic tune and then you can play around with it and make it your own. I was surprised when I went to the first rehearsals of *Les Misérables* for my run last year, I couldn't believe the amount of people that were actually having to have their music notebashed for them. They were there with tape recorders to record what lines they had to sing, but it's such a different world. In opera, when you turn up for the first day of rehearsals, you're supposed to know all your notes, all your music. You don't have to be off-score particularly, but it does help if you can be.

Still, there's a lot to be said for learning something by ear and making it your own. A year or so ago I met Fran Healy from Travis at a concert we were both singing at, and I was chatting to him about songwriting, which I'd really started getting a buzz for. I said, 'You know what, mate, I would love to be able to learn the guitar so I could just sit down and play.'

And he said, 'If I can give you any advice about songwriting – the less you can learn the instrument, the better for the songwriting it is. If you start learning hundreds and thousands of chords it can get confusing. The best songs are simple, two or three chords. And if you make a mistake, that takes you down another little avenue. It's like map reading. Sometimes you don't want to memorise your journey on a map because you're ignoring all the little side streets. If you struggle to find your way to where you wanna be a bit randomly, that's the most interesting way forward. And it's exactly the same when writing a song.' Which is a great point. Having to learn everything by ear in my early years was of great benefit, I think. And to be honest that way of learning is more emotional than learning technically, because you depend on your natural instinct with the music, rather than your technical skills. If you know the rules, you stick by them. If you don't know the rules, you're breaking them all the time.

Often when I'm singing I'm focusing much more on the acting side and the words and the text, rather than the actual notation. Even when I was doing *Les Misérables* I would think of what I was saying, the character and the mood and the emotion, rather than the notation, and that's exactly what Claude-Michel Schönberg, the composer, taught me to do. He said, 'Imagine this being like really good jazz, play around with the rhythms, play around with the notes, make it your own.' And I believe that's what many of the big classical composers, if they were around today, would say to you about their scores. Make it your own. The score's a guideline. Claude-Michel played piano on 'Bring Him Home' for a couple of concerts on my last tour and he played it very differently, and beautifully.

I sang on a floating stage at the Henley Festival in 2008. That was a great day. First of all because the rain was battering down and Natasha Marsh, who was also singing, had to wear these bright pink wellies with her evening dress. But also because I got to sing with Courtney Pine, which was incredible. He accompanied me on a Neapolitan song. The opportunity to play with him was a real step towards what I'd been trying to achieve, to work with musicians who play instinctively without having to have it spelt out for them. People who make you work with them rather than against them. When you're in a classical situation you have a structure, and that keeps you all together. But when you're with somebody who improvises around the song and what you're doing, it gives you so much more freedom to embellish and to extend, to try new and different things. It's a wonderful gift, and working with Courtney gave me that experience. We were still kind of constrained by the orchestra, but Courtney managed to open it up and set it free. Blew everybody's minds. What a player, and what a gent.

So I had all that to master, years of studying and learning, getting it all down, learning all the rules so I'd know how to break them. And getting a place at the Royal College was thrilling, but because my D'Oyly Carte tour was coming to an end, I'd also auditioned for *Phantom* in the West End, to play Raoul, and they'd liked me and sent me a script, they wanted to see me again. That was a fantastic opportunity, and I thought that could be it, I'd be working, I'd be a singer. But then I was offered my place at college, and I had to weigh it up. And ultimately I really did want to study. I wanted to be confident, I wanted to have the skills, I wanted to be legitimate. Then I could explore. So I decided on college, and I'm really glad I did.

However. Neil Mackie said he wanted to give me options, and sent me to see another teacher, Edward Brooks, before I decided on him. And I liked Edward Brooks. He seemed more personal, and made me feel more confident about my singing. A very different teaching approach. Edward made me open up my voice, he made me feel like I could sing better. So I chose him as my teacher. And I'm not sure exactly what behind the scenes shenanigans were going on, but there was some sort of hostility between him and James Lockhart, and James apparently put his foot down and said I had to go with Neil Mackie. And Neil asked me to do so, even though he'd sent me to try with someone else. So I went with Neil, because I wanted to get the place. It was very, very strange. My very first taste of opera politics. Ha. That was nothing.

Chapter Eleven

THE WEST LONDON
KARAOKE MAFIA

It's amazing how empowered people feel when they're handing out money for tuition. I won a few scholarships for the Royal College, from some really sweet, supportive folk, but not everyone who gives scholarships is a kindly benefactor, as charitable as they may be. Early on I went to sing for Peter Moores, who was chairman of Littlewoods Pools and has given a lot of people opportunities in the opera world. He was real cocky, thought his money spoke. When I auditioned for him, he said, 'What's wrong with your fingers?'

I said, 'It's this thing called clubbing.' Just slightly thicker fingers.

He said, 'Well it's horrible, I'll pay for an operation for you.'

I said, 'I don't want you to.'

Then he said, 'Your name, Boe, it doesn't work, you're gonna have to change it. It sounds weird.'

Mum and Dad were there waiting for me, and at one point Mum just flew at him, because he said, 'We all know Alf's a bit silly, a bit simple.' She went crazy, nearly hit him. She floored him with that crazy Irish temper she's got, he was practically on his knees apologising.

He offered me a scholarship but said, 'I'll only give you the money if you go to the Royal Northern College of Music.'

I said, 'I don't wanna go to the Royal Northern. I've got a place at the Royal College. Why would I want to change already?'

He said, 'Well that's the only way you're gonna get the money.'

I said, 'I don't want your money then.'

I won't humour people just because they've got money. As I said though, there were some very supportive people who helped me out, no strings. Doreen Lofthouse married into the Fleetwood family who'd founded Fisherman's Friend in the 19th century. She turned it into a global business. She's done a lot for Fleetwood: she donated a statue of Eros to one of the roundabouts – it was up for nearly a week before someone nicked the arrow. She helped me out. And there was a wonderful fella called Martin Harris. I think he was a patron of the college. He saw me in a concert and paid for all of my education there, all my tuition fees. I didn't even know about it till later. I met him a couple of times. He was an absolutely lovely man, and I wondered who he was until my singing teacher said, 'That's the guy who's paying your tuition.' So humble, and so generous. He died while I was at college, bless him.

I had time to kill that summer between D'Oyly Carte and Royal College, so I got some work at Fleetwood Freeport, an open-air shopping centre on the waterfront, running kids' rides, go-karts and all that. I got really fit because some of the go-karts wouldn't work, so I'd have to put the kids in them and run around the track pushing them, yelling at the kids to steer left and right. I had to dress up as a pirate once, big foam head

Mum and Dad
get married.
Fleetwood,
March 31, 1954.

My manager Neil and I with
our first cars. I've always loved
my cars.

Me and Dad in the summer house we built together in the back garden. Our family would sit out there all night eating dinner and hanging out, it was wonderful.

Me and most of the Boe clan on holiday in Keswick, the Lake District. We went there every summer for years and years – I'm very fond of Keswick.

That's me hanging from our garden swing, our neighbour Colin demonstrating the correct usage. I used to sit on that swing and wait for Dad to come home from work.

As Joseph in the nativity play, four years old. 'Yes, I said he would be born in a stable,' was my one line, which I just about got right. Don't worry by the way, that was a plastic baby.

Me, aged nine, as Paddington Bear at the Fleetwood carnival. Despite being hidden inside that fur head you can still kind of tell how uncomfortable I was. Hot? You have no idea.

Ah, my first Guinness. At my sister Anne's wedding. I was 11 – she gave me a quarter pint with lemonade. I loved it!

On the drums in my first band! Michael Gawne there on guitar – he's a great guitarist, still plays in Fleetwood.

With Mum at my Royal College of Music graduation, 1997.

On my beloved white drumkit that Dad bought me. Couple of hired hands posing with me on the brass there.

ging Neapolitan songs with a busking band in azza San Marco, Venice 1998. I'd st Mum and my brother Michael d got up to sing to attract their attention.

Singing at Castle Howard, August 1997, during my Royal College days.

With baritone Sam McElroy, Scottish Opera Go Round, 1999. Fantastic tour.

Performing in *Don Giovanni*
Royal College of Music, 1997.

Clockwise from top left: Me, my
brother John, Mum, Sarah's Mum,
Sarah. Christmas 2005 in Fleetwood.
Sarah and I had been in Strasbourg,
Sarah had a haircut she didn't like
and kept going to get it fixed until
there wasn't much left. I thought it
looked cute.

Dad and me at home in Fleetwood, 1994.

In *Kismet* at the London Coliseum, 2007. The horror.

Singing 'Stranger In Paradise' on *Parkinson*, London 2007.

In *La Traviata* at the Millenium Centre, Cardiff, 2009. I'd bulked up to 14 stone as I had to spend quite some time topless.

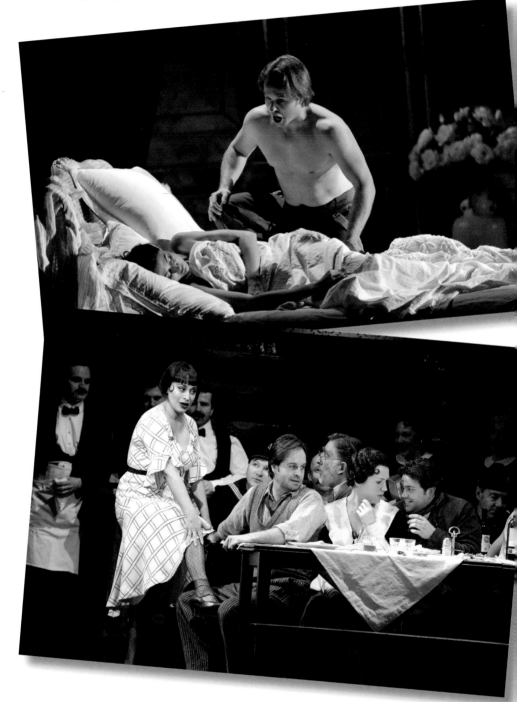

As Rodolfo in Jonathan Miller's *La Bohème*, London Coliseum, 2009, one of four *Bohème* productions I've performed in.

thing, greeting the kids at the door. Most of them were pretty scared unfortunately. And then off I went, rented a car and drove down to my halls of residence in Shepherd's Bush. It was a really exciting time, a new beginning, going to college in London, moving into these halls with lots of pretty musician girls. It was awesome.

The Royal College of Music looks like Dracula's castle. On our first day all the freshers were brought into the main hall, and Janet Ritterman, the director of the college, sat us down and said: 'You are all in an establishment of fine art. It is an honour to hold the title of Royal College of Music student. You should all be proud of where you are and of what you are going to achieve here.' I quickly found home at the college bar. Big long-haired hippie barman, Kerry, real salt of the earth. You could go in and tell him all your troubles. I loved hanging out in that bar. We'd drink a lot, play pool, 40p a game. We'd collect 20 pences all week long so we could play pool, and I was getting pretty good at it. That first year was really solid, there were real characters. People said later on, rose-tinted or otherwise, that that was the last year the Royal College of Music had such an eclectic crowd, that it got all a bit public school after that. But when I was there, there were certainly people from all different walks of life – it was a really crazy mix. I made some real strong friendships pretty quickly – I'm still friends with some of them. Tim Gunnell's a percussionist in my touring orchestra now, he was there with me. I had a lot of girlfriends too, or one night stands at least. I was part of a group of postgraduate boys who decided to get through as many freshers as we could in that first week. I think I clocked up six or seven. Shocking behaviour. Poor girls. I went to the summer ball with five dates, which I wouldn't advise anybody to do – it wasn't particularly smart. I told three of them I'd meet them there because I thought there was a chance only one would come through. I wasn't fussy. And they all came. They were all in different parts of the place so I just worked my way around these five girls – one was in one room, one in another, a couple in the ballroom. I was playing them off each other all night. 'Let me go and get us some drinks,' and I'd go off and see another one. 'Let me go and get some drinks . . .'

The Royal College world that Janet Ritterman tried to drum into us on the first day didn't come naturally to me. I never felt like I could fit into that. I didn't fit into it. But I didn't let it intimidate me. I just tried to be myself, which I've tried to do throughout my career. I worked incredibly hard there, always did well at my exams – distinctions and firsts. I chose to focus on opera, so from my postgraduate course, which would take me through my first two years, I'd move on to an opera course for another two. They actually devised a vocal course for me, a lot of which was learning languages, learning to sing in the languages, learning different styles of music, oratorio, the lead songs, opera, early music. I had tons of coaching, movement classes, whatever was needed to turn you into a good stage performer. I had to learn music overnight because I was so behind everyone else. I studied languages like mad: Italian, French, German, Russian. Although it was more about learning how they were structured as opposed to having to speak them fluently, I had to understand how they worked. I had to learn repertoire. My locker was piled high with music books. I've got a bad back now because my bag was full of music books all the time. Had to learn Strauss, Schubert, Handel. Coaching lessons, acting lessons, technical lessons. Learning about music, about performance, composition, how composers wrote, why they wrote what they wrote, what influenced them. I found it fascinating. I loved the fact that I was acquiring all this knowledge.

But the big thing for me was learning how to read music and rhythm, really understanding it, learning how to conduct time signatures, which you have to have an understanding of in order to understand rhythm, and where the notes slot in in that time signature. I'd mark down all the beats on my paper with a line where all the beats were, and I'd memorise what came in-between those beats. Then I'd play around with the rhythms, which used to really annoy some of my teachers, because it's not to the book, you're improvising, and with classical music you're supposed to be precise.

It was tough work. A lot of people at college had breakdowns, fell apart because of the amount of pressure. I walked into the canteen one day and they were filming a *South Bank Show* documentary, cameras everywhere, and Melvyn Bragg was there interviewing this really wired guy who was running around the place. And this guy came up to me and said, 'Wow, canteen food, ooh look at that, it's a mystery, man, it's crazy!' He threw his arms around me. 'Music's amazing, it's a wonderful thing!' And it was David Helfgott, the Australian pianist. He won a scholarship to the Royal College in the late 1960s and had a nervous breakdown of sorts, partly because of the pressure he was under, although he was already unstable, I think, and had issues with his family. They made that great film *Shine* about it, with Geoffrey Rush. He was studying Rachmaninoff's Third Concerto, and collapsed on stage while he was playing it, during his final. When I met him there he did a recital, and while he was playing, all of a sudden, sat there in the concert hall, sat in the exact same position that he was in when he had his nervous breakdown, he stopped, and stood up, and he just looked at the piano. He said: 'I like that! I like that a lot!' And he sat down and carried on playing. I thought, that guy is so focused on his music, his art, he wanted to recognise and acknowledge something that made him feel that he was in a different world. He acknowledged the piece of music. And I thought, that's it, that's what live music is about. There's no regime or routine to your performance, you can do whatever you want, make it your own. He made that night his own. That really inspired and influenced me. If I start a song and I'm not ready to sing it . . . it happened a few times on my last tour, I'd be enjoying the orchestra's intro so much I'd get them to play it again. It creates something new, brings something pre-determined to life.

Socially, I wasn't one of the singers at college. I've never been like that. There was always a specific table at college that was just for the singers, and I never sat with them. There were singers I got on with, but I never went out of my way to be with them. I hung out with the brass players and violinists. There was, however, karaoke. When I came back from Fleetwood one Sunday evening, everybody was standing outside halls of residence, 'Alfie, Alfie, come round to The Eagle, they've got karaoke on, come along and sing.' I was a bit depressed coming back to London, I was missing home a bit, so I thought it would get my mind off it. And we went to The Eagle round the corner and I did 'New York, New York' and 'He Ain't Heavy, He's My Brother'. I didn't even realise it was a competition, but it turned out they were trying to find the pub representative for the West London Karaoke Championship, and I won. £500, which we all quickly blew on beer. So before I knew it I was representing Shepherd's Bush's Eagle pub in the West London Karaoke Championship. Then we did the semi-final and I won that, through to the final, which was in the Goldhawk pub on Goldhawk Road.

Me and a couple of lads from college got there early, walked in and there was a fella in there, bit of a gangster – it was a real old London pub. He came up to me and said, 'Our representative is in the final. Representing this pub. Our pub. You better be careful, because if you win, lad, you won't be able to use your legs to walk out of here.' For crying out loud. I just wanted to sing a song. Nobody had told me about the karaoke mafia. So I was hoping somebody else from college might turn up, but they didn't. The competition started and a few other people got up and sang, and then it was, 'Right ladies and gentlemen, it's time for our finalists to come on board, here we go, the West London Karaoke Championships nineteen ninety-five.' Some guy got up and did his turn, and then this Goldhawk girl got up to sing. And just as she did, 50 or 60 people from the Royal College of Music walked in wearing Royal College T-shirts, all beered up, all wired, holding banners saying 'Go Alfie!' And this guy looked over and his eyes just said, 'Bloody hell,' he just sank. And I got up and I sang 'Suspicious Minds', and 'He Ain't Heavy', and 'New York, New York'. And I won, and everybody went absolutely mental. What a night.

I had a lot of good times at college, and a lot of really shitty ones. My second year was tough. I'd moved out of college halls and into a flat in Gloucester Road with three other students. These guys were real druggies, massive pot smokers, acid, every-thing, and I was never really into it. I'd had the odd spliff but because I was a singer I couldn't afford to do anything heavy, even if I'd wanted to. Two of them had been left a lot of money by their grandparents, and they basically threw it away on that stuff. One spent £150,000 in a year on drugs – he was just off his head. He missed his final recital three times because he was stoned. I went out on the town with him one night and we drank from 11am till 2am. In one bar two guys offered us into the toilets for a fight because we were eyeing up their girlfriends. They were two massive big bruisers, so we legged it. I couldn't find him at one point; he'd ended up getting into a fight with a

busker in Leicester Square who gave him a black eye, cut all his
face. So much for being part of a fine art establishment.

I was running out of money, I didn't have any work, my rent
scholarships had run out, travel and food were becoming a
problem. I was living on overdrafts because I refused to get
student loans, I never went in for that – something Mum had
always drilled into us: never get yourself in debt. I didn't want
to leave college with £100,000 in student loans to pay off. So I
never did it, I tried to make my own way and deal with the over-
draft situation.

I couldn't handle living in that flat, in that spliff fug, although
I did have one somewhat bizarre experience myself. Some time
around then I did a gig in Amsterdam. I had sung for an agency
called Askonas Holt, who later represented me, but at this time
they were following my progress through college, sort of looking out for me in an unofficial capacity. And they got me this
gig in Amsterdam, my first time there, working with a German
guy called Thomas Quasthoff, who's a lovely man and an amazing baritone, in the Concertgebouw, stunning old concert hall.
I had the day free so I went into a coffee shop, went down to the
cellar to play some pool, I was really into pool. People were
smoking away and I was playing with them, hanging out, and I
had some coffee and some cake and cookies. I didn't know they
were hash cakes and hash cookies, I'd never been to Amsterdam
before. I soon knew. As soon as I walked outside it hit me. It felt
like it took two days to walk over a bridge. I got back to my hotel
and got changed for my performance; getting dressed felt like
hours. I somehow snapped out of it enough to do the gig, inevitably ultra-relaxed, but I'd been nervous anyway, and was now
extra paranoid that the crowd didn't like my singing. I was
thinking, 'They hate me, they hate me, they hate me.' I don't
know how I pulled it off, but I did, it went well. We went straight

to dinner afterwards and I was still buzzing, still stoned, still paranoid, and Thomas came up to me to say goodbye and give me a hug just at the moment I got up to go to the bathroom. Thomas is a thalidomide sufferer, he's 4ft 4in. So as he threw his arms around me, I stood up and inadvertently lifted him off the floor. I was stood there with him hanging around my neck and I was thinking, 'What's happening?! What's going on?!'

But that was Amsterdam. I couldn't live in that haze of second-hand smoke every night at college. Every single evening I'd come back and they'd be sat around the table and I'd be thinking, 'Please, please, please don't start smoking.' But it would only be a matter of time before the cigarette papers came out and they'd start rolling joints. And at 11pm the beers would come out, drugs would be flowing, dealers would be knocking on the door at 4am demanding money . . . I couldn't deal with it. So one night I said, 'I'm sorry fellas, I've got to move out,' and I just left there and then, moved in with a mate of mine for a few nights who lived round the corner. But although I'd escaped the drug pit, he and his lot were into porn. Lots of it. Porno movies all over the place. And that was just miserable. I didn't know what was worse, that or sitting down every night with the acid-swallowers. I was really depressed, I just felt sick. I had no money coming in, was working myself to death at college, my living situation was dire. It really was not a positive time. And I just walked out. I wanted to be on my own. So I went and slept on a bench in Hyde Park for a few nights. It wasn't quite what I'd envisaged for my life at the Royal College of Music, but at the time, it seemed like my best option.

Chapter Twelve

CLIMBING OUT OF THE HOLE

My temporary homelessness didn't seem all that dramatic to me, though that may speak volumes about my perspective back then. It wasn't a great time in my life by any means, but it was the middle of the summer, it didn't get dark till late. I could leave a lot of my stuff in my locker at college and spend my evenings drinking in the bar till 11, or later if they extended it. Then just after midnight they'd lock the doors and I'd go over the road to the park with my sleeping bag, settle down on a bench and attach my rucksack to my ankle to stop people trying to nick off with it. Had to hide from the wardens if I saw them. And in the mornings I'd go back into college as soon as the doors opened at 9am, shower, have breakfast, shave and have my first lesson at 10. I could wash my clothes there too – the wardrobe department had laundry facilities. I spent a lot of time in that wardrobe department. There was an element of fun to it, being able to party and just collapse on a bench at the end of the night. A few of us used to drink in the park anyway. I hardly had any money and preferred to spend what little I had on food and drink rather than rent, it seemed to make more sense when there was a bench available for free.

I was being really stubborn about work – I wanted to be a singer, and with the occasional gig coming in like the Amsterdam thing, I thought I should be able to make a living doing that, which in retrospect I clearly couldn't. Getting some other job wasn't an alternative, at least the way I saw it. But it was a stupid thing to be doing. Mum went absolutely crazy when she found out. Somebody from college found me there and sent me to a counsellor, who sent me to a hostel on Cromwell Road. Mum was really upset that I hadn't told her, and I felt really disappointed with myself. I wasn't trying to be a martyr. I didn't think much of it at all really. I was just doing it, and it was fine.

I was drinking a lot. Drink has always been a bit of a problem for me, or at least it was. I used to have massive binges from time to time. It frightens me now to think of it. I got myself into some states in my life where I really scared myself. I went to Ronnie Scott's one night and drank myself stupid, threw up all over myself in the back of a cab, woke up face down on the floor in the college halls, really scared, really freaked out about the state I'd got myself into. I didn't want to be like that. Just the other night I was in a bar and somebody was buying Jägermeisters and asked me to have one, and I didn't. I don't touch that sort of stuff, I can't do it any more. I shook it in America when I was trying to get my career on track, and I've never really gone back to any of that.

Once I moved into the hostel I started to see sense. It was a Catholic hostel run by a Catholic priest and I had a lot of counselling there – we'd talk a lot. I had to go to church and to Mass, and I had time to meditate and think about things, and pulled myself around a bit. There were a lot of times at college when I was really deeply depressed, really, really down. Having no money, not knowing what was going on career-wise, if I was wasting my time. Really wanting to achieve, and people like Russell Watson were getting out into the world, people who were discovered in pubs and were making it and doing what I wanted to do, to an extent. I was really working for it, really working, and I had a vision of where I wanted to be and it wasn't happening. There was a lot of frustration and angst. I tried to never let it show too much, I didn't want to mope and moan about it because that sort of thing can always bite you in the arse. But deep down I was extremely frustrated. I knew I had to be patient, and I had some optimism somewhere in the back of my mind. That was the first thing Richard Van Allan, who helped me get into college, had taught me – don't try to jump the gun. And as discouraging as my situation was at that time I held on to that, tried to stick to it, and I'm glad I did, because he was right. And I think I'm in a much better position to handle it all now, I don't think I could have coped with things back then, I was too young, I don't think I was psychologically equipped.

And a few good things started to happen. There was an external engagements office at college – you'd put your name down and they'd offer you a gig, singing in a restaurant, the odd little concert, £250 or so. I did a few. There were demo jobs, and I volunteered for all of them. They were great. When a singer, a recording artist, needed a sound test or a sound check and couldn't turn up, the likes of me would go along and do it for them. And there were a number of projects going on at Abbey Road at the time where they needed a singer to test out this old recording method, cutting a record into wax discs, making old 78 records. I did the pre-tests, so they used me as a guinea pig to figure out how to do the recording. As a result I have a load of records at Mum's, me on old 78s, and they sound beautiful, like genuine vintage records. I loved all that sort of stuff. When I was doing that I sang into the same funnel that Enrico Caruso sang into when he recorded his albums – a real thrill. Wonderful experiences, and I learnt a lot about recording.

I was going into Abbey Road Studios quite often doing all these demo recordings. I did one once for Queen, or for their sound engineers at least. They were doing a project where they were getting classical artists to sing or play Queen songs. Andrea Bocelli and Sarah Brightman were involved. Those two did a duet on her album around that time. I know she covered 'Who Wants to Live Forever', but I'm not sure if the Queen album ever actually happened in the end. But I went and demoed 'The Show Must Go On' and 'Who Wants to Live Forever'. Mum's got that recording as well at home. It was awesome. I was in Studio 2, The Beatles' studio, which reeked of history, and I was singing Queen! It was moments like that that kept me going. Moments like that inspired and encouraged me, kept me thinking, 'Something's happening. I'm getting there.'

I was still living at the hostel, and I finally decided it might be a good idea to earn a regular wage, and got a job as a waiter at the Covent Garden Brasserie. Late one night I was serving two guys their pasta and just as I was putting the plates on their tables I caught sight of a rat running past, stamped my foot on it and said 'Enjoy your meal' as I dragged its carcass back to the kitchen as subtly as I could, leaving a trail of blood on the floor. I think I got away with it. They didn't leave anyway, munched obliviously on their lovingly prepared microwave pasta. We used to save the food that we didn't need, or that hadn't been eaten, and feed homeless people at the end of the night. I was always the one who had to tell them to leave when they were begging the customers. I was always the one sent out to tell them, 'Come on guys, come back later on, we'll make sure you've got something in your belly.' Always me. There was one guy who used to come around all the time, a boxer who'd split up with his missus and hit the bottle and moved down to London. His daughter had left home as well, left her mother in the north of England to come and live on the streets with him. They used to come to the café late at night and we'd make sure they had soup, sandwiches, pasta, whatever we had left. He showed me pictures of himself as a young boxer, sparring with Muhammad Ali. It was incredible to get to know people like that who'd come off the rails, to hear their stories.

After the Brasserie I got a job as one of the security guys at the front of concerts at Shepherd's Bush Empire, looking out to see what trouble was going on, who was fighting, who was fainting, trying to drag Julian Cope back from the throng after he stage-dived. I saw, or at least heard, what with my back to the stage, some great gigs too. I became a big Marillion fan after they played there. It was an odd double-life, studying classical music by day and having my ears blasted at these rock gigs by night. And ironically, after some time doing these jobs, towards the end of my second year I started entering singing competitions and I realised I could make some sort of living by singing, certainly by winning those. The first big one I did was in Munich. James Lockhart put me forward to take part in Lyric Tenor of the World. I was chosen to represent the UK, had to learn seven or eight different operatic arias, and got through to the final with three other tenors. A German guy won and he was really outstanding, he had a beautiful voice. But I came second, and to have done that, in a competition that started with 2000 people, was great, and I also won the audience prize, the audience vote, which I was really chuffed about. I've always felt like I've had a connection with the audience, throughout my career.

I won about £5000 for that competition, which as a student was immense, my word. That set me up for a long time, it really helped me through that second year and into the third.

I won the Clonter Opera prize. There was a singer in that who said, 'Well done for winning, Alf, but I won the audience prize, which really outshines the first prize. That's what really matters, pleasing the audience.' He's still cocky now, that guy. I thought, 'OK, you walk away with your eight hundred pounds, I'll walk away with my fifteen hundred pounds.' That's not what it's about and that might make me sound just as cocky; I was delighted with my audience award in Munich. But that was one thing I couldn't stand about college, people who came through the establishment because of their standing, where they were from, with attitudes like that. A lot of singers there held that mantel pretty high and made everybody well aware of it. And I never did, because I was from Fleetwood, and happy to be so. I think that's why the classical world grates on me so much, because of people like that. It's not that my face doesn't fit, because I've been in it and I've done well in it, I've held my own. But the arrogance of some of those people never ceases to amaze me.

That second year ended magnificently. The Royal Opera House was closing for refurbishment that July, and there was a big screen in the Covent Garden Piazza showing the closing gala performance, a big shindig, opera, ballet, the works. I was drinking in the area with my friend Joe Shovelton. It was a boiling summer's day, we'd bought some wine from a restaurant and were knocking it back rather enthusiastically. And I guess I was full of Dutch courage because I decided we should hustle our way into the Opera House and gatecrash the after-party. I was still in touch with Paul Griffiths, the head coach there who'd taught me 'Che Gelida Manina' a couple of years earlier, and I knew some of the door staff so it seemed within the realms of possibility. We were so wired. And we got to the stage door, walked over all these TV cables and just went in. That easy. I just waved at the doorman and he said, 'Good to see ya!' and we walked in. I knew how to get to the stage, so we made a beeline for it, because I wanted to nick something from the Opera House as a souvenir – they were tearing the place apart and I wanted a piece of history. But these really famous opera singers appeared, started walking past us, and we got to the stage and found ourselves at the end of the line-up, which wasn't part of the plan, but we went with it. I still had my bag over my shoulder, big old RAF canvas bag my brother John had given me. And there was Thatcher, Prince Philip and John Major, getting closer and closer and closer to us. Joe was whispering, 'They're coming this way, they're coming . . .' and I was saying, 'Just go with it, make something up.'

John Major materialised in front of us. He said, 'Hallo, boys!' And we said, 'Hello!' And then the line dispersed, mercifully. And there were all these people on the stage, and I somehow found myself chatting to Plácido Domingo, right there in the middle of the Royal Opera House stage. I was full to my eyebrows with wine, RAF bag still on my shoulder, and there was a huge circle of women surrounding us. I said to Domingo, 'I'd love to sing for you one day, mate.' He could clearly tell I was drunk as a fart. And I think that's always stayed with him, because I have worked with him a few times, sung for him a couple of times, and there's always a look in his eye that seems to say to me, 'Oh yes, you were that drunk idiot.' Still, he got his manager to give me his card, and all these women came up to me asking me what we talked about.

Then we did somehow blag ourselves into the party and these women in ball gowns came up to us asking if we were in the show, and I said, 'Yeah, we're ballet dancers.' And Joe, who's a scrawny little tenor, suddenly straightened himself up, attempting to look tall and lithe and proud. They asked us what part of the show we were in, and I said, 'We were in the second half, it was hard work.' They said, 'OK . . . lovely.' It turned out there hadn't been any ballet in the second half. Wayne Sleep came over and said, 'Look at these three lovely boys!' There were only two of us. He'd clearly been enjoying himself too. Bryn Terfel was there, and his eyes certainly said, 'OK. Here we are. Two drunk idiots.' Chris Maltman, who'd just won the Lieder Prize in the Cardiff Singer of the World competition, could also see that we were smashed. But what the hell, we were having the time of our lives.

When we left I walked into the auditorium and saw workmen ripping the place to pieces. Straight away they were working on the place. It was a sad sight and I wanted to save a piece of it. So I leant over the balcony and took one of the little red lampshades, shoved it in my bag. I still have it at home in Fleetwood. It's on my wardrobe next to my clogs that I had as a kid.

Chapter Thirteen

SPACE OPERA

I can't remember who put me in touch with Clint Boon. Clint was the keyboard player of Inspiral Carpets, who'd split up a couple of years earlier in 1995. I grew up listening to all that British indie music when I was at school and I liked the odd track they did, 'This Is How It Feels', 'Dragging Me Down', although I was more into The Stone Roses and The Charlatans. I think one of my friends at college knew him, and my name had come up in conversation. Clint called me, then sent me a demo tape of some tracks he was working on, and asked if I would improvise on some of them. I didn't know what it would lead to, there wasn't any sort of plan, but it was nice to be asked and I thought I'd have a go. Clint had a good history of recording and making records, a history in the business. I thought maybe something cool could come of it.

He drove over to me in Fleetwood one Saturday and took me back to his house in Milnrow, just outside Rochdale. I expected the signature long moppy hair he had in the Inspirals, and he'd cut it short, but he was still very obviously Clint Boon – he's got a pretty iconic look. We went upstairs and then up a little ladder into this tiny little attic studio, which was just about big enough for two people. We had to crawl through a really tight little space to get into it. I found out recently that Elbow did their first demos in there, which is quite cool. I'm a big Elbow fan. They're good mates, Guy Garvey and Clint. That Manchester scene is kind of small really, everybody seems to know each other, a lot of them grew up together. I came downstairs one day and Paul Gallagher, Liam and Noel's brother, was on his sofa – he'd written a book about growing up with them. The Oasis boys were the babies of that early '90s scene, and before they formed Noel had been a roadie for the Inspirals. Clint says he's like the Forrest Gump of the indie scene, popping up and overlapping with all these other bands.

Initially he didn't really say what he wanted from me, but he did have a vision for what he was working on, this music that was within the realms of indie pop, but with a dance element to it, more psychedelic than the Inspirals, and a bit of opera. He later described it as "space opera" in fact, which kind of makes sense when you listen to it. He played the songs he'd sent me on the tapes and I just started improvising, no words, just some la la las around the tracks, and he recorded it. Then he'd play it back and I'd harmonise with myself, and he'd play that back and I'd do more. So I was overdubbing my own voice on it as well, improvising around the tracks. And we started hanging out more and more, and recording more. He'd ask me to sing arias of sorts, ad-libbing. Sometimes he would do the lead vocals, and sometimes I'd harmonise with him. The only time I did the lead vocals was a version we did of 'This Is How It Feels', which was great, and never released. It's on YouTube somewhere. And it was all really exciting, because it was a new direction, something fun that I thought might really work, and so different to what I'd been doing. It was pop music!

We became mates, having beers and going out in Manchester, and he came over to hang out with my family in Fleetwood. It was a bit of a tricky time, because Dad was suffering with his illness, he wasn't long out of hospital. I wanted to spend as much time as possible with Dad, coming home to Fleetwood on the weekends, but my college schedule was flexible, and sometimes Clint came down to London during the week. Towards the end of my time with Clint, Dad was really poorly and it was difficult for him to socialise with anybody. He couldn't really handle any intensity around him, and Clint's a very active guy. One Saturday night we were having dinner at his house after recording all day. I was staying over for the weekend. We were having a good laugh and started singing Elvis songs, because we both loved Elvis, and we were breakdancing, if you can call it that. And he was doing some move, trying to hold himself up on one arm, and crashed down onto the coffee table and broke his rib.

When the music was starting to sound pretty good and songs started coming together, Clint got a band together, The Clint Boon Experience. We had a female trumpet player, guitarist, bassist, Clint on his keyboards, and a drummer. And I was Opera Dude, that was my official title, that's how I'm credited on the albums, the first of which was all compiled from his attic, on his own system – he produced it. We were gigging before anything was released, testing the music out, playing some bars, great dark sweaty little places like The Barfly in Camden. And they were really fun gigs, very different to what people might have expected from the Inspirals association. There'd be a guy playing the tuba while Clint poured beer in the top of it, there was a reindeer on the front of an organ, and me singing opera.

I was juggling it with college, joining the band on the road whenever I could. We were only doing 40-minute sets, supporting other acts. I'd be on for half an hour or so and come on and do a final song with them to end the night. And the gigs were wired, incredible atmosphere, we were really building up a fan base, and I got to meet a lot of those indie rockers, the Shed Seven lot, Carter The Unstoppable Sex Machine – later we supported Shed Seven and I did a few of those bigger tour dates, Manchester Academy, Brixton Academy.

It was wicked, it really was. As Opera Dude I used to get a lot of attention, it was very cool. There were rockers and moshers and screaming girls, a couple of groupies, it was bedlam really. Some girls would join us in the green room or in the crew room or backstage, or we'd have a private room at the bigger venues. I wasn't going out with anyone at the time, I was having fun. I think I came onto Shed Seven's drummer's girlfriend one drunken night. Unsuccessfully.

And I was constantly recording new stuff, new vocals for them, while we were touring. 'Alfie, I need a line on this, I need a line on that, can you harmonise with this . . .' So there was lots of material that I did for him, some of which went on the second album. I didn't really tell anyone at college what I was doing, certainly not teachers, because the more you told them, the more you'd give them ammunition to say, 'You shouldn't really be doing that. It's not right for the voice or for your career. If you want to be an opera singer that's not the way forward.' A lot of times I would get told things like that by professors and teachers and critics, 'You shouldn't be doing this,' even with the biggest and best things I've ever done, *La Bohème* on Broadway, *Les Misérables*. But I've never really turned anything down that I've had a strong gut feeling about doing. I've always just gone for it. And being part of that scene with Clint really stoked my fires. It was a world I wanted to be in and stay in. I love my rock music. I've always wanted to be in that world, to have that sort of response from an audience, while staying faithful to my own voice. And the more I perform and sing now, the closer I feel like I'm getting to that world.

It was really fun, lively music. And fair play to Clint, he knows how to write a song. He was the main songwriter in the Inspirals really. He wrote 'This Is How It Feels', great song. Back then, I think, he'd made his name as an artist, and wanted to build it up again, because the Inspirals had finished and his career had sunk a bit, he didn't have a record contract after that and really wanted to get back in the game. And there was a hell of a lot of affection for him from the crowds. I think that was one thing that put up a slight wall between me and Clint, the attention I started getting from the audience – they liked what I was doing, they liked my singing. I had a black suit on and a bow-tie and these big black wraparound shades, and my hair all greased back. And my following grew the more we gigged, there were more and more cheers when I walked out. I hadn't established myself as an artist, I was still at college, so I think when Clint saw me getting some acclamation it possibly freaked him out a little bit, because he wanted the attention.

One night when we played The Barfly in Camden, the crowd went crazy for me when I walked out, lots of cheering. And after the gig I was having a really fun night, chatting away to Sean Hughes, the great Irish comedian, he was a captain on *Never Mind the Buzzcocks* at the time, and Clint came over and joined in the conversation. And he leant over to me, whispered in my ear and said, 'Don't forget – I'm the bloody star of this show.' I thought, 'Wow. OK. Time to get off the horse.' And I went my separate way. It wasn't a big deal, I just think his ego got the better of him a little bit. I didn't really say anything, I just decided to stop gigging with him.

And the band got pretty popular, they played *TFI Friday*, which I would have liked to have done. The album got Record of the Week on one of the Radio 1 shows – it was the first time I ever heard myself on the radio, and that was a thrill. Then I heard myself on TV – Clint also licensed one of the songs, 'Comet Theme Number One', for the theme tune to the footy show on Granada television, but he hadn't asked my permission. I didn't have a contract with him, but he should have asked. My voice was on there, and I could hear it every week, watching that bloody footy show. I spoke to him a few years ago. He got hold of me through myspace.com I think, he was working as a DJ for Xfm radio in Manchester, I think he still is. So I phoned him up and we chatted, and it was fine. We've all grown up a bit. We kept in touch, he's come to see me at gigs a couple of times when I've played in Manchester. I've no hard feelings against him – it's water under the bridge. Rock and roll I guess.

Chapter Fourteen

DAD

Dad could do anything. I was in awe of him as a kid. I've got loads of pictures of him and me together. If he hung a picture on a wall, the wall would fall down before the picture did. He'd build a shed in next to no time. He did everything properly and he did everything securely and with intent. Whatever he put his mind to he would see it through. We built this little summer house in the back garden where we could all sit outside and have dinner. We had a couple of really warm Indian summers, the sun setting slowly, and we'd all sit out there till 11 at night and just chat, as a family, and take it all in. It was wonderful.

Even when he was working nights, he was never too tired for his kids, never miserable, always joking around. He always had time for us. I used to sit on the garden swing in the mornings and wait for him to come home. I'd see him cycling down the road, and he'd come in and do handstands. I spent a lot of time with him, more than my other brothers and sisters did, because

I was the last, I guess. I was spoilt in that sense, having that time with my parents. It's something I really relish now. He loved family life, and when he retired from ICI in 1990, at 55, he said it was the best time in his life because he got to spend it with his wife and kids at home.

For a year after retiring he made toys for the grandkids. Carts, cradles, trains, dollhouses. He made toy boats and put them on the boating lake. Some sank. He took up a lot of hobbies, especially woodwork, and he was good. He made fruit bowls. Everything was wood at one point. Bowls all over the place. 'Look at this, Patsy, look what I've made now!' Brilliant. Mum would paint and decorate the furniture he made, the dollhouses. What a team. Dad bought a new circular saw and one day managed to practically cut his thumb off with it. He came running into the kitchen going, 'I've cut me thumb, I've cut me thumb! Don't tell your mum or she'll take my toy off me!'

He was a solid role model, and as a teenager you don't see that – you just think your dad's a pain in the neck, you think you know it all and you get embarrassed by your parents. I was a real spoilt brat sometimes, and I regret that. I grew up a lot in the 10 months we had him while he was ill. I wish he was around now so I could show him how much I appreciate how he loved and cared for me. Because Dad did *anything* for me, he really did. He'd not bat an eyelid if I asked for a lift somewhere. If I needed a ride to band practice, before I could finish saying, 'I need to get my drum kit in the car,' the drum kit was in there. And he'd drive me to somebody's house or to these dodgy old sheds in the middle of nowhere, where we'd set up and play. He'd sit outside my singing rehearsals all night, two or three-hour rehearsals, he'd just sit there in his car. He was hard of hearing, so loud noises really hurt his ears, but I wish I'd said,

'Come in and sing along, Dad.' Or, 'Come in and have a listen to the drums. Come in and have a listen to the band, see what you think.'

We started to notice little things that summer before my third year at college. He was getting a bit forgetful, forgetting names of things, forgetting what he'd done yesterday, getting bad headaches. He'd been at my graduation, and at one point when I was on stage I looked over at him and he was asleep. We didn't know – nobody knew, at the time, that he had this brain tumour, and it was just knocking him out.

After an initial period in hospital he was transferred to a neurology unit in Preston for a biopsy. I had to perform an opera in Aberdeen for a couple of weeks, in Haddo House, and as soon as I was done I drove straight back to the hospital. I pulled off into a service station to get him a present and bought this thing I thought might make him laugh – this stupid little frog that sat down on the edge of the table, it had a fishing rod. It was kind of cute and funny, and I just wanted to do something. Just *something*. I didn't know what to do to help . . . all I could think at that point was to buy this stupid thing. He'd had his biopsy, and I walked into the room and said, 'Hi, Dad . . . good to see you . . . I've got you a little gift,' and I put it at the side, and he just looked really blank, glanced at it, and said, 'Thanks, Alf,' expressionless. He didn't show any disappointment, but I knew it was just pointless, and I felt like an idiot. If I'd just trusted in the fact that it was enough to simply be there with him.

We were waiting and waiting for the diagnosis. It killed us to go in every day and wait for 10 hours for the doctors to tell us what was happening. Eventually they took Mum and Dad and Theresa into a little room and told them before me and Fran and Maria were invited in. And I walked in and saw Mum, Dad and Theresa all in tears. About as heartbreaking as it gets. Mum said, 'There's nothing we can do for your dad.' In that moment, I didn't know how to react, and I turned away. I tried to cry and show that I was sad, but it just wasn't something I could fathom. I didn't know what to think. I was absolutely numb. There was probably an element of disbelief, denial: 'This isn't right.' But mostly I just couldn't feel anything. I didn't know what to feel or how to be. And I seriously regret turning away, and not facing Dad. I snapped out of it and turned to him and threw my arms around him and knelt on the floor, and he said, 'I'm sorry, son. I'm really sorry.'

I said, 'Dad, don't apologise for this!'

The hospital asked us if we wanted to take him home or have them put him in a convalescent home to be looked after. We said, 'No, he's coming home.' And he spent his last months at home. This was August. They said, 'Enjoy Christmas, because it won't be long after that.' And he lasted through until May. He was a tough old boy.

It sounds odd but there was an element of excitement in how I was feeling. Our family adjust to things like that, that's how we work, because we believe there's more going on than just the life we experience down here. And we were being shaken up, something *new* was happening. But it hit me later on. *Bang* did it hit me. I was floored. Like somebody had smacked me in the face with a spade, knocked me out. I was all over the place. I couldn't believe that what had happened had happened. I couldn't believe that my dad wasn't gonna be with us any more. It took his death to really make me realise I was gonna be without him for the rest of my life. That's so hard to get to grips with, and I feel it every single day, I really do. Because I miss him so much. And I have these really uncomfortable panicked feelings sometimes, that he's not around any more, he's not here. I can't touch him and I can't see him and I can't talk to him.

I was spending more and more time with him. I could always juggle around my coaching lessons at college and have longer weekends at home here and there. It was really sweet and understanding of them to give me that flexibility. Every weekend I went home, and every weekend I saw this slight decline in Dad's health. His mannerisms, his responses to things. And his looks, because he was having radiotherapy, he was on morphine and retaining water, he was puffed up. It was difficult to see him decline like that, this Action Man who used to hop over the garden gate to the shops across the road. And his memory was going, he forgot names of things, he'd say, 'Can you pass me that ... can you pass me that ... whatsit, whatsit called?' Moments like that were really upsetting.

It was a slow and steady deterioration. Towards the end he couldn't sleep upstairs so we made space for him down in the dining room, and we'd sit with him. We had nurses in the mornings but we stopped that because some of them weren't very affectionate, and we started just caring for him ourselves, those of us who were around. John was with the RAF in the Falklands. Maria and Michael were living out of town, so they didn't come round every week. Week in week out it was me, Mum, and my sisters Annie, Theresa and Fran. Towards the end of his life we were having to sit up with him quite a lot, and we had to sit with him during the night because he was waking up shouting out for his mum, my nana, Evelyn. That really surprised us, and at some points he did display signs of being youthful and somehow sprightly again. Slight little things. If you were feeding him he'd wink at you or do something where you could see the playful side of him still in there. We even thought, 'Wow, he's really turned a corner,' a couple of times.

But when you see something that comes across as an improvement it's often a sign that they're close to dying. I think it's nature's way of giving them an element of their health again, showing them how it could be. You *are* gonna feel healthy again, you're gonna feel young. This was the prime time of your life and once this pain is gone this is how you'll be. That's my interpretation of it.

But he was really regressing. Towards the end it was terrible. I came home one weekend and he looked so bad, my goodness, it was a real shock. He was unconscious a lot of the time and he would shout out, but his eyes would be closed and he'd be sat up, it was like he was in a different world already. And we'd have to hold him and stroke his arm. You couldn't touch his head because of the tumour, so you'd just try to calm him, pat him, relax him.

One weekend I came home and I said, 'Mum, I'll settle with Dad tonight, you go and get some rest.' We finally got him to sleep at about 9pm. Mum went to bed and I sat up watching TV for a bit in the living room, and every time I heard him cry I'd be up and I'd be in there to check on him. I'd stroke his arm and he'd settle, and I'd go back. Around 4am I heard him shout out like crazy, 'Mum! Mum! Mum!' And I ran in and I sat with him, and it was the closest thing I'd ever done with him. I sat with my dad in my arms and I had a flashback to when I sat in his arms after my nana, his mum, had died, when I was four. I remember being sat on his knee and him saying, 'I just want you to know, Alf, your nana's gone to Heaven and she's happy now, she's not poorly any more.' It was really cool. And now I was sat with my arm around him, stroking him, this incredible role-reversal. And I stayed sat up with him the rest of the night.

Mum woke up about six and told me to go and rest. I went upstairs and got into bed but I couldn't sleep, so we had breakfast and decided to go for a walk. Our Annie came round to relieve us, to look after him and bathe him, and me and Mum went up to the beach. And we had a really bizarre walk. It was like being in a bubble, in some sort of dome, a sort of protection, an aura. It felt like we were being protected. And as we were walking up to the beach it started to rain, but just on the other side of the street. There were enormous black rain clouds on our right, and on the left, where we were, bright sunshine. And we didn't say a word to each other. We've spoken about it since and she said she felt exactly the same. Like we were being protected.

We got home and Mum said, 'Alf, would you go to church and fill up this bottle with some holy water.' So I jumped on my bike and went to the Catholic church down the road, and while I was filling up the bottle at the font at the back, I looked into the church, and it was empty. I walked up to the front with this bottle, straight down the middle aisle to the altar, and I said, 'Please, give him his rest. He's suffered enough. Please give him his rest.' This was three o'clock in the afternoon. And he died two hours later.

I came home. It was Annie, Mum, Theresa, me and Dad. Annie told us to hold him, she knew what was happening. She's a state-enrolled nurse and has been a district nurse to the elderly. She'd nursed a lot of sick, dying people. We were talking to him – whether he could hear us or not I'm not sure – but his breathing was getting very shallow, and then he'd take a big breath, and then it would be really shallow, then he'd take a big breath again . . . and it was slowing down, slowing down, getting slower . . . slower . . . and shallower and shallower . . . and then he sort of frowned, and one little tear rolled down his cheek. And he took a breath . . . and he never let go of it. And that was it. He was gone.

I was holding his hands, I was holding his shoulders. And I felt him leave. It just didn't feel like it was my dad any more. I was holding the image of him, but not the person. He'd gone. And I never thought I would have to do this, but everybody else left the room, I was left there on my own with my dad, and I had to close his eyes. I lowered my dad's eyelids. And that was the last time I saw his eyes. An amazing moment, an amazing feeling, something that I'll never ever forget being a part of. There are people in the family that weren't there, and I was fortunate enough to be one of those to experience the last moments of my dad's life. I feel very blessed about that.

The funeral was amazing. It was such a beautiful bright day, and there weren't many tears. Mum wasn't crying. I was carrying Dad's coffin with my three brothers, and as it was being lowered down to the grave, a handle broke off, one of those awkward moments when everyone freezes. But Mum looked at me and I leant over to her and said, 'That wouldn't have broken if Dad had put it on!'

The church was rammed, and there were people coming up to us after the service, people we didn't know, saying things like, 'I met your dad, he picked me up in the pouring rain and drove me home, he didn't even know me.' Another: 'Your dad collected my groceries from the market and brought them home for me when I couldn't get out the house.' All these things were coming out about the type of guy Dad was, and it was lovely to hear, because he never spoke about stuff like that, he didn't come home and say to Mum, 'Do you know what I did today, love? There was this little old lady at the bus stop in the pouring rain and I offered her a lift and took her home with her groceries.' He never did that. We heard lots of stories like that after he died.

We all came back to the house and talked about Dad, reminisced. Afterwards, one of our neighbours said to Mum, 'I was looking out at your back garden, Pat. Is it some Catholic thing that you do when somebody dies, throwing all those white feathers up into the air?'

Mum said, 'What white feathers?'

He said, 'I was looking from my window, and all I could see were these white feathers flying up in the air.'

We haven't got a clue what he was on about. Weird things like that surrounded that whole period of time. Soon after Dad died, every so often the doorbell would ring and there'd be no one there. My brother-in-law Phil, who's an electrician, said it was probably loose floorboards hitting the wire, so we got a new bell, new system, but it kept happening. Then when me and Sarah were living in Oxford years later, we had a toy for Gracie that used to chime if it was picked up or shaken. If you just left it on the floor it wouldn't make a sound, but around the time of Dad's death in May, the same month as Grace's birthday, it would always go off on its own. And I'd phone up Mum to tell her and she'd say, 'The doorbell's been ringing again.' So it was just like these little messages. I'm sure there are explanations for it all, but moments like that make you think a little. Even if there are practical explanations, I don't think there's any harm with it making you think. It sparks off thoughts and memories. I love things like that that you can't explain. Death shouldn't be a depressing thing. Dad spent 63 years on this earth, and he spent 50 of those years with my mum.

About three or four months before he died we were talking about family and we were all a bit down, depressed, because it had been a heavy time, we were going through a lot with Dad. At that point he was still pretty savvy when it came to talking and communicating. He was always aware of what was happening, he knew he was dying and he dealt with it. He took it on board, he didn't start feeling sorry for himself or getting angry or moping about. And out of the blue, he said, 'You know what, Alf, one day, you'll see me. You'll see me again.' Simple as that. Didn't lead on from any previous conversation. I didn't know what to make of it, I didn't know what to say or what to think. After he died I realised what he meant. I saw him in my own actions and mannerisms, and I never had before. I do believe my dad's spirit and soul still exist. Certainly in me. I see that every day. Just the other morning I was stirring the coffee and rattling the spoon in the cup, exactly the same way he did. With vigour. He did everything with vigour and I'd like to think I inherited that. I like to think so. And it was like he knew I'd experience that after he'd gone, that I'd have a new perspective on what it meant to be his son. I finally realised how much I was really like him. And it made me realise what I had to do for my own family. I wasn't married then, I'd not met Sarah, but from that point I knew that when I had my own family I'd be as good with them as my dad was with me. Family is now my sole responsibility and I want to make sure everything is right and secure for them. I'm not going to be around for all of my children's lives, and I think about that a lot, because Dad died at 63. I'm 40 next year. He was very ill, but . . . he'd be 77 now, and it's gone so fast. So fast. He left us all feeling secure, and instilled a lot in us, but after he went, some of the family had some rocky times. Midlife crises, divorces, heavy drinking, myself included. John was hit hard by it. He said to me, 'Alf, my best mate's died. You'll have to take his place.'

If Dad was around now, I know he'd be loving my gigs. He'd be on the road with me, he'd drag Mum up. 'Jump in the car, Patsy, we're off to see our Alf.' And he'd drive to Birmingham, Manchester, he wouldn't think twice about it. And Mum would go with him. She can't go out on her own now, she doesn't like going anywhere too much, and I understand that. When she surprised me by turning up in Liverpool to see my concert at the end of last year I was amazed. It was lovely. She'll come with Annie to see me in London occasionally. But because Dad used to do that sort of thing and not think twice about it, she doesn't really think anyone else can for her. I totally understand that. It's like she doesn't want to be taken out by anybody else. She just wants Dad to take her.

Chapter Fifteen

ON THE ROAD

My third year at the Royal College was really tough. I'd graduated at the end of the second year with a first, distinction, and this was the first year of what was supposed to be two years of the opera course, but I was getting itchy feet. I wanted to move, to get going, to step up my game. Dad was getting really ill, and I was having big problems with one of my teachers, who just wasn't giving me the time I was supposed to have with him. It was a heartache, and it stressed me out. My living situation wasn't great either. I was in Fulham Broadway with two other students, and the place was so cheap, I'd open my bedroom door and it would hit the bed. I had to crawl around the door to get into my room. I started feeding a rat outside the window. It was the best friend I had. He'd crawl underneath my window and I'd throw biscuits out. That was the highlight of my day.

The day after Dad died in May I had to come back to the Royal College to do my final opera scenes for my exam. My brother Michael was doing his exam for his sign language course in London, and it was the only chance he'd have to get his qualifications as a national interpreter, so we came down together, and it was so bloody depressing, really hard for us. I did my performance that afternoon and got marked very badly by the acting teacher. Musically I got a distinction, a first, but my acting teacher slated me in her report, said I wasn't all there, I wasn't quite in it. Difficult to be completely in it when your dad's died the day before, and she knew about it.

I felt like my life was on pause. And I didn't want it to be, I wanted to keep firing ahead, keep working. I still felt inspired and encouraged about things, because the Clint Boon thing was still happening, I was doing demo recordings and winning competitions, and even Dad's death seemed like it was part of my story, a part of life that I had to get through. 'It's all in the art of growing up, son,' that's what he used to say. But his death did hit me really hard. I was feeling aggressive all the time, and I spent a lot of time out and about in London knocking back the drinks, mostly on my own. I'd go into a bar with genuine intent to learn music. I'd have a score in front of me and I'd go through it, get a beer and listen to the music, learning it bit by bit, and another beer would come . . . and the wine would come, and then I'd get a whisky . . . and I'd be mixing and mixing and mixing and before I knew it I was on the tequila, and whiskies turned into double whiskies . . . I was drinking far too much. I'm not blaming Dad's death for me going out and getting absolutely sozzled. But I had to find some escape.

I wanted to get the hell out of the Royal College – I was running into problems there with some of the authorities, standing my ground, and I just decided to leave. I'd spoken to Richard Van Allan, who was Director of the National Opera Studio, and after an audition there he'd taken me on. And that was a whole different scene, I loved every minute. It was a year's course at Morley College, Lambeth North, an adult education centre. They rented out a few offices and a rehearsal studio, there'd be pottery classes in the next room, that sort of set-up. My first day there, we all sat in a room, and I thought, 'Here we go, another lecture about how proud we should all be to be there.' And Richard Van Allan said, 'Right, the library's on the second floor, there are some rehearsal skirts over there, a few swords and props there – let's get to it!' And I thought, 'Yes! At last! Human beings! Human beings running an establishment.' Fantastic. *That's* what this business is about.

Richard Van Allan died a few years ago, sadly. He was a working class, down to earth guy, who came from a traditional background in Derbyshire, didn't have to go to Oxbridge to learn his trade. He was a real guy who just sang songs. He was a policeman at one point, and he got into opera singing, as a bass baritone, and he worked all over, worked with Pavarotti, worked in Milan, Covent Garden, Metropolitan Opera. Great fella. And that's what I'd been looking for, somebody like that to teach me what the business is about. It was great, a huge relief. I was back on track. The pause button had been pressed and was playing again.

By this point I was determined to earn money solely through singing, and I was finding I could, to an extent. I was doing some small concerts, and also I was playing with a little jazz band we'd formed at the Royal College. We played old nostalgia songs, 'All of Me', 'Autumn Leaves', "A Foggy Day (in London Town)', all that stuff. I said, 'Why don't we call ourselves Nostalgia?' and they said, 'No, let's call ourselves The Royal College of Music Jazz Band.' What can you do?

I was on the drums, I had a tiny little cymbal and snare, and I sang. A guy called Tim Carlston played trumpet, Justin Woodward on the vibraphone, and a double bass player called

Richard Pryce, who'd been arrested for hacking The Pentagon and changing everybody's salaries. He'd done it from his bedroom in Colindale when he was 16, for a laugh. Called himself Datastream Cowboy. Scotland Yard had turned up there at his parents' house and arrested him. He had the CIA and FBI on his case, the US Senate said he was the number one threat to US security, he was fined a grand or so. He was a bit of a nerd, obviously, but played the double bass like a dream, amazing bass player. I've worked with him since, he's played in some orchestras with me, done some concerts. And we did a few little jazz gigs with that band, museums and the like, the opening of the bar in Harvey Nichols.

At the National Opera Studio I did a masters in operatics, singing, vocal studies. I was learning roles, having solid coaching, learning tons of music. It was some of the most valuable training I ever had, because it taught you how to deal with the actual job, to get out there and perform, work through a rehearsal process, learn to work with conductors and directors. It was just a great establishment that trained you how to be an opera singer. We had a week's residency where we'd go into an opera house somewhere, and for me it was Welsh National Opera. We went to Cardiff for a week to see operas, sat in on musical rehearsals and technical rehearsals, production rehearsals, and at the end of the week we put on an opera gala concert in Swansea. The whole thing about the NOS was to learn how to build up your stamina. You'd cram as many operas in as you possibly could, and learn as many as you possibly could.

I was living in this old fella's house in Barnes. He lived in South Africa. I think he owned South African Airlines. It was like Miss Havisham's house, it was a throwback, a bit spooky really. I had a little bohemian attic room with a single corner sink and a single-burner stove. No TV. I wasn't allowed to use the rest of the house, but his nephew lived there too and he and I got on pretty well. He said I could help myself to some of the wine collection – i.e. not the dust-encrusted vintage section – so I'd grab a bottle sometimes. I lived on lumps of cheese and digestive biscuits for weeks, it was all I could really afford to eat. The kitchen was so old, the knives and forks were ancient, the guy had spent no money on the place, and it was freezing, so we'd walk around in thick jumpers. His nephew would invite me down to eat with him and we'd light a fire and keep warm. All very bohemian.

I liked Barnes, I'd hang out with college guys in good little country pubs like The Sun, and The Bear. Michael Ball lived in the area and I used to catch the bus past his house quite a bit. I really wanted to meet him and ask him for advice, so I shoved a letter through his door one day. Never heard anything back. I told him about it when I did his radio show a couple of years ago. I said, 'You never got back to me, ya bastard.'

He said, 'Well, would you?! Would you?!'

I said, 'Of course I would, if someone put a letter through my door, I would have at least written back.'

He said, 'Well I don't.'

Fair enough.

At the end of the course that June we performed a number of different opera scenes at the Royal Festival Hall, and got to sing to a lot of casting directors and agents. Askonas Holt, the agency who'd been watching my progress and had sent me to that concert in Amsterdam, signed me, which was really thrilling. A lot of people from opera houses watched us perform too. Steven Naylor, the head of music at the Glyndebourne opera house, thought I'd be suitable for a production of *La Bohème* there, as Rodolfo, the lead, so I was brought in for an audition. I sang for him, and David McVicar, who was directing it, and a few other people, including George Christie, the head of Glyndebourne. The guy who auditioned before me was your typical opera singer, wearing his scarf. I lolloped in: 'Alright!'

And immediately David McVicar said, 'He's the one. I want him.'

They said, 'What would you like to sing?'

I said 'I'd like to sing "Che Gelida Manina" please.'

They said, 'Whenever you're ready.'

And I waited, and they waited, and finally the pianist said, rather drolly: 'Where's your music?' I'd left it on the radiator outside, which set David off laughing as I bounded out to get it. The pianist sighed and said, 'It's OK, I know it . . .' And I sang it, and got the job, and also bagged the lead tenor role in *Don Pasquale* with Scottish Opera Go Round. My first two big jobs.

So I went on the road with Scottish Opera Go Round, which was an amazing thing to do. We basically sat in a van for a few months, six or seven of us, travelling the highlands and islands of Scotland, performing four times a week. One night you'd play a 500-seater theatre and the following night you'd play a church hall or scout hut to 60 people. Once there was a dog in the audience, just sitting there barking at the back of the audi-torium. Another night there were kids in the front row, less than 2ft away from us, opening packets of crisps while I was singing my aria; it sounded like the crackling of an old record, so I started singing like an old 78 album, jerking my voice. That's what training's about, you get to work with so many different audiences. It develops you as an artist, to be able to deal with things like that. Kids throwing up in front of you. It was a great experience to do that, to travel around and put on an opera basically anywhere, just to open the doors out of the back of the van and perform to whoever wanted to listen.

We were living in the moment, getting heckled; it was unpredictable and organic. There'd be a line in the show where one of us would be asking a question, and you'd invariably get someone in the audience shouting out an answer. And there'd be a laugh and the opera would stop and you'd work with it, so you'd be interacting all the time. At one point I was in the middle of singing an aria and a kid at the front cracked open a can of pop and it went everywhere. I walked off-stage, got a cloth and cleaned the mess up, singing throughout. Things like that were fun, we'd turn it into a joke, and that sort of interaction helps you as a performer, to be able to work with the crowd.

Ernesto's a great role. I loved it, although there was one point where I forgot the words in the aria. The first line was, 'I have nothing left to live for,' and I sang that line over and over again for the whole song because I forgot the others. 'I . . . have nothing left to live for, I . . . have nothing left to live for, I have nothing left to live for . . .' Yeah, we take it you've got nothing left to live for, mate. And the shows went down so well, full-house every night. We played the big theatres in Edinburgh, Perth, Inverness, 500- or 1000-seaters, but by their nature they were more organised, more routine. The best nights were in places like Galashiels, Glenuig, Thurso. Little islands like Kirkwood, on the Orkney Islands. Tiny little halls, church halls, scout halls, town halls. People would come out and see it because it was easy for them – they could just walk out of their house and cross the village square. And they weren't opera fans particularly, just people who wanted to be entertained.

I found that fantastic. It showed me that this country and the people in this country *do* have an interest in classical music, it's *not* considered boring, you just have to take it to them. It's not enough to just expect people to come and see you in an opera, or to offer cheap tickets. 'You can have the nosebleed seats for ten pounds, cos that's all you're worthy of having.' It's not good enough to do that – you've got to get off your arse and take the music to the people. D'Oyly Carte was good like that too. But it's really the amateur companies that give people access to classical music, and it's a huge shame. Because the big opera houses have a responsibility to make it accessible, I think. People feel like they need to have been educated in a certain way to appreciate opera, and that's not the case at all. They're intimidated by it, because of the image opera can project of itself, and they shouldn't be. The music's the thing, and if it's done well it can emotionally affect anyone. It needs to be more accessible, but there are certain people in the industry who like to keep it to themselves, like a kid with a toy that doesn't want to share it.

We'd end up going to the local village pub after the show for a couple of pints, then the following day we'd drive to the next venue. We were living in bed and breakfasts. Meeting the villagers in beautiful little places like Glenuig with a loch right in the middle. You never knew what to expect, driving through that country. You'd go around a corner in this big white minibus and you'd be faced with half a dozen highland cattle blocking the road, and you'd have to manoeuvre through them really slowly. It was brilliant. And everybody got on because we were doing something really fun, really productive, and you never knew what you would be greeted with from one night to the next. The driver, David Monroe, was also the pianist, and we became really good mates, partied a lot. At one point, we stopped off at a petrol station and I bought a tape of the Royal Scots Guards Highland Bagpipe band. It was the only music we had for the van. Well I thought it was funny. After 13 hours of this bagpipe music all the way from Thurso to Glenuig, David finally whipped out the tape and threw it out the window. A couple of guys didn't get on and had a fight at one point, but when you're living on a bus for three months that's gonna happen. On the whole it was one big party, I have very fond memories of that time. And after I finished I signed up for another Scottish Opera job, another two months on the road, doing an opera gala concert. And that was fun too. And then I went on to Glyndebourne, to do *La Bohème* for the first time.

I've done *La Bohème* four times now, and in some ways I've connected to it more than anything else. I'm a firm believer in the notion that those roles find you, it's not something you can calculate. You know when the right one comes along.

The first time I'd heard *La Bohème* I was 7 or 8. My brother Michael, who was in his early 20s, had bought a highlights album of the Thomas Beecham production, an old 33, with Jussi Björling and Victoria de los Ángeles. Michael was a big opera fan, he was the only one in our family who was really. He's a sign language interpreter now, but he'd gone off to the seminary to be a priest when he was about 19, and it was there that he discovered he could sing, because he joined the choir. And he brought his passion for opera into the family – a lot of Maria Callas, but I specifically remember him playing me this *La Bohème* record. It didn't quite compete with my burgeoning love of Elvis but I really enjoyed listening to it, I loved the singing. Then later, when I was in the D'Oyly Carte and had to study 'Che Gelida Manina' to get into the Royal College of Music, I bought a specific *La Bohème* CD that somebody had recommended. It was exactly the same recording Michael had played me, it transported me right back to our living room.

La Bohème happened for me. My voice was suited to the role, I identified with the character, and with that bohemian existence. At the time, when I got the job at Glyndebourne, I was a pretty poor young student, living in that Miss Havisham attic in Barnes, which was very *Bohème*. Rodolfo actually comes from wealth – he talks about his millionaire uncle; if he's struggling for money he knows he can write a letter and get some sent from his family. But I could certainly identify with that bohemian life those guys live, trying to make do with stuff, nicking food. During the third year of Royal College, me and my flatmate Simon would go into the supermarket on the way home, and shoplift basically, because we were broke. We stole a whole chicken once. Rodolfo and his friends like their wine, and they get excited about a big fish for dinner. We had beer and a big chicken.

At Glyndebourne, David McVicar moved the story from 1840s Paris to a contemporary London bedsit – it was a great new interpretation of the piece. I have a lot of respect for David for doing that, taking that risk, because it was relatively early in his career as a director. In the scene with the fish dinner, he had everyone snorting coke as well, just to make it a bit more relevant to today's students. Rather than just everyone going crazy for a bit of fish. Colline comes back with some coke, and everyone has a line and they all burst into this ecstatic dance – the music tells the story. So they're all wired up, and Musetta walks in and tells them Mimì has collapsed and is dying. And it heightens the tragedy, instantly flipping from excitement and joy, this crazy release of energy, to absolute disaster. And during rehearsals, the singers in the show, you could tell they'd not really had any experience with coke because they didn't know how to react after supposedly snorting it. A couple of them acted like they were stoned.

I'd done coke once or twice so I had more of a clue. There was one ridiculous night with a friend of mine a few months earlier, during our National Opera Studio days. It was the last day of the football season, and we drank ourselves silly in Soho, ended up in someone's flat in Walthamstow, slept on the floor, and the next day we went to this dodgy old pub to play pool. My friend had some coke and I snorted a line on the top of this toilet cistern, then came back to the table and said, 'Do you know what mate, this doesn't really do anything for me. It really doesn't do anything for me at all, it doesn't affect me, I mean I'd rather just drink beer, I'd rather have a pint, a pint makes me feel more excited than this, this doesn't do anything for me, I can't see the fascination at all . . .' And I just carried on talking like this all the time, a million miles an hour, 'This is rubbish, it has nothing to do with me, I can take it or leave it,' it just went on and on and on. We were there all night. We got a tube to White City to go home to my friend's flat, came up the stairs, sat on the pavement for a bit and just crashed out. We woke up there on our backs, the BBC studios across the road looming over us. All a little surreal. So I knew something about coke, but I didn't say anything in the rehearsal, just danced erratically on stage on my own, which was kind of bizarre, and David McVicar told the rest of them to stop acting stoned.

I played Rodolfo very subtly in that production, quite youthful. The audience could watch the beginning without assuming the story would go down his path. Marcello was played as a boisterous sort of rocker, Schaunard was a complete clown, and Colline was very suave and sophisticated and brash, the guy who played him was pretty muscular too. My Rodolfo was more submissive, a little timid, a studious, shy and retiring sort of guy, hiding behind these three dominant characters. I've not played it like that since. That's the beauty of *La Bohème*, the beauty of the writing, and the beauty of working with a good flexible director. You can do so many different things with *La Bohème*, you can set it in so many different time periods, in so many different arenas. You can do it in a bohemian flat, you can do it in a travelling circus, you could do it as a rock band on tour. Each time I've performed it differently. The second time, for Baz Luhrmann's production on Broadway, I played him pretty rocky, quite wild, scruffy, messy. And years later for the ENO, I'd aged and played him stronger, more dominant. Also of course it depends on who you're playing with, it depends on everyone else's interpretation, how you react to their portrayal of their characters, all of that. You read that when you're just rehearsing with somebody, you develop it and you find your character.

I'd love to do a *La Bohème* movie. Everyone thought Baz would do one, but *Moulin Rouge* was a sort of homage to it anyway. There was a silent one in the 1920s, and there have been films of the opera, but the story is so strong and the music is so good, you could actually do it with the orchestration and have the dialogue translated and spoken as well, maybe some songs here and there. 'Musetta's Waltz' would bring the house down, there's a lot you could do with that cinematically. I've been working on a script with Sarah. Still a lot of work to do on it, a lot to rethink, but I know where I want the production to go, that's what I've been concentrating on. It's set in contemporary London. With the recession wreaking havoc, people out of work, the immigration issue – to me it all fits with *La Bohème*.

So I've always connected to *La Bohème*, and doing it on Broadway changed my life. But working with David McVicar on that first one was great, he was really supportive, and Glyndebourne went fantastically well – it was my first real major role in an opera, and what a role to do. I learnt it inside out and had a lot of coaching on it, a lot of training. Glyndebourne's quite an event, it's beautiful. You make a whole day of it, get your spot in the field, middle of the countryside, watch an opera, and then there's a 90-minute interval where you have a picnic and then come back drunk to see the second half of the performance, inevitably making for a more wired atmosphere. The Christie family, who run it, are wonderful. I've played there three times I think, and it's always a good time, it's like being on a holiday camp. I loved that production. I felt I was really starting to make a name for myself, and to work for Glyndebourne on that level was immense. It was also filmed for Channel 4, it went out on Christmas Day, which was even a bigger deal than I knew. Because, unbeknownst to me, Baz Luhrmann's people were watching, and they were making plans.

Chapter Sixteen

BACK TO THE
DRAWING BOARD

At the time I thought my Rodolfo was a good performance, but in retrospect it was pretty juvenile, my voice hadn't yet grown enough to suit that repertoire. Technically, structurally, emotionally. Add to that the fact that I was a nervous wreck because it was the first big thing I ever did, and because I just wanted to do it correctly all I was really singing was an imitation of what I'd heard on the CD. More or less. Now I feel I've made it my own, I can sing it my own way. When I did Jonathan Miller's production in 2009 my voice was in a completely different place. That's just how the voice works, how it grows, which is why opera singers are invariably older than the characters they play, and keep singing into their 70s, because their voices need time to mature for the music. I found a great singing teacher while I was working in New York later on, Bill Schuman – he's been an incredible help. He was giving me lessons every week while I was there and he seriously turned my voice around, he made singing easier for me, with little techniques and tips I

hadn't had before. It was really nice to have these little suggestions which unlocked certain doors in the voice that I'd been
working on for years. He just had a different way of explaining
things, and he gave me challenges, to reach certain goals by
certain times, practising scales and exercises for specific ways of
singing. Stuff I'd wanted to learn at college. Bill just knew the
voice inside out. He developed a sound and a technique for me,
it was really eye-opening. Whenever I go to New York now I call
him up and get a lesson. He has his opinions on what I should
be doing career-wise – 'Why you doing *Les Mis*?', he was saying
last year. But didn't they all.

The assistant to the conductor for David McVicar's *La
Bohème*, David Gowland, took me through the opera, he kind
of took me under his wing, I'd meet him for half an hour at
10am every day before rehearsals. During that period he was
appointed to run a two-year course at the Royal Opera House
called the Vilar Young Artists Programme, and he asked me if
I'd be interested in joining it. The way he explained it to me, I'd
get to study roles and perform principal roles on stage at the
Opera House, which would be a fantastic foot in the door for
me, to be staff there, a house singer. I'd always wanted to work
at the Royal Opera House. He did say he wasn't entirely sure
what it was going to consist of, there wasn't much in the way of
a plan yet, but it was an exciting opportunity and I auditioned,
got in. It turned out to be absolutely disastrous, and one of the
most traumatic periods of my life.

There were eight of us. We had our induction week, where we
presented ourselves to the company, to the house, got to sing to
some of the house singers, to introduce ourselves as singers. But
they had us doing master classes with people, language classes
with movement, and it was like going back to college. Not what
I thought it was going to be at all, it was a real step back. Because

I'd done all that, I'd done the Royal College of Music, I'd done the National Opera Studio. I'd been on the road as a singer. I'd played in opera houses in Belgium, I'd done *Bohème* in Glyndebourne . . . and this was back to the drawing board.

The person running the programme with David Gowland was an Australian woman, Tisi Dutton, who was really hard, really tough with the girls. And they said their intention with the programme was to break down these young singers, strip them of the techniques they'd learnt in the past, and over the two years rebuild them and mould them into an idealistic image of what an opera singer should supposedly be like. David Gowland told me that. Instead of realising what abilities we had, and working with those abilities and nurturing them, it seemed to me like they basically wanted to slam us on the floor. I'd worked too damn hard to get to where I was for that to happen to me. I'd done a lot of training and a lot of studying and a lot of work to develop myself as an operatic artist, and I wasn't going to wreck it all for the sake of their programme and their egos.

They wanted to put everybody in their place. They told us how to act, how to hold ourselves, to come in every day in shirts and ties. Utterly unnecessary. I rebelled against that as a matter of principle, jeans, T-shirts, hoodies. Another guy, Grant Doyle, did the same. They didn't say anything about it. I wasn't trying to rock the establishment or be a troublemaker or even be awkward, I just wanted to sing without anybody getting on my back. A lot of people want you to fit in with the idealistic world of opera singing, more so in this country than anywhere else, possibly with the exception of America. Europe seems to be much more relaxed and open to classical music, because it's something they've grown up with. It's mainstream. In Italy, operatic songs and classical Neapolitan songs have been played to kids from a very early age, it's ingrained in their culture. It's party music for them and it's treated as such, all the festivals blast out *Aida*'s 'March', everybody dancing to it down the street. There's food, the wine's flowing, and everybody's having a good time, everybody, *everybody*, not just the rich geezers who can pay for seats at the opera houses – the farm workers, the fishermen, the townspeople are all out there having a laugh. Yes you have the establishments like La Scala, Verona. But even then Verona doesn't just attract a rich crowd, it attracts everybody. It's a spectacular venue, and sitting in an old amphitheatre in the middle of the summer is incredible.

The attitude they wanted to drum into us on the Vilar programme didn't sit well with me at all. Really bureaucratic, people trying to change, or at least hide, who we actually were as people, for the sake of their establishment's image. I really don't like it, I think it's a low blow to the common man. You should be able to stand there as who you are, where you're from, who your ancestors were. I auditioned for New York City Opera in 2009. I sang my heart out that day, and I sang really well. People who were listening in the wings were very flattering. The pianist said it was the best audition he'd heard in a long time, and the feedback we got from the company later on said yes, I had a very fine voice but I'd auditioned in jeans and a T-shirt. They said I wasn't dressed correctly. I don't get it. If I get a gig, obviously they're gonna shove me in a costume. Why should I dress like a prima donna for an audition? They can hear my voice whatever I'm wearing. I don't know, maybe I just didn't appeal to them on that day, but the fact that they'd given me such positive feedback about my voice, it's just weird. They said they'd looked into my work history and I wasn't right for them. I'm not sure what exactly, my fallings out with teachers at the Royal College, or the fact that some of my work had been mainstream, performing on Broadway, making albums. Albums are a big deal, because once you start singing songs that aren't classical, or you're making records that appeal to a mainstream audience, they look down their noses at you. Until their theatres are empty and they want you to sell seats for them.

In that induction week at the Opera House, the BBC came in and interviewed us about the new programme, and we were all told to turn up smartly dressed. I turned up wearing a sweatshirt with a Duffer logo on it. Didn't shave, had a few beers the night before, just to make a point. The BBC certainly didn't have a problem with it. And at the end of the week David Gowland said to me, 'Alf, I want to let you know, I'm gonna flip my lid and shout at everybody, because I think everybody's been really rude, really obnoxious, really arrogant about this whole programme. But it's not aimed at you.' That automatically put me in an awkward position. I was part of the group, so as far as I was concerned, it *was* for me too. And he brought us all into a room and we stood in a line, and he and Tisi Dutton asked us what we thought of the induction week. A couple of people commented on what they thought was negative about the programme and what they thought could be improved. They were asked for their opinions and they gave their opinions, commented constructively on what was wrong. Because some things *were* wrong. And these singers were adults, they weren't kids, they can say what they damn well like. But Tisi Dutton and David Gowland took it badly.

David slammed his piano lid down and he said, 'RIGHT! *I* want to say something. Every single one of you singers in this room, every single one of you is arrogant and spoilt, and *none* of you are capable of being here, none of you are capable of getting up on that operatic stage and being in the Royal Opera House. And until you are, you know where the doors are.'

Well, thanks. Welcome to the Royal Opera House, this is you for two years. And from that moment I thought, 'I'm not gonna do this. I'm not gonna work in this environment.' I wanted to be a junior principal singer there, and I would have been satisfied if I could have had that opportunity, not even to do major roles. I would have been happy with second and third tenor roles. I wanted to develop myself as a singer, as an artist. But I wasn't being given that opportunity. The list of roles was distributed between us all, between eight singers for the next two years of productions, whatever David Gowland deemed appropriate for us all at the time. And I got grave-digger, spear-carrier, soldier on the left. With one line to sing here or there. I couldn't spend two years doing that. It was so frustrating, a total waste of time. The only role I was looking forward to was Pong in *Turandot*. There are three clowns, you work as a trio, it's a great little role and I would have enjoyed that, but that was really it.

There was another tenor on the programme, and David gave him so many opportunities in that house, so many major roles, covering other singers, and he was going on to perform them on stage as well. Proper dates in the diary for him to perform these great roles at the Royal Opera House. Alfredo in *La Traviata*, Nemorino in *L'elisir d'amore*. I thought everything would be distributed equally, everybody should have the same opportunities as each other on a small programme like that, there shouldn't be favouritism. I asked them why this was happening and they said, 'We just think he's more suited to those roles than you are, you'll get the chances.' And I said, 'Well I'm not getting them, am I? Look at what I'm doing. I'm carrying a spear and pretending to dig a fucking hole.'

Those young artists programmes don't equip you with anything other than the experience of playing one stage. The classes they run, movement classes, acting classes – if students haven't had that education by that point, they shouldn't be on a young artists programme. They should send them around the UK to perform for different audiences, take productions on the road, play small theatres, church halls, scout huts, town squares in the middle of the summer. Just get out there and take the music to the people, and give everybody in the cast a specific role. Scottish Opera Go Round was the best education I could have had in that respect, it showed me how to handle different audiences, how to work in different venues, how to cope with acoustics, with different sets, different spaces on stage. Simply playing the Opera House stage is not what this business is about. And I always thought it was. Get to the Opera House and you've made it. I got to the Opera House and I hated it, because of that programme. I'm not the only one who's had such an experience, far from it. Maria Callas got a lot of criticism from opera houses, she got a lot of stick for her appearance, for her singing, she'd been fired for being a diva, but she just knew what she wanted. She moved fast. She knew what life was about, she knew what singing was about and what audiences wanted. She was a great actress. That was what shone, even more than her voice. People criticised her voice, but her acting was what *made* her voice, the emotion, her honesty. And that counts for a lot. The Royal Opera House Covent Garden, such hallowed ground. It's a bloody wooden platform. No better than the Marine Hall in Fleetwood.

Chapter Seventeen

ROCKY ROAD TO BROADWAY

I started to hear mutterings about a new Broadway production of *La Bohème* when a girl I'd been seeing was auditioning for it. It was generating a right old buzz, everybody was talking about Baz Luhrmann. Who? I didn't know who he was, then somebody told me he'd directed *Romeo + Juliet* and *Moulin Rouge*, which had come out a few months earlier. I asked my agent about it and he said, 'Well, is it really something you want to be doing?' Well, yes.

Part of my requirement on the course was to watch productions and dress rehearsals, which I'd often take advantage of as a chance to take a nap. I'd smuggle in a cushion from home, find an empty box and have a lie down. Unfortunately my audition for Baz happened to coincide with a dress rehearsal for *Parsifal*, a Wagner opera that goes on for five hours. The only time I could do it was in the hour interval, so I jumped up, ran out, tubed it to Waterloo and legged it to this studio they were rehearsing in, turned up sweating like crazy, wet through.

It was Baz, his assistant, his wife Catherine Martin – everyone calls her CM – producers Noel Staunton and David Crook, and the conductor, Constantine Kitsopoulos. I did 'Che Gelida Manina', and while I was singing Constantine was nodding and smiling at Baz, while he was conducting, which was encouraging, and at the end Baz said, 'That was great, can we do it again? Let's try it like this . . .' They opened the fire doors and they sat me there, cross-legged, in front of Baz's assistant, and asked me to sing to her. It was quite something, because it was a bright day outside, but quite foggy, and this fog was flooding in, and I was singing away . . . it was really beautiful actually. Like Baz was directing the weather. And he was really sweet, he said, 'Well done, that was great, great. Hey, they have really good coffee here, go and try it. And we'll see you soon, we'll be in touch.' And that was it. So I cleared off, and I felt really good about it. Shot back to Covent Garden for the start of the next act of *Parsifal*, and all I could think about was the audition, it was going round and round in my head. I was thinking, 'Please, please, please.'

My agent got a call a couple of days later from the casting director's assistant asking me to go to New York for a second audition, they'd fly me over and put me up for the weekend. Well. At that time I was supposed to be learning a repertoire for a recital, and Tisi Dutton brought me into an office and said, 'I hear you've got a second audition for Baz Luhrmann's *Bohème*.'

I said, 'Yeah, I've got to go over to New York.'

She said, 'Well not yet! It's up to us if we let you. You can go if by Friday you've learnt all of your recital, from memory.' Nearly 20 songs. 'I want you to sing through your recital stuff with David and I want you to have learnt it.'

I said, 'OK.'

She said, 'Do you think you can do that?'

I said, 'I'll try my best.'

She said, 'There's no trying your best, it's either *yes* or *no*! A simple *yes* or *no*.'

It was that aggressive, man! So I said, 'Yes then.'

It would usually take three or four weeks to learn all that, I had about four days. Didn't sleep much, brainwashed myself with the music. And Friday came, and I sang through it with David, and it was fine.

It was my first time in New York and I was absolutely buzzing. I just wanted to stay there. I was blown away by everything. I walked out the airport, I was blown away by the yellow cabs. We drove over those bridges, I was blown away by the bridges. I saw Manhattan appear on the skyline, blown away. To sum up: I was blown away. I was grinning from ear to ear, my heart was pounding . . . I just felt *alive* again, I felt really alive! And happy! Really happy! I loved holding a dollar. I loved ordering a coffee and a pretzel and a burger and fries and sitting in a diner. Everything I dreamt about America when I was a kid in Fleetwood looking out to sea seemed to be coming true.

They'd booked me an arty Times Square hotel where every room was a different colour – mine was yellow. Bright, bright yellow, the bedsheets, the floor, the walls, the pictures . . . it was like living in an egg. I walked into Times Square that evening, overwhelmed by the lights and sounds, and I couldn't sleep that night because I was so excited about my audition the next morning. And when I got to the rehearsal studio I was met by Baz, and the producers, and the assistant casting people, and they were really pleased to see me! They wanted to see if I could work with the soprano they'd chosen to pair me up with, to see how well we would work together. A girl called Wei Huang, from Shanghai, and we seemed to click. That evening, Baz's assistant called me: 'Alfie, I just want to say you did really well today, well done.' I thought, right, this doesn't sound good. She said, 'I just want to hand you over to Baz.' My heart was pounding. 'Hey, Alfie, how you doing? Well done today, mate, you did really, really well, great audition. I just wanna say that I think that you'll be ideal for our show and I'd like to offer you the job.' I almost cried. And I spent the night so excited thinking about working on Broadway, about starting a new journey. I wanted to be there so badly.

I was still on a high the next day, still dazzled by New York. 'I'm gonna fly from JFK!' Then when I got to JFK, it hit me. I realised, 'I'm flying back . . . to shit. I'm flying back to my life at the Royal Opera House. Back to being treated like crap by the Vilar programme.' And I knew the Broadway gig wasn't going to go down well with them. I had to give three months' notice, and those three months would be absolute hell, quite possibly the worst three months of my life. I didn't *want* to say that I was leaving because of *La Bohème*. I *was* leaving because of *La Bohème*, but I wanted to get out anyway because of everything else. And I was getting a lot of pressure from the other singers to be the spokesperson about the programme, because they didn't want to speak up. I felt this pressure from all angles. We were having singers meetings, I'd confided in them that I was going to leave and they were saying, 'Alfie, you have to tell them what's wrong with this programme, fight this for us.' But I couldn't, because I had Baz saying, '*Please* do not say anything bad about the Royal Opera House. Just hand in your notice and leave.' He knew what I thought about it all, but he didn't want to get his hands dirty, and I think there was talk of his *Bohème* coming to the Opera House – he didn't want to burn any bridges. So I went to the top and just said I was leaving because I wanted to go off and do *La Bohème*.

The Director of Opera there, Elaine Padmore, couldn't give me enough support. She was wonderful. She said, 'There comes a point in every singer's career when enough study is enough, and it's time to go out and do the job. I know you've done the job before and you have the opportunity to do this. I wouldn't miss it, go and do it.'

The Music Director, Antonio Pappano, said to me, 'Can you really imagine yourself singing act three of *La Bohème* three times a week on Broadway? It's a tough old scene, can you imagine doing that three times a week?'

I said, 'Yeah, I can.'

Then I told David Gowland and Tisi Dutton, and they gave me such a hard time. I had so many meetings, there were so many times where I had to sit in a room with them and explain why, why, why I wanted to leave the programme to go to America. I didn't tell them what I thought about the programme, but I was nevertheless threatened by David Gowland. 'If you *EVER* say *ANYTHING* negative about the Vilar Young Artists Programme I will be down on you like a ton of bricks.'

I said, 'You know what mate – I don't take kindly to threats, and if you're threatening me, let's have it out now, let's do it now, let's sort it out.'

Tisi Dutton said, 'Guys, please, calm down, calm down!'

But I was gonna smack his face in in that room, I really was. He's still running that programme now, it's called The Jette Parker Young Artists Programme, because Alberto Vilar, the investor, didn't fulfil his financial commitments. He went to prison for fraud.

You'd think they might have been proud that one of their students was going off to do this amazing job, starring in a huge production of *La Bohème* in New York. But the thing is about the operatic world, if an opera is not put on on an operatic stage like the Opera House or the English National, La Scala or Metropolitan, then it's not an opera, it's not legitimate. To them. If they'd investigated a little further they would have realised that Baz Luhrmann started out his career as an opera director. The *La Bohème* he did on Broadway was originally on the stage at Sydney Opera House, in 1990.

I was a mess. I was sick every single day, physically sick. From the stress of simply going into the building – I was scared shitless going in there every day. I was shaking, my nerves were shot. It was awful. I almost lost it, I was really unstable. I lost so much weight. I was living in a room in a house in Clapham North, and thank God I'd bought this little vintage drum kit. I'd sold my last kit, the one from the Whisky Train era, years earlier, and didn't have a kit until this new one. I set it up in the bedroom, and every night for three months I bashed all hell out of my drums in my little sanctuary, blasting out *Bridges To Babylon* by The Rolling Stones on my headphones, smacking my drums just to get my mind off my mental torture. I can't listen to that album now because it takes me back to that eerie time. It's a funny old thing that.

Later, I even found out through Baz's production team that they'd been contacting my agent months before I knew they were auditioning, because they'd seen the Channel 4 broadcast of the Glyndebourne *La Bohème*, liked the way I'd played Rodolfo, the innocence, and wanted to see me. My agent had been turning it down without telling me, saying they didn't think it was right for me. They probably didn't want to rankle the Opera House by having one of their artists leave their programme. Either way I was furious when I found that out, that they'd not given me the option to make my own mind up. My agent did attend meetings with the heads of the programmes and defended me to some extent, explained that this was something I wanted to do, but there was still an element of him sort of siding with the house, that it was possibly not what I should be doing. They'd turned down other offers too, they weren't sending CVs and photos out to people when I was asking them to. They weren't on the same path as me, so I left them soon after. Even at that stage I wanted to do records and to play to more mainstream audiences. I wanted exciting jobs! Jobs that inspired me and took me into different worlds. I wanted to shake up the classical world, I wanted to work with that European feeling, opera for the masses. Because England is very insular when it comes to classical music, they keep it very much to themselves, very much protected.

There were a couple of lights in that tunnel. That January there was a Royal Opera House production of *Tosca*, with Pavarotti. His mother died during rehearsals and it wasn't clear if he'd go through with the production, a four-night run. But he did, and I got to watch him from the wings, he was absolutely amazing. He played Rodolfo there in the 1960s. David Gowland arranged an afternoon for me and this other tenor, the guy he was giving all these opportunities to, to sing to Pavarotti in his hotel suite. But I didn't go, because I was just so shaken up about everything. My confidence had gone and I just couldn't do it. But it's one of my biggest regrets, not doing that.

Also I was in a production of *Tristan and Isolde*, playing the shepherd. I was brought out of class to rehearse it. That was wonderful because I loved singing that music, and I loved working with Bernard Haitink. I actually did his last performance at the Royal Opera House, and to do that made up for all the crap I'd been through, he was a fantastic conductor and he was lovely. I had a tiny little line in the piece, and I sang it to him, and I sang with the rest of the chorus, and he was really supportive, he gave me a lot of encouragement and spoke to a lot of music staff about me, he really acknowledged my voice. No one else there did, and he was a major star. I thought, 'Wow man, this is great, Bernard Haitink likes my singing!' Working on that show with him meant a lot, it was very precious to me.

I left soon after that. I finished my final recital, and at the end, the head of opera came up to me, and the head of the programmes, and the casting director and the company manager, and one of them said, 'Alfie, that was really good! Did you enjoy it? You looked like you did!'

I said, 'You know what? I hated every single minute. I hated every single minute of that. And I promise you, I will never do it again.'

And I've never done a recital since. It wasn't the music or the performing, it was just all the pressure they'd added. I wanted to get out. They were doing a final Vilar performance, and I said, 'I'm not coming back, I'm not doing it.'

They said, 'Well, we'll only accept your resignation if you do.'

I said, 'You can't. I'm resigning. I'm leaving and I'm not coming back. And I'm not gonna do the final concert.'

And I didn't.

There was no farewell, needless to say. And they were very quick to black out my face on all the promo posters and flyers for the Vilar Singers. Like I never existed. When I won a Tony award – the principal cast of Baz's La Bohème all won Tony awards – it was amazing how quickly I was resurrected as one of the Opera House's artists. But as awful as those few months had been, I was kind of loving it, sticking the rebellious two fingers up at them. Yeah, I wanted to fire it up a little bit. I wanted to be a fox in the chicken house, you know? And I was, I did kick up the dust a little bit. I don't make decisions lightly and I wanted to prove I was something different. I've ruffled some feathers in the industry over the years, but I think you've got to do that. It keeps them on their toes! And if I'd turned down *La Bohème* on Broadway and stayed on that programme, I probably wouldn't be singing today. I certainly wouldn't be in the position I'm in today, because Baz Luhrmann's *Bohème* brought a hell of a lot to me.

When I was doing *Les Misérables* last year and I was living in a flat in Covent Garden, I'd often walk past the Royal Opera House, and I'd always feel an element of relief that I didn't have to go in and be part of that programme any more. And it felt *great.*

Before going to the States I had to do Benjamin Britten's *Albert Herring* in Glyndebourne, and I had three months to kill before that, so I went home to Fleetwood. I needed to recuperate. And I practically locked myself away in that house, sat in my room, because I was just a mess, mentally and physically. I'd really been put through the mill. Mum was there for me, she was great, she gave me the time I needed on my own, and consoled me, and fed me well! I felt safe at home, really, really safe, and so relieved to be there. I was thrilled about America, it was the only thing keeping me going. But I was upset, wrestling with my decision to some extent, a little tormented about what I was doing, concerned about not being able to sing again in the Royal Opera House after everything that had gone on there. Mum said, 'What's your gut feeling?' and I said that I wanted to go to America. She said, 'Well go. Do it. And you *will* sing at the Opera House again.'

There was further madness, I was having problems with someone who was calling me up and giving me a hard time about some gossipy opera nonsense, and I'd had enough. And Mum got my phone, switched it off and hid it. She said, 'I don't want you to talk to anybody, I want you to recover. Get yourself back on your feet.'

Chapter Eighteen

PINCHING MYSELF

I had to really turn everything around over the summer. And *Albert Herring* really built up my confidence again because I threw myself out there, used all the emotion that had been coursing through me, and it paid off.

Britten premièred *Albert Herring* in Glyndebourne in the 1940s. The title character's a young kid who's governed by everybody and he bows down to them all. Bosses demean him and he's very humble about everything, quite an unassuming guy. He's under the thumb, he does what he's told, and he gets humiliated, because the villagers can't find a suitable woman to play Queen of the May for the May Day festival, so they choose Albert instead. I related to him at the time – I couldn't answer back, I didn't say what I'd wanted to say, I'd sucked it up, I'd shut up and retreated. He's even given Foxe's *Book of Martyrs* at one point, the book my mum used to read to me in bed. The nightmare machine, my old nemesis. It's supposed to be a comedy, *Albert Herring*, but it's quite an emotional one to play, it certainly was for me, and I took full advantage of my state of mind to do it. Saying that, I also based him on David Jason as Granville from *Open All Hours* and Pike from *Dad's Army*.

We performed *Albert Herring* in August, seven shows, and I pulled it out of the bag. I got a standing ovation every night, got great reviews and won the John Christie award. John Christie started the Glyndebourne festival in the 1930s and died in 1962, and good old Richard Van Allan won the John Christie award in 1966. So I was really chuffed to win that, it was a big honour and meant a lot to me. And it was one of the best productions I ever did, I really loved it. *La Bohème* on Broadway, *Les Misérables* in the West End, and *Albert Herring* at Glyndebourne – those are the productions that changed my life. My last performance went down a storm because I was so adrenalised, so excited to be leaving for America the following day, I was on fire. The whole thing was something of a slap in the face for the Vilar people – I'd left their programme, done a major operatic festival, got outstanding reviews and won the John Christie award. Although even some people at Glyndebourne were saying, 'Why are you doing this *La Bohème* on Broadway?' Why not? That was always my answer. 'Why not?' They'd say it was a controversial production. I'd say, 'What's controversial about it?' And they could never answer because they didn't know. I think it was just because it was on Broadway. There was nothing different about the opera, it was in Italian, it was the full score, we hadn't cut anything out.

The morning after my last *Albert Herring* show off I flew to New York for our first music rehearsals. A friend of mine had a flat, excuse me, apartment, in Inwood, north Manhattan and had gone away, and I stayed there. I felt like my life had begun again, I had a good old time in the bars and diners, I was in my element. We did a TV commercial in a massive warehouse in

Yonkers. We played against bluescreen. I couldn't believe I was on this film set, making a TV ad for a Broadway show, working with Baz Luhrmann. My word. We had publicity shots taken, I've still got the pictures of me and Wei Huang, who starred alongside me as Mimì. The photographer was Douglas Kirkland, he'd done that great shoot of Marilyn Monroe wrapped in the bedsheet. Moments like that, I had to pinch myself. And I really enjoyed the rehearsals, 10 hours a day. I loved Baz's take on *Bohème.* He wanted audiences to be able to instantly identify with it, just as Puccini's audiences did when it was first staged in the 1890s. He brought it forward to 1957 Paris, because that was a specific period of time where bohemian life was really blossoming there, and the social and economic situations had parallels. It was a magnificent production. It had transvestites and drag queens, prostitutes, a right motley crew. Parpignol, who sells toys to kids, was a clown, there was a jazz band in the café, it was hilarious, so much fun. And Baz had glitzed it up a lot more than his Sydney production, he had more money to spend on sets and lights. It was really dazzling.

There was nothing controversial about it. Some purists grumbled about our use of microphones, but they weren't for amplification, they were for voice-enhancement, it's a different technique. We were put through the same system as the orchestra. The musicians were miked because they can't afford to keep an 80-piece orchestra running all the time, so they cut down the size of the orchestra considerably and used synths to double strings, things like that, to make it sound thicker. And because they were put through a sound system, we had to have voice enhancement. If it wasn't for the mics it would have sounded ridiculous. Saying that, nine times out of ten, my mic would fall off, down my back, no matter what I did. So I was singing it acoustically anyway, and everybody could hear me. The sound guy would come up to me and say, 'Your mic fell off again, didn't it?' Sometimes I told him to just take it off and I did entire shows without a mic. Baz had gone by then. I don't think he knew.

I mentioned this in an interview for *The Scotsman* newspaper a few months ago and there was a bit of kerfuffle about it, because I said microphones have also been used in the English National Opera. A few people piped up online and said I was talking nonsense. For the record, we used mics for *The Merry Widow* in 2008, for the dialogue. On *Kismet* in 2007 we used mics for the whole lot, dialogue and singing. Some people just don't wanna hear about that. Sure, they might not have ever used microphones, but I certainly have, and I know that other people in other productions have. It's frustrating when people try to protect the industry like that, it's very hypocritical and really weird. They're very blinkered. They don't see what they don't want to see.

Anyway. If you're comparing what Baz was doing with what critics would call legitimate opera, those were the only differences, that we were playing Broadway, we were playing to a mainstream audience, and we had some voice enhancement. There was something of a rivalry between us and the Metropolitan Opera, because they were performing Franco Zeffirelli's production at the same time, an absolutely stunning production. Very different to ours. But critics were always comparing them, reducing it all to: 'This is the real deal, on the Metropolitan stage, compared to the Baz Luhrmann farce on Broadway.' Baz's perspective was very similar to the way I feel about opera. He made a point of saying, while he was promoting the show, that Puccini made it for everyone, from the street sweeper to the King of Naples, and Baz wanted his production to be accessible to everyone, not just the opera elite. It was amazing to meet someone who was so respected and so estab-lished in their career, and who shared the sentiments I had.

My Rodolfo was rougher than how I'd played him in Glyndebourne, and quite different to the other two actors who were sharing the role with me, David Miller and Jesus Garcia. David and I were both doing three evening performances a week, Jesus did the two matinees. I have so much respect for those guys. David played him in a very suave, romantic Italian style; that was David, he's a tall good-looking guy, he's got a beautiful romantic voice. He's a good guy, he's in Il Divo now. Jesus Garcia's performance was very subtle, he's a beautiful singer. More studious, timid, somewhat similar to how I'd played Rodolfo in Glyndebourne. This time I played him quite forceful, strong, but pretty deluded. A bit thick really, basically kidding himself, because as I said he comes from a wealthy family and they look after him, they make sure he's comfy, make sure he's safe, with enough money. And Baz encouraged every-one to interpret their roles their own way, which was evident in his choice to cast three very different people. Smart too, because people could watch one performance and come again and see someone else do it differently. And that's what happened, we got audiences coming back to see us all do it, paying three times to see the same show.

I was nervous at first, but I knew the piece. And the first thing Baz did was to get everybody to write the opera in their own words, their own translation of the piece. Rewrite it in our dialects, so how I would say that dialogue as Alfie Boe from Fleetwood. We'd start off slowly, singing it in Italian, then the following day he'd say, 'Now do it in your own words.' We had to change just like that, so we got to know it inside out, we really understood what we were saying. Then he had us tag-teaming, interchanging the actors with the actresses. Because the main roles of Rodolfo and Mimì were shared between three couples, in these rehearsals Baz would keep mixing it all up, it was brilliant. He was nice with it too, if we fell apart, we fell apart, and he'd go, 'Let's try again, guys, back up.' So chilled, so cool, so relaxed, no pressure, no anger.

There was one time when there was a bit of upset. Wei Huang, my Mimì, was straight out of music college in Shanghai and she wasn't that experienced with working with a guy. And I found it a little frustrating because she would never hit her mark, and she would never do the direction that Baz gave her. So I'd take her and I'd gently move her, physically move her. Baz pulled me aside one day and he said, 'Listen, Alf, you can't move Wei. You cannot do that, you can't correct her mistakes.' I apologised. And then he had a word with Wei, told her to trust me. The other two couples were fine, but Wei just wasn't comfortable with me, she was incredibly nervous and didn't quite know how to react in an affectionate scene, to the extent that when I would give her a kiss or a hug, she would nip me and pinch me. At one point I had to kiss her and whenever I did she bit my lip, because she was that nervous. She bit me so hard one day she made me bleed. I thought, 'How can I turn this around, how can I win her confidence, and show her that I'm not going to pressure her?' And I decided to just make her feel special. The next day I went into work with a box of chocolates and I said, 'Wei, I was just thinking about you, I know you're a long way from home, so I bought you some chocolates, I hope you like them.' She was gobsmacked. So every morning after that I did something like that, bought her some chocolate or some biscuits, brought her some coffee, schmoozed her a bit. All through rehearsals, San Francisco too. And it was working. It worked! And we turned out great together. When we were on Broadway, *Time Out* and the *New York Times* both said Wei and I were the couple to see.

And months later when we were in LA, during the third run of the show, Baz visited to see the show, and we were asked to go into his dressing room. And he turned around to us and he was in tears. He said, 'You guys just blew me away. That was the most emotional performance of *La Bohème* I have ever seen in my life.'

Chocolates and biscuits.

Chapter Nineteen

FALLING IN LOVE IN SAN FRANCISCO

Rehearsals continued in San Francisco, where the show would be opening for a few weeks before Broadway. I spent most of my spare time in the first couple of weeks hanging out with Ricardo and Radu. Ricardo's 3ft 6in, he played a switchblade-wielding pimp in the show. He hadn't acted for years before that because he'd broken his neck while trying out for a stunt job on *Howard the Duck* in 1985. Small guy, huge personality. He smokes cigars, so the first thing I said to him was, 'Do you know what, mate, that'll stunt your growth.' He said, 'I love you, Alfie, I really love you. We're gonna get on well!' And we did, we were best friends. We dressed the same, we used to go to these biker shops on the Sunset Strip and wear the same jeans and T-shirts and walk down the street together. He used to let me drive his car, a Mazda Miata, which had extended pedals for him, so my knees rubbed my chin. Radu meanwhile is a 7ft Romanian kickboxer who played opposite Ricardo. Radu drank an entire bottle of olive oil every day, said it was full of the protein and nutrients he needed for his body. He's built like a brick shithouse, very muscly. He was too tall to fit in the Mazda, so Ricardo would take the top down for him.

For those first couple of weeks I was renting a room off a woman who would bring guys back all the time and get into some really violent arguing and shouting, four in the morning, hell it was loud. Then at breakfast I'd see them and it would be like nothing was wrong. I couldn't live like that, so I got out of there and found a cool little apartment room on Pine and Mason, a lovely part of San Francisco. My apartment was pretty high up, it overlooked quite a lot of the city and I'd stand out on my little balcony and survey it all, in love with the place. Eating fantastic Italian pizza every night, going to great bars and drinking proper American beer, I felt like I was in a movie all the time. And rehearsals were going great, it had all really kicked into gear, we were singing with the orchestra now, feeling it all come alive. We were in the American Conservatory Theatre on Geary Street, an actors' college, and because of the triple cast I'd sing the first section, then David would do the same, and then Jesus. One gorgeous hot day, I finished my aria, got past my big high C, I'd done 'O Soave Fanciulla', the last song of Act One, and I walked out to this kitchenette to get a cup of tea while David did his bit. The only cup I could find was one of those Thermos ones with a huge base and a tiny narrow top. I busted three teabags trying to shove one into this idiotic cup. Then as I walked out of the kitchenette I looked up and saw this girl, and she looked at me. Sarah. And I know this is about as corny as it gets but the song 'Dream Weaver' came on in my head. 'Dreeeeeam weaver ...' Everything else disappeared. Total tunnel vision. Slow motion, the works. She was glowing, absolutely glowing. She had a white vest on, tiny blue shorts, she was tanned like nobody's business, luscious long brown hair, beautiful. I thought, 'Right. You're the one.' I made a beeline for her, went straight over and sat down. I said, 'You can't get a decent cup of tea around here,' which may not make it into the pantheon of great chat-up lines. Stupid, stupid thing. I felt an idiot. I thought, 'What the *hell* are you saying?' She said, 'Lovely music in there,' and I said, 'Yeah, it's *La Bohème*, by Puccini.' She asked me what I did and I said I worked on the show, and she assumed I was stage crew. I asked her out within five minutes, told her to get some friends together and come out with some of us that night, and she said yes. Jessica Comeau, who was playing one of the Musettas, had come over and started talking to her, and was apparently reassuring her that I wasn't some crazy person.

We met up for a drink that evening, in the Union Square Sports Bar and we had a great time, although she told me some time afterwards she'd thought it was a dive. She brought a friend, Alex, with her and we played pool. I put Steve Miller and Aerosmith on the jukebox and was horsing around with the pool cue, spinning it on my foot, playing air guitar with it, basically being a bit of an arse. The '80s alien sitcom *ALF* was playing on the TV, and Sarah couldn't get a handle on that being my name, so she called me Alfred. Everyone there called me Alfred anyway. In London it was Alf or Alfie, but in America, always Alfred. Some of Sarah's family still call me Alfred. Her grandmother calls me Alford.

I was drinking Guinness, accidentally knocked into her and spilt it all over her back, her white vest, so that was good. Again, I felt an idiot. I've felt an idiot since I first met her. I still do now. I apologised, and she wanted to go home and get changed, funnily enough. I practically begged her to come back out later to a blues club with a few of us, and gave her enough cash for a return cab journey, to make sure she did. She seemed to think that was chivalrous, a kindly act by this exotic Englishman. American boys, or at least the ones she'd dated, didn't do that, she later said. More fool them. I met up with Ricardo and Radu and grabbed a cab to this awful Indian restaurant where David Miller was having a party for the singers. I'd asked if I could bring Sarah and he insisted it was cast only, so Ricardo, Radu and I thought we'd show our faces for a bit while she was off sprucing herself up. We turned up, Ricardo said, 'This is the biggest pile of crap I've ever seen Alfie,' and it was. We had a poppadom, some lime pickle and then cleared off. Those two weren't even invited because they weren't singers. That's what it was, singers knitting together. That happens in college, in opera houses, it's something that just seems to go on in the professional classical business. There's no other music world that has that cliquey group – you don't find that in music theatre or pop music. It's all so segregated in that world. So. We went to this blues club, Biscuit And Blues, I used to go there to see bands all the time.

Sarah and Alex were acting students at the American Conservatory Theatre and had class at 9am, and this was around 11pm, but Sarah had bribed Alex to come back out with the promise of cute guys, as I had said I was bringing friends. Radu had disappeared to a massage parlour, so when they turned up I was just sat with Ricardo, who dresses like a Mafia boss. He was wearing a trilby, a three-piece suit and a badge that said 'No shit, I'm short.' Alex, visibly, wasn't impressed; I guess she wasn't into older married guys who were 3ft tall. I thought she was gonna smack me silly. She made it clear that she needed to get home to bed, and I asked her to stay, I told her my other friend was on his way. Soon enough Radu appeared, and Alex kind of lost it. Guess she's not into 7ft Romanian kickboxers. I thought I'd arm-wrestle Radu, which is a pretty stupid thing to do unless you're also enormous and a kickboxer, and I am clearly neither. I was actually managing to hold him up, but I couldn't move him. And suddenly something cracked. It just went, and my arm died. Completely lifeless. I had, it transpired, snapped a ligament, and it killed – my elbow has never been the same since. I can still feel it, and whenever my elbow twinges it reminds me of Radu. But I wasn't going to let it ruin my night; we were having fun, we were dancing. Me and Sarah got some time to ourselves, we talked a lot, connected really quickly. I was wearing a ring that Dad had bought me and she asked me about it, so I started talking about him. That was a big deal because I hadn't properly opened up about him to anyone, not even my family. It was a real release.

We left the club together and walked down to the main road, past the theatre we were playing in, The Curran, and Sarah looked up and saw the poster, which featured me and Wei in an embrace, with our names on it. She said, 'That's you! I thought you were stage crew! I thought you shifted boxes!' We kissed goodnight – cordially – and I put her in a cab home. And I was on cloud nine. Those San Francisco hills were really small, because I was flying over them, I really was. I'd never felt like that before. I got back to my apartment, opened my balcony doors and took in the skyline, the moon shining. Everything at the Vilar programme was behind me, and I just felt happy. Really, really happy, really warm, really content, really satisfied with my life. It was an absolutely beautiful moment.

Sarah and I met up again the following day. She was living by herself in an apartment in Pacific Heights, she'd begun her masters programme around the same time as I'd arrived in San Francisco, a couple of weeks earlier. We spent a lot of time together from that point, practically every night, hanging out, listening to a lot of music, Led Zeppelin, Tom Waits, Steve

Miller. She got me into Led Zep's *Houses Of The Holy*, which I hadn't really explored before. They're a big band for us. We danced to 'Rain Song' song in my apartment, so later on we had it as the first dance at our wedding. Sarah was with me when I met Robert Plant in a bar last year, and in the studio with us when we recorded 'Song to the Siren' together. Robert's sound-tracked our relationship in a sense. And that honeymoon period in San Francisco was magic, she was wonderful. She bought me tea and biscuits for my birthday to remind me of home – it was really sweet, nobody had ever done anything like that for me before. Got it slightly wrong though. Peppermint tea and chocolate chip cookies. Cute.

We just connected on every level. The first time we kissed was at a *Bohème* party Baz put on at the W hotel – a really lovely rooftop party, full of celebs. We were both dazzled by it all, the boy from Fleetwood and the girl from Utah. And she kissed me, I was so shy with her. I soon asked her to come to New York with me for the Broadway run. She was unhappy at college; to some extent her situation mirrored my frustrations at the Opera House. She'd spent the previous four years getting her bachelor's and wasn't feeling particularly inspired to continue studying. It was no small thing for her to be at that college; there were 15 in her class from 2000 auditions, but she quit, on her birthday.

Gala Night in San Francisco was such an event. TV crews, press, red carpet, the works. It was a big deal, Baz was such a big deal, *Moulin Rouge* had only come out that summer and was so huge. Nicole Kidman was there, Kevin Spacey was there, Baz had a film crew getting audience reactions to the show. He did that a lot, he's amazing at creating a buzz, generating hype. The Curran is a beautiful theatre, 90 years old, and Sarah had never seen an opera before, she brought her friends with her. I really loved singing that night, knowing that she was out there with her friends.

We recorded the cast album in that period in San Francisco, at George Lucas's Skywalker Ranch, and Sarah came with me. I'd had a show the night before and had to get up at 7am to drive up there. My voice was wrecked, because I'd not had time to recover from the show, and I had to sing 'Che Gelida Manina', which I didn't feel in any fit state to do. So I recorded everything else I had to do first, and me and Sarah spent the night there, in a guest ranch near the studios, so I could do the aria the next day. The land there actually looks like something from *Star Wars*. There are CCTV cameras in the rocks, which moved around, and he lives in a massive old colonial mansion at the other end of the valley. We were in the Norman Rockwell Suite, which had beautiful Rockwell paintings on the wall, and we settled down for the evening. Sarah went to have a bath and I lit a fire; I thought I'd make the room nice and romantic, but she came out of the bathroom prematurely when she saw smoke coming under the door. The fire was properly blazing and I was trying, failing, to sort it out. She said, 'Did you open the flue?' I didn't know anything about a flue. Sparks were flying onto the carpet, some were dangerously close to the paintings, and we worked it out in the nick of time, opened the flue, but it was a hairy moment. I'm glad we didn't burn the place down. Nobody wants to be the guy who burnt down Skywalker Ranch.

Chapter Twenty

SINGING ON BROADWAY, SLEEPING ON LILOS

The first few nights on Broadway were a whole other level. I went to the toilet during the show on opening night, I think David Miller was on, and I found myself next to James Gandolfini at the urinals. I said hi.

'Alright, mate?'

'Yeah. How are you?'

'I'm cool thanks. Never pissed next to a gangster before.'

'Neither have I.'

Then Harvey Keitel walked in. In the interval, Baz grabbed me and introduced me to Leonardo DiCaprio and Rupert Murdoch. Hugh Grant was there, Cameron Diaz. Drew Barrymore was thrown out midway through Act One because she and her boyfriend, the drummer from The Strokes, were caught being a bit too amorous in the ladies' toilet. And at the after-party at the Hudson Hotel I ended up playing pool with Leonardo DiCaprio. Nice guy. Shit at pool.

The next day, *The New York Times* said it was the coolest show in town, and it absolutely felt like it. It was amazing singing on that stage and looking out at the audience and seeing the likes of Tom Hanks, Steven Spielberg, George Lucas. Sigourney Weaver came to see it one night. I had a massive crush on her when I was a kid, because of *Ghostbusters*. Stunning. I still do a bit, she still does it for me. Sarah knows, it's all above board. I invited her backstage to say hi, and she was lovely, beautiful. I was a little awestruck. Sting came. I was at home one afternoon, David Miller was on that night, and I had a phone call from someone in the cast saying, 'Alf, you're a big Sting fan, he's in tonight watching the show, why don't you come in and meet him and ask him to come backstage and meet us all?' So after the show I went up to him, introduced myself and asked him to come back. We walked through the pass door and he said, 'This *bel canto* stuff is great, I love it,' and he started to sing. I'm in this empty theatre, walking across a Broadway stage next to Sting, and he's singing. Another of those moments. I met him a few years later at the Classical Brit Awards, he was nominated for his lute album. I reintroduced myself and he said, 'Yeah, I remember you, what are you doing here?'

I said, 'My album's up against you in Album of the Year.'

He said, 'Really? Cool, cool.'

And he just backed away. I didn't stand a chance, I was up against him and Paul McCartney. Macca won it.

We were selling out, every night we had a full house. Us three Rodolfos were all very different. David Miller has a beautiful voice, and Jesus Garcia's is lovely, a very *bel canto* Italian sounding voice. There was a bit of a competition between us all though. We all wanted to fight for press, we all wanted our faces on the posters, we all wanted to be the stars of the show. The producers wanted to find the star couple as well, something to pin it on. Baz didn't care, he wanted to spread the love equally – we all had press nights. But for much of the promo the producers went with David Miller and Ekaterina, because they were a very beautiful couple, the pretty boy and the blonde Russian. Deservedly so though, they were great. Sometimes we'd have to swap partners if somebody was sick, so a couple of times I played with Ekaterina. She was a bit of a diva, she performed with me one night when Wei was off sick and started demanding things from me on stage. I had to remind her to consider the rest of us. She only wanted to play with David, I think. He actually married one of the Mimì understudies. It was a soap opera in itself.

I was living with Sarah in The Ansonia Building, a grand old gothic mansion on the Upper West Side, 73rd and Broadway, over 100 years old, used to be a hotel. Caruso stayed there, Stravinsky, Mahler. Babe Ruth lived there, some of the apartments cost millions of dollars. Big building, big reputation. Our apartment, on the other hand, was tiny. About as big as this page. I think it used to be the maids' quarters. It was like a wind tunnel, a hallway. Sarah arrived from her family home in Salt Lake with a suitcase and a TV-video combo. We had no furniture, our bedside table was a little box with a napkin for a tablecloth. We didn't have a bedside light, but we had a tiny little fridge by Sarah's side of the bed, so she would open the fridge door and use the light to read books at night. I say bed, it was a blow-up mattress in the corner that we had to inflate at 4am every day because it would deflate during the night. We'd set the alarm for 4 and pump it up again to see us through till morning, otherwise we'd end up basically lying on the floor. The characters in the show had better living conditions – you could say I was taking method acting to its extreme. We even had a dog, Guinness, still got him. Sarah's parents' dogs had

pups, so her mum sent us one, for crying out loud. It wasn't
very practical. I'm glad she did though, he's a good old dog.
And winter was freezing – it was a crazy winter, two weeks of
blizzards, so cold and snowy they shut down Broadway for two
weeks; the theatres were dead. We went out one day, me, Sarah
and Guinness, and walked through Manhattan – it was a ghost
town, hardly any people, no cars, fantastically romantic. There
were people having snowball fights in the road, we went into
Tavern on the Green and had Irish coffee, it was beautiful. But
man it was cold. A lot of musicians on Broadway lost money
because of the weather that winter.

It was all a bit of a shock for Sarah, leaving college without a
plan, leaving her family to be with me in glamorous Manhattan,
but living in this tiny room. We made the most of it. She'd buy
clothes from Neiman Marcus and keep the tags on and return
them. She wore her prom dress to opening night. I bought her a
dress from BCBG. But it was an odd double-life, partying with
A-list stars and going back at the end of the night to this box; I
was starring on Broadway and sleeping on a lilo. But as hard as it
was, we had a romantic time of it. I proposed to her there in New
York. She was working in a casting agency, Mackey/Sandrich,
doing secretarial work, and I dropped her off at work one morning then went into town to check on the engagement ring I'd got
for her, then went hunting for a restaurant to propose in. Every
restaurant I wanted to go to was closed for refurbishment. Green
Room, Rockefeller, Greenwich Kitchen, they were all shut. I
bumped into Alvaro Domingo, Plácido Domingo's son; they
both had some sort of connection with *La Bohème* on Broadway,
and we went for a drink. I told him I was struggling to find a
restaurant, and he told me he and his dad owned a restaurant in
Midtown East called Pampano, a Mexican seafood place, and
suggested I take Sarah there for dinner. So I phoned Sarah at

work, told her I was going to take her to a burger joint, and I got myself suited up. She came home, said, 'Why are you wearing a suit to get a burger?' I told her to get her glad rags on and we went to Pampano. I always used to do napkin tricks with Sarah, Charlie Chaplin gags with my fork, and when she went to the bathroom I put the ring underneath her napkin. I said, 'Pick up your napkin, I've got a trick to show you.' And she lifted it up and there was the ring. That was a year after we'd met.

The Tony Awards were in June, and at first there was talk of an award only going to the couple who played the leads on the first night, but Baz, bless him, didn't want that. So the Tony bigwigs created an honorary award and a few of us got one for best performance, best principals. I got one, Wei got one, all of us from the principal ensembles, the three Rodolfos and Mimìs and Musettas and Marcellos. And it was great, we performed in Radio City, did a section from the show. I was stood on stage with Wei and I was *screaming* it out, and the mixer got the level just right, my voice was flying. Radio City's absolutely huge, it's massive, it's like an arena. It's incredibly glamorous, very art deco, very high, seats for miles, up to the heavens. It's proper New York, you just know you're singing into history, the amount of legends that have played there. That night was a bit of a conveyor belt though, because those things are run like clockwork, and they didn't have enough space for all the shows to be hanging out backstage so they had to keep moving everybody through. We turned up on a bus, walked through the stage door, were pushed on stage, came off the other side, out the pass door, back onto a bus and back to our theatre. The highlight for me was meeting Christopher Reeve – he was in his wheelchair in his dressing room, we all met him. I had so much respect for him, and he was really sweet, and very complimentary to us all.

Soon after that, after nine months on Broadway, the show closed. It wasn't long after 9/11, so people weren't coming into the city as much, and there had been that crazy winter with no shows, and also a musicians' strike, so money was lost there too. And the *La Bohème* cast was big, they couldn't afford to keep it running there. So it moved to LA. I had nothing to lose by going back into it. I loved the production, it was a great opportunity to do it again, a great chance to be in LA, and I thought it might give me the opportunity to develop some relationships with an agent out there, to get some film and television work.

The first few weeks were a little nomadic, we lived just off Sunset Strip, in the hills, for a couple of weeks, moved into a friend's house for another week, then settled in Santa Monica with some of Sarah's family friends, which was lovely, by that great beach. Owen Wilson lived across the road from us – we used to see him and his girlfriend on their bikes. We'd only ever see him on his bike and he'd only ever holler, 'So where do you ride?!' His brother Luke nearly ran me over with his Porsche. I was walking down the alleyway behind the houses with Guinness and he pulled out of his garage, nearly knocked us over. You bump into people – not so literally – like that everywhere in LA. Oh, that's David Schwimmer in front of me in Starbucks. There's David Hyde Pierce walking down the street. Quentin Tarantino eating next to us in a Thai restaurant. I was in an Italian restaurant on Fairmont Street once, sat on a table next to Steve Austin, the WWF wrestler, bit of a thrill. A bit. I was kind of a WWF fan. I prefer the old-fashioned British stuff, the beer drinkers. I used to watch the wrestling on a Saturday morning, Big Daddy and Giant Haystacks. I loved Giant Haystacks – he played the Marine Hall in Fleetwood. He was such a big guy he couldn't make it up the stairs to the stage, so they had to put a little dressing room for him on the auditorium floor, which was kind of sad really. I loved those wrestlers. To see Big Daddy and Giant Haystacks fight on *Grandstand*, on the telly on Saturday afternoons . . . it was like watching King Kong and the T-Rex. Nothing could break the boulder of Big Daddy's belly, but Haystacks came close.

There was this pool hall we used to go to in Santa Monica. I got into playing pool in America quite a lot. I used to go there to chill out on my days off, and I played with some dude called Frank. He must have been in his '80s. I got to know the guys behind the bar and I said, 'What's his story?' Because behind the bar there was a photograph of him with Paul Newman, back in the '50s or '60s. They said, 'That guy is the reason they wrote *The Hustler.*' *The Hustler* was adapted from a novel, but I never got to the bottom of it, I never asked him. But I used to play pool with him all the time and he was bloody good. He used to kick my arse like crazy, he'd clear up all the time. I never said, 'Are you the guy they wrote *The Hustler* about?' It might be a pack of lies, but I'd rather live with that than investigate it – it doesn't matter if it's not true. All I know is I played pool with him a lot and he taught me how to play.

Elaine Padmore and Antonio Pappano from the Royal Opera House came to see me in *Bohème* and were very complimentary, it was wonderful to see them. Meanwhile I could see the show coming to an end, it was only a limited run, and I was desperately trying to figure out how we could stay in LA, we loved it there. I sang to loads of opera houses while I was there. One night Danny DeVito and his wife Rhea Perlman came to see the show. I really wanted to meet them, so I asked the company manager to invite them back, and after the show we walked to our cars together, Danny was such a solid, down to earth guy, and Rhea was a diamond. I mentioned that I was looking for an American agent and he told me about his agent, Fred Specktor, Vice President of CAA. I did already have an American agent but he was doing bugger all. I did nine months on Broadway and he didn't bring anybody to see me, and he'd rarely return my calls. I put a lot of trust in that guy to help me with my career over there, to get me in front of people, and he achieved nothing. So I wrote a letter to Fred Specktor, inviting him to the show, and he came along, then asked me to come for a meeting in his office in Beverly Hills, and he was really cool. I asked him for advice, because I really wanted to get work in LA, acting work.

And Fred was incredibly helpful, he set up meetings for me with casting directors on the big studio lots. I went to see some at Twentieth Century Fox, DreamWorks, three or four of them. One of them was really enthusiastic until she realised I wasn't who she thought I was. She checked the headshot of the person she was supposed to be meeting and said, 'Oh, you're my three thirty appointment.' That was a bit of a letdown. But that was really good of Fred, to do that for me. We keep in touch, I talk to him every now and then. He's a big deal, but what a nice guy.

La Bohème finally reached the end of its life there in LA, and we went to Salt Lake to get married. We were living in Sarah's family house with her parents, and a month before the wedding, Mum and my brother John came out to stay with us. Sarah and I took them to Zion, the national park, for a weekend break, took them around Bryce Canyon, stunning red rock. We wanted to show them where Sarah was from. Mum was a real trooper, she loves hiking. But my goodness, our families are as different as it gets. Bit of a culture clash. Sarah's friends threw some themed wedding showers for us, guests had to come and gift both of us, and one party was themed 'lingerie and tools'. I think Mum was a little taken aback. Sarah got some pretty underwear, I was given a bum-bag with a toilet-roll in it and a trowel.

I wanted to do something really simple for my stag do. Eat some chicken wings and chill out with everyone, play pool or something. We ended up in a strip-club. I didn't want to go in the slightest, but others did, and I succumbed, I even invited the priest along. He didn't come, funnily enough. Probably a good thing, because it was exceptionally horrible. The amount of people who so easily adjust to being in that environment, it's really something. I'm not a fan. One of the girls was attempting to pole dance with me and I was saying, 'Please don't. If you don't mind.' Mainly because she was pretty disgusting. But she was laughing her head off, she thought it was great.

We had a few parties, including one the day before the wedding where, inevitably, I was asked to sing. At the time I was getting ready to go on a tour of America with a big band, singing old Broadway songs, so I sang Sinatra's 'Luck Be a Lady'. I went up to Mum after and said, 'That was fun Mum, wasn't it!' She said: 'You should not be singing that stuff, Alf. I don't like it.' Ah man. Mum had quite specific views on what I should sing back then, she likes the classical rep. 'I'm sorry, Alf, but no.' I was so upset, because I was really looking forward to singing different styles, breaking into different genres. It was new to me and I was feeling pretty sensitive about it. I didn't know what to say, so I just walked out of the house in tears, and kept walking, and I punched a tree, broke my hand. When I got back, Sarah's mum brought me and Mum into a room – she's very positive like that, Sarah's mum – and got us to talk it out.

My hand's still damaged now, my knuckles are kind of flat. Because trees don't move. So I got married with a broken hand. You can see it in the wedding photographs, because I didn't want to get married with a cast on. It's ridiculous. I'm shaking people's hands and you can see the pain in my eyes.

Chapter Twenty-One

DISCOVERING AMERICA WITH THE JAZZ CATS

In retrospect I maybe shouldn't have got married in a kilt. It was Mum's tartan, Irish Tartan, County Mayo. A kilt and a broken hand. There are a few things we could have done differently – we might have turned it all down a notch. Sarah had eight – eight! – bridesmaids, because she was 24 and one of the first of all her friends to get married so made them all bridesmaids. All of Sarah's girlfriends were enamoured with John and he scored with one of them – there's footage somewhere of her dancing kind of inappropriately with him in front of Mum and the priest.

It's my fault because I was in charge of getting the music sorted, and I did too good of a job. Somebody had put us in touch with this DJ, big tubby guy with a handlebar moustache and little bow-tie. He said, 'We'll do the Christina Aguilera song, we'll do "The Shoop Shoop Song", we'll do some Britney, we'll do the *Grease* medley . . .'

I said, 'You know what, mate? No. None of that. Listen carefully. Do not bring any of your records. I'm going to go home and I will make you sixteen hours of music, and that's what I want you to play.'

He said, 'Well, if that's what you want, but I don't think people are gonna dance to your music.'

I gave him a big pile of CDs, rock songs, Celtic music, some good Irish jigs, the floor was packed all night long. It was very pretty, the reception was in Red Butte, gorgeous botanical garden, and Sarah looked stunning, she was glowing just like she did the first time I saw her, more so – she looked so beautiful. She always does. And it was a great month. Despite the cultural differences, our families had a lot of fun together. Some of my sisters came for the wedding, brought their kids, and John had a blast, he stashed loads of beers in the garden so he'd never have to go into the house to get one. Sarah's family were still finding them months later.

We couldn't have our honeymoon till almost a year later because I had too much work to do. After the wedding I had to come straight back to London to do Britten's *A Midsummer Night's Dream* for the ENO, which wasn't a very good production, awfully modern. I didn't particularly enjoy it. Ridiculous wig they had me in. The people in the opera house were saying it was such a classic one to do, but it just wasn't fun at all. And it was my first run-in with ENO, because on the first day of rehearsal I made a couple of musical mistakes, in one of the most difficult parts of the show. I'd sung every single other part correctly, but there was a tricky ensemble moment where I needed a little bit of help, a bit of coaching on it. John Berry from ENO phoned up my agent in New York, and said they were very worried about my learning process. My agent phoned me and said, 'We've never had this said to us before, by any opera house about any artist. This is a very worrying thing, Alfie.' I said, 'Listen, I made one mistake and I needed a bit of help with it and that was it. I sang the rest of the piece perfectly.' They should have been worrying about the conductor – he cracked open the score and didn't know it all. He spent most of the time while he was conducting the rehearsals on his mobile phone. One singer was so incensed he just walked off in the middle of the piece. And it didn't help that ENO had set me and Sarah up in a shed in the bottom of somebody's garden in Kilburn. And I do mean a shed in the bottom of somebody's garden. Metal roof. Massive spiders. It had been converted into a bedsit of sorts for this lady's father-in-law, who'd been ill. We moved in and she said, 'I hope you'll be happy in here, my father was. He died in here a week ago.' £250 a week too.

From that we went to Brussels. I went straight into another production of *A Midsummer Night's Dream*, but a much better one, directed by David McVicar, who I'd worked with on *La Bohème* at Glyndebourne. It wasn't cartoonish like the ENO production was, it was pretty spooky actually, in a lovely way. It looked like the set for *Edward Scissorhands*. We had a cute little flat there, it was our first Christmas as a married couple. We had a pair of my hiking socks for stockings, the Boe DIY skills serving me well. Sarah really wanted a tree so I bought one and walked back with it, trekking through the streets of Brussels with this 6ft Christmas tree – all you could see was my legs underneath. This tree walking down the road. I glimpsed through the branches at one point and there were some Japanese tourists taking my photo. Well, not my photo, a photo of this walking tree.

I then went on this 10-week tour of America, which was unofficially affiliated with the Boston Pops, some of our orchestra had played with them. It was called *Broadway: The Big Band Years*; we were doing 1930s and '40s musical theatre songs, the big band stuff, Frank Sinatra, Cole Porter, Gershwin, Lerner and Loewe, all of that. At that point I was really into that sort of music, I loved listening to a bit of Sinatra, and it was relatively easy to sing, although it was a slog – we did a gig practically every single night for two months. There were about 20 of us driving around the United States in a coach. We went right round the curve of America, starting in California playing the universities, down to Palm Beach, all the way along the bottom, Arizona, Texas, South Carolina, North Carolina, Virginia, up to New York, Boston, Connecticut, down through Ohio and Indiana. Mostly smaller regional places. It took us three days to cross Texas. We hit border control at Mexico and I didn't have my passport with me, I didn't have a green card at that point, and the bus driver said, 'If anybody comes on board, hide under the seat.' Are you kidding me? I was scared stiff, picturing this border cop getting onto the coach and dragging me out. I was ready for it, crouching under this seat, the only Brit there, thinking, 'What the hell am I doing? I'm a *singer* for crying out loud, I just want to sing!' But they just let the bus through.

It was really eye-opening, seeing so much of the States. We went through Louisiana and Mississippi – the Mississippi river was a knockout. It was a constant carnival there in the south, the energy of the place and the vibrancy of the people really inspired me. But there was some dark stuff there too. A couple of buses overtook us there, one said 'Whites Only', and another said 'Blacks Only'. There were a lot of Ku Klux Klan symbols around, it was a bit of a shock to be in the presence of that, to be faced with it. In those smaller more insular towns, there's still a lot of that going on, and when you're driving through and you catch a glimpse of it, it's brutal. Just keep on driving, don't stop. We drove through some of the poorer regions to get to the venues, a lot of rundown places that had been hit by big corporate companies that had basically shut down towns. Walmart

As Tybalt in *Roméo et Juliette*, Royal Opera House 2010. The first opera I did after performing *Les Misérables* at the O2.

As Camille in *The Merry Widow*, London Coliseum, 2008. That was a wonderful production. I loved singing all the Lehár/Tauber music Dad used to play on Sunday afternoons.

The Pearl Fishers, London Coliseum, 2010. The one that nearly killed my spirit for good. I basically felt like I look in this photo.

As Valjean in *Les Misérables* at the Queen's Theatre, 2011. An incredible five months.

Singing 'The Impossible Dream' with Matt Lucas at the Royal Festival Hall, London for the *Bring Him Home* tour, December 2011. I asked him why he'd come dressed as Toad of Toad Hall; he told me he'd come dressed as someone wearing a tie. Touché.

Soaking it up at the *Les Misérables* 25th anniversary concert, the O2, October 2010. One of the best nights of my life.

Onstage and in my dressing room. Who am I? I'm Jean Valjean!

With Sarah at the opening night of *Betty Blue Eyes*, 2011. Just guests!

Me and Neil with our *Bring Him Home* gold disc!

My managers Neil and Jilly with their beautiful Pointers!

...inting in Fleetwood with Mum. We're ...th keen painters.

Sarah, Grace, and Sarah's brother Alex in Salt Lake, looking down at the canyon. One of my favourite places in the world.

With Prince Charles at Buckingham Palace. In 2007 I was made an ambassador of The Prince's Foundation for Children & the Arts, which means so much to me.

Getting all Christmassy on ITV's *This Morning*, 2011.

Promo, promo, promo . . . chatting and singing on *Daybreak* and *Loose Women*.

As Nanki-Poo in a revival of Jonathan Miller's *The Mikado*, London Coliseum, 2011. Inspired by Stan Laurel on this one!

With Grace at the O2 for *Les Misérables* rehearsals.

[O]n the edge of Hotel Caruso's [in]finity pool, Ravello, Italy. I [rea]lly wanted that shot for the [ba]ck of the *Passione* album! Was [ter]rifying, but worth it.

[Ar]riving at the Laurence Olivier Awards at the Theatre Royal, London, March 2011. I presented a couple of gongs and sang 'Some Enchanted Evening'.

Photo by Neil Ferris! At a Decca shoot for the *Alfie* TV commerical.

had opened a strip mall and the small-town businesses had had to close. Bakers and butchers had just shut down because everybody was at Walmart. It's such a shame that that happens with America, people all shopping under one big roof – it patronises it. We drove through real shanty towns in Cleveland, proper poverty, people living in shacks and huts. And we played everywhere, we did it all. We played a retirement community home in Florida, which was like a holiday camp, a little prisoner of war camp for old people. Kalamazoo was a riot – I'd only heard of the place before in that Glenn Miller song, we did some good partying in the bars there. Some places weren't so inspiring. One motel we were in, me and Sarah were in bed watching that film *Sideways*, and the guy in the film was in a similar motel watching TV, just as we were watching him, and his bedspread, that generic American bedspread, seemed to blend from the TV into our bedspread in our room. The mundanity of those places is overwhelming.

The culinary situation was pretty dire, food was bad on the road. In the venues in the north part of the country, the Women's Legion would cook for us, which was very sweet of them, and it was great to have home-cooked food, but it would always be lasagne. Always lasagne. Why? In the south, it was gumbo and rice, jambalaya, which was great, except for one time in Louisiana when I was really looking forward to some nice southern food, and what did we get: lasagne again. I hate it now.

The crowds were awesome, full-houses, and again I learnt a lot about how to interact with audiences, how to work with them, shades of D'Oyly Carte and Scottish Opera Go Round. We got a great response from them, we'd joke with them, we'd talk to them about the songs. It was good training, and that's stuck with me all the time. Doing my own individual little gigs in the years after that was good experience too – you learn a lot from crowds when it's just you and a couple of musicians. Invaluable experience, great training for what I'm doing on tour now. I'm still learning. I was kind of using the *Bring Him Home* tour last year as an opportunity to see how far I can go with what I'm singing, in terms of variety and spontaneity. I want to always keep changing things on the road – it keeps everyone on their toes. Not just the musicians, whenever I change something it means the lighting guy has to change something, the sound guy has to change something, the projectionist. They have to keep up. But it's nice to have that freedom. I don't want my shows to be rigid, I love the spontaneity, and I want to translate that intimacy and informality to the bigger venues I'm starting to play.

It was a hell of an experience, travelling America on a bus with 20 musicians. There were two hammocks swinging away, and some seats had been removed for bunk beds. The highlight of the day was playing Scrabble. Most of the guys on the bus were great. The drummer, Gregg Gerson, used to be Billy Idol's drummer. He's a reformed alcoholic, very strong-willed, very proud of the fact that he'd not touched a drop for 15 years, got his medallions for it. Very LA, rides a Harley, lives on the beach in San Diego now with his wife and son. The first time we rehearsed together, when the first song finished he jumped off his drums and walked up to me and said, 'You're a monster. You rock. I love you. Gimme a hug.' I love him to pieces, he's been through a lot, he's a real character. We got on like a house on fire and hung out a lot – he was a real saving grace for me on that tour. We're still good friends – I want to use him for some of my gigs in America. We used to go to In-N-Out Burgers together to avoid some of the grottier food that was on offer on that tour. In-N-Out was half decent food. That was the place for us. I bought him an In-N-Out T-shirt and insisted he wore it. But because he was a rocker, he didn't fit that big band jazz mould, the cats, as they called themselves on that tour. They didn't like what he brought to the table, his style of drumming – it wasn't jazzy enough for them. He left and they brought in a jazz drummer. They were nice enough to me though, and there were some really good players. Great trumpet player, great jazz guitarists, really solid, knew their stuff. Although they had hired a cellist to play bass, which Gregg said was like spitting in front of a fan. It was a real shame when he left, because I got on better with him than I did with anyone else. But he was pretty miserable about having to play with that band, it wasn't working for him. He called it purgatory.

Keith Levenson, the Artistic Director who was leading the whole thing on piano was a conductor on Broadway. He had a drink of whisky on the side of his piano at all times. He'd have conversations during my songs with the other singer, a girl called Robin Skye, who'd sung in some Broadway shows. Actual loud conversations. I'd be up there singing 'A Foggy Day (in London Town)' and Robin would come and sit on the end of his piano stool while he was playing and they'd have full conversations with each other – you couldn't quite believe it, couldn't quite fathom their ignorance. Robin was really sweet though, other than that, and funny. At one point her hair extension fell off, in the middle of a show, and she just picked it up, put it back in and carried on singing.

Keith was seeing Mackenzie Phillips, the daughter of John Phillips from The Mamas & the Papas. She was another big drinker, heavy smoker, proper 1970s party girl, and could get herself into a bit of a state, which was a shame because she was a nice girl, you could have a decent conversation with her. She just seemed to be vying for attention a lot – it was difficult to believe half the things she said. I don't know what went on in her life, she's had a heavy time of it by all accounts. Near the beginning of the tour, me, Sarah, Mackenzie and Keith, an odd bunch to begin with, stopped overnight in a resort called Two Bunch Palms, near Palm Springs. Al Capone built a compound there in the 1920s – apparently he used to go there with his gang and party with the Hollywood elite. He had a tunnel system built – it's blocked off now. They had an Al Capone suite, with a meeting room and a private restaurant at the end. It's quite a place, pretty creepy, but Mackenzie and Keith liked it, we had a fun time. Mackenzie used to go there with her family, the Phillips clan, when she was a kid.

That tour was depressing for Sarah though, on the road with 20 musicians, only a couple of other women – she said she felt like she and Mackenzie were groupies. She only lasted a week – she left after California, didn't want to go through Texas. And then she joined me in South Carolina, stayed until Virginia, and then went back to Salt Lake. And it was getting heavy for me too: we did something like 97 shows in two months. I was getting really tired, really fed up, and really bored of being on that bus. There was a guy there called Brad who was really good at Scrabble, beat everybody, the reigning champion, and towards the end I started beating him. And I thought, 'Shit, I'm beating this guy. I've got to get off this tour.'

Chapter Twenty-Two

BREAKING IN

We lived on the road for a few years. It was tough, moving around from job to job, no stability, borrowing money from our parents. And that was before we had kids, we had the freedom to travel about together. Each job fed the next, tiding me over financially for the rehearsal and performance periods until I got paid again at the end. That's why you get a lot of opera singers on the road all the time. I performed in *Otello* at Glyndebourne a few months after the *Big Band* tour, and I asked a fella if he was going home for Christmas, and he said, very matter of factly, that he wouldn't get home for two years. And that's not uncommon in opera. I couldn't live like that. Even now it hurts, it's hard when you have a family at home and you can barely get to see them. It's really quite lonely. You hear of lots of affairs and divorces in that world. Sarah was a rarity – the wives weren't around much. She got to know a lot of the female singers. The idea that you'd be away from your family all the time offended me. I really wanted kids and I refused to believe that it couldn't be done, that you had to sacrifice your life for your career. I was always looking for a way to do that, to have the luxury of your family life and the beauty of your kids along- side a good career, and in a sense I'm still looking for a way, because I'm still on the road so much. While the kids are young they can come with me, but it's a huge frustration for Sarah because we don't have a base, our living situation is never set in stone. It can change at the last minute, at the drop of a hat. Plans suddenly don't work and we have to make new ones. It's been a tricky time.

We were finally able to have our honeymoon a year after we got married, and as well as our little three-day camping trip in Zion, we went to stay in Sarah's grandma's condo in Hawaii. I'd never been anywhere like Hawaii before, some- where that tropical and that hot, where when you stand in the sea, you can be up to your chest in water and still see your feet clearly. In the sea in Fleetwood you can't be up to your ankles and see your feet. We went snorkelling, which I hadn't done before, and I was a little jittery having to throw myself off the side of a canoe into the sea, a mile from shore. Sarah was off like a shot, swimming away, thanks a lot. I was on my own, panicking. The guy on the boat behind me was having a panic attack – his wife was trying to calm him down. But it was extraordinary. At one point the sun hit my back and I felt this glorious warmth all over my body, and it was like somebody had flipped on a light switch, the sunlight illuminating the whole of the coral. Another reef, I walked out and went under and the sea was a little rough, couldn't see much with all the sand swirling about, and then again it suddenly cleared and settled, and I looked around and there were these bright green giant turtles next to me, quietly floating there. So serene. They were like these ghosts that had just appeared from nowhere. It was such a wonderful feeling to be there with them.

Around this time my first album deal began to take shape. Record company rumblings had begun with a false start back in 2003, towards the end of the *La Bohème* run on Broadway. James Morgan, who I'd met a couple of times, got in touch with me. I'd worked with his wife Juliette at Grange Park Opera, an outdoor opera festival, sort of a mini Glyndebourne if you will, I did *The Mikado* and *Così fan tutte* there and Juliette was in the chorus. James was working as a record producer, he'd worked with a number of artists including Katherine Jenkins and Elton John. So he had dealings with Universal Classics and Jazz, he knew people in the industry, he had the contacts and was able to get me in front of people. He'd been taking note of what I'd been up to, especially on Broadway, and wanted to present me to record companies, set up some auditions for me.

He introduced me to Mick Cater, a manager who was interested in looking after me. Mick was very supportive but couldn't really do much and he didn't officially take me on but said he'd get into things once I'd got a deal. Mick used to manage Bob Marley and The Wailers. He told me this story about a time Marley was playing in Africa. The concert venue didn't have a big enough power supply, so Mick went and got authorisation from the electricity board to reroute power from a village to the gig. Well, authorisation might not be the right word, but he paid the guy. And he stood on top of a hill and saw this village fall into complete darkness as the gig started up. He was a character Mick, he used to look after Robert Palmer. Nothing really ended up happening between me and him. I met Sony, BMG, Warner Bros and EMI, all to no avail; a chap at Sony said the world didn't need another tenor. Really? OK. That's it now, we have all the tenors we need for the time being. Sorry, folks.

I came back to the UK to meet Universal Classics and Jazz. I sang for Mark Wilkinson, the General Manager, and Dickon Stainer, the Managing Director, at the Royal College, and they were great, took me for a drink after. They asked me what album ideas I had, and I basically outlined everything I've ended up doing and still want to do – a traditional opera album, the Italian Neapolitan repertoire, some Lehár, rock, pop, blues. I told them I wanted to do it all. It all blends for me – when you listen to an Ozzy Osbourne song you can hear a symphonic reference in it, it stands up next to an adagio. They were interested but they were focusing on Katherine Jenkins and Russell Watson, wanted to pool their resources into promoting them. That classical repertoire that I would have been doing for them is kind of limited – there are only so many versions of 'Nessun Dorma' you can throw at the public. You know, that one's been recorded by everybody from Pavarotti to Kermit the Frog. So it didn't go any further, and I was at a bit of a loss. By this time I'd been singing to record companies for 12 years, since I started in the D'Oyly Carte, and failing to get anywhere was really discouraging. I was getting opportunities, making opportunities, to get seen in front of people, to sing for them, and I just didn't know how I was going to break in. It seemed impossible. I was frustrated, James and Juliette were frustrated, all of us desperately trying to make it work and just not hitting it.

And then in 2005 Darren Henley from Classic FM approached me. I'd known him for some time through an old college friend who worked for them, and Classic FM, who up to that point had just put out compilations, had an idea for an album series with Sony called *Classic FM Presents*, and were looking for an artist to launch it. So I sang for Classic FM and one of the Sony BMG bigwigs, in the basement of the Royal Albert Hall; they were doing their *Classical Spectacular* performance that night so got me in there for a bit. A boiler room, no less. Freddy Krueger's digs. I sang a Neapolitan song, an operatic aria, and Pink Floyd's 'On the Turning Away'. They liked the first two, but Darren had a problem with the Pink Floyd song, he said it wasn't the sort of thing I should be singing. It's a wonderful song and I still want to record it one day, but fine. It all fell apart anyway because Sony pulled out of the partnership to some extent – their guy didn't have any balls, he didn't want to take any risks – and the Classic FM series looked like it might not be happening.

So I was unsure about everything. I didn't know what to do, I didn't know if I wanted to properly get back into opera, I didn't know if they'd even have me back after Broadway and the Big Band stuff and everything else I'd been doing. But I was getting job offers, ENO were offering me work, and I went off to Strasbourg for a few months to do *Così fan tutte* for Strasbourg Opera, working with David McVicar again. That was a really cool job, although David was hard work on that one. He's a phenomenal director, very naturalistic, and incredibly passionate about what he does, he tends to get consumed by it. If things don't go his way he freaks out a bit. And he's very flamboyant, he sometimes gets carried away with all the operatic grandeur, he can be kind of volatile. But he's been very good to me over the years, he's given me a lot of work, a lot of great opportunities. And that production was great. I skived off rehearsals one night for a Bob Dylan concert. I wanted to treat Sarah to something for her 26th birthday and we saw a poster for this gig. We're both big Dylan fans – he really got me into folk music. I bought tickets before realising it was actually in a place called Amneville, a two-hour drive from Strasbourg. We didn't have a clue where it was. David had planned a rehearsal for that evening, which I needed to wriggle out of, so I said, 'You know

I'm trying to get an album deal. Well there's a guy coming into this town who's connected to the music industry, and this is the only opportunity I can get to meet him, is there a chance I could be released from the rehearsal?' Don't know if you'd call that a white lie or just an out-and-out lie, but it worked for me, and David let me go. So we rented a car and drove to this gig and it was great. He did Sarah's favourite, 'Shelter from the Storm', and a blinding encore, finished on 'All Along the Watchtower'. Worth bunking off for.

Sarah found an amazing flat with a great open-plan kitchen. This lady basically gave it to her for nothing because she felt sorry for us, this newly married couple with not a lot of cash. She certainly gave us a great deal on the place. We were seven storeys up and overlooked the square in Strasbourg – it was something else. And we loved that flat, we had amazing dinners in that kitchen. There was another couple living there, a baritone, Franco Pomponi, and his wife, who'd been in the chorus of Baz's *La Bohème*. Neither of them wore underwear. The kitchen table had bench seats, and every time we'd walk out of our room for breakfast we'd be greeted by these two builders' bums. Good morning.

There was one incident in that flat that sends an awful fear shooting through my body whenever I remember it. We were having a party and one of the actors from the opera brought a couple of crates of beer up – really strong French beer, I might add – and we didn't have enough room in the fridge for it all, so because it was the middle of winter, we thought we'd put the crates on the ledge outside the living room window to keep them cool. And as I was lowering a crate onto the ledge it slipped out of my hands. Seven storeys up, top of the building. And it happened to be the switching on of the Christmas tree in the square, so there were hundreds of tourists below, all gathered around the tree, and the crate toppled off. I went, 'NO!' and heard a huge smash and immediately thought, 'I've killed somebody.' I bombed it downstairs and ran out to the square and the beers were everywhere – they were tinned bottles, so they weren't really damaged – and there were loads of homeless people pointing up to the sky, cracking open these beers and drinking them, shouting, 'Joyeux Noël! Joyeux Noël!' Pointing up to the sky like the beers had come from Heaven.

There was a bit of a void after that. We spent the next six months unemployed and disheartened in New York. I was with a theatre, TV and film agency called Hartig Hilepo, but nothing was coming through and I was getting sick of not having money, of not getting any work, not knowing where things were going. Sarah wasn't getting acting work either; it was very difficult for her upping sticks all the time – Strasbourg, Brussels, London – we just weren't settled, and my agent said I had to be in New York to stand a chance of anything happening, so we'd made the move. It took us four days to drive there from Salt Lake in a U-Haul van, sleeping in motels. We had Guinness, our dog, with us, and $1500 in our pockets – that was everything. We were only just married and still getting to know each other really – it was all new to us both. We didn't know what was going on, we were really worried about everything, wondering what the hell we were doing, we were fighting a lot. A day away from New York, there was an awful snowstorm and we both had a meltdown, massive fight, and Sarah got out and just walked off into the storm. I grabbed Guinness and walked after her, trundling after my wife through the snow, the dog in my arms.

And that was about as good as it got. My agent still didn't manage to get me anything. *Les Misérables* was being revived on Broadway, and I pleaded with them to get me an audition to play Valjean, but the guy said they didn't think *Les Misérables* was right for me, that the part wasn't suited to me. Even spun me something about them going down an ethnic route with the character, which was nonsense. I would have loved to have had a go, but they wouldn't even get me an audition. The irony. I got one gig, a *Phantom of the Opera* concert in an embassy. That was my only gig in six months, a three-day job. I think I got $800 for it, which was nothing to sniff at back then. We were living in an apartment on New York's Upper West Side. Sarah got herself a job as a restaurant hostess.

That was the first time I seriously considered packing it in, the singing. I started looking around for other careers because I was feeling so dejected about not making it, I thought I was wasting my time. The record thing had gone quiet, and I was really tired. I was thinking of going into catering school, becoming a chef, because I love cooking. I looked at a number of different catering schools in New York, had a few tours of facilities, some really lovely ones, looked into the training. I was really considering it. But it would have cost $100,000 for five years of catering school, and I didn't know where I would have got that from, or if I could stomach going back to college for another five years. I wouldn't have been happy and I knew it, but I just wanted to earn a living. Apart from the *Phantom* gig I hadn't had any singing work for six months, I wasn't getting anywhere. The only stability and security I found any comfort in was Sarah's family in Salt Lake. We spent a month with them and it was really quite warming. Sarah's family are a tight unit, and it was a godsend actually, having that solid American family home that we could always go back to, especially as I was so far from Fleetwood.

Thankfully the Classic FM situation spluttered back to life. Darren Henley got back in touch, back on track with the album idea, with Sony taking a lesser role, marketing and distributing for them. He wanted it to happen but said I really needed a manager, and asked if I was still in touch with Neil Ferris. I'd met Neil in Oxford a couple of years earlier; a friend had introduced us in a pub. He used to be Managing Director of EMI and has worked with David Bowie, Prince, Depeche Mode, The Rolling Stones, just a ridiculous roster of legends. We'd gone back to his house that night to hang out with him and his wife Jilly, who works alongside him, co-manages with him. And a very impressive house it was. Oliver Cromwell's old hunting lodge, don't you know. Helicopter pad in the back garden. Huge gym. Big room with all these gold discs on the wall and a huge snooker table. Me and Sarah were like, 'Damn.' Medieval art collection, including a painting of Henry V, painted on wood, that Henry V actually sat for. Neil had basically retired by that point, but we talked about music, I told him the sort of things I wanted to do and we seemed to connect, and stayed in touch. So when Darren mentioned Neil I called him, told him what had been going on with Classic FM, and we talked about him becoming my manager. He said, 'I think this might work, Alfie. I always knew that there was somewhere we could go. I'll see what I can do. I'll make some phone calls.' And he's never stopped making phone calls. He fought for that deal, got me signed, he made it happen. We're a great team. He's been such a support, and such a lovely fella to have on my side. He knew from day one that he wanted to build up my career and look out for my interests, and I'm so grateful to him for that. The last night of the *Bring Him Home* tour in January, in Gateshead, I cajoled him into coming on stage with me and duetting on 'The Impossible Dream', which was hilarious, because by his own admission he's tone deaf, but I wanted to publicly thank him, because he means the world to me.

I couldn't wait to get back to the UK to get started on the Classic FM album, to start recording. It was good timing too, because it turned out the guy who sub-let us our flat in New York had dropped us in it. Everybody sub-lets in New York, and we thought it was all above board, we thought the super who looked after the building knew who we were. We wondered why he was always giving us sceptical looks, and this guy had apparently told him he'd sub-let the place to a little old lady. Not this young couple with a dog called Guinness. It was illegal for him to sub-let at all, we thought he owned the place. But by the time that all exploded we were ready to go, and we shifted.

Classic FM wanted an operatic arias album, and I chose ones that suited my voice at that time, some Donizetti, Bellini, bit of Puccini. Instead they went for all the opera pops, songs they thought would sell an album, which was a little frustrating, but fair enough. 'La donna è mobile', 'Nessun Dorma', 'Vesti la giubba' – the problem with a song like 'Vesti la giubba' is you've got to be 40, 50 years old before you can really do it justice; it's a mature song to do, vocally. But I knew a lot of this rep and learnt it, and was flown over to Brno in the Czech Republic to record with their Philharmonic Orchestra, where we had literally two days to record the album, seven hours each day, which was a challenge. I'd have to sing each aria three or four times, and there are 14 songs on that album – 42 arias in two days. Really tough. 'Jerusalem' was problematic – they didn't get the right arrangements or the right key for me, and there wasn't time to change it, so I had to adapt to what they had. It wasn't a lavish recording, cost a few grand, you can hear the shuffling of feet, chairs moving and creaking. You can hear a string player drop his bow at one point. The orchestra weren't entirely used to the recording concept. But everybody in that band was really sweet, lovely musicians to work with, and very respectful of what we were doing. And it got the ball rolling. I got a bit of cash, rented a little flat, some gigs started to come in.

That was the first time I ever had to do any TV promotion as well, which was mildly terrifying. Singing 'Nessun Dorma' on *GMTV* at 8am. I was a bit naïve about it all, didn't know how to act, always ultra-polite, answering questions politically correctly, being a good boy. I thought that everything hinged on these moments for me. And that remained the case up until last year really, when I started to speak my mind a bit more. There was a TV interview I did in 2008 where they asked if I was encouraged at school, and I said, 'Yeah, yeah, all my teachers were really supportive and told me to be a singer,' which wasn't the case in the slightest. I wasn't even given the opportunity to play music. Then they asked Jeremy Irons, who was on the show too, if he was encouraged at school and he said, 'Was I hell.' That really hit me. After the show I said to Neil, 'Why can't I tell the truth like that?' But I just didn't, for years. I always said what I thought I should say. I think EMI, who I signed with after Classic FM, might have told me not to say anything controversial in interviews, and I still had stuff etched on my psyche from the Royal Opera House era, when both the Vilar people and Baz Luhrmann were telling me not to say anything negative. At that time I was so scared of saying things, the wrong things. Now I say what I want. More or less. That first round of promotion was fun though. I sang at the Blackpool Illuminations opening night, which was a cool little homecoming thing to do. Didn't get to actually turn the lights on of course. They gave that honour to Dale Winton. I was supposed to do an album signing at HMV there too, but me and Neil got stuck on the M6 for six hours and missed it. There probably would have only been 10 people there anyway.

Chapter Twenty-Three

REQUIEM FOR A SQUEEZEBOX

A couple of weeks after the album came out Sarah and I flew off for a three-week ordeal in Macau, which was disgusting on many levels. I try not to think about it much today. Just revisiting it now gives me the heebie-jeebies.

A friend in New York was trying to start her own agency and said, 'There's a job going if you need some extra cash.' And we really needed some extra cash. It was two weeks' rehearsal and then four performances at a festival, run by a rather odd Chinese opera singer. He was incredibly self-important and seemed to be jealous of any other tenor on the programme. He wanted to be the star of the show and he wanted everyone to know it. I was playing Beppe, the second tenor role, in *Pagliacci*. Of course this guy gave himself the lead role, to boost his own career and ego. In Macau. Well done.

The Chinese audiences were amazing, sitting deadly still throughout the whole piece then absolutely erupting at the end. But Macau itself: not so fun. It's incredibly polluted and not wholly welcoming – the hotels have barbed wire along the top. Ours was called The Ritz, which I can only assume was the owner's idea of a joke. Our window looked out onto a brick wall. We found the English TV channel, it showed a lot of *Midsomer Murders*, which ended up getting us through the month. That was all we watched. Three weeks of *Midsomer Murders*. It was a lifeline. Sarah wore a tank top one day and she got gawked at by everyone – you don't see many women around there and she was really uncomfortable, as was I. We didn't feel safe at all.

The food was largely inedible. We didn't really eat for those three weeks, we stocked up on bread and fruit and cheese and lived on that. One night the guy running the festival took the cast to dinner. Sarah was feeling ill and I didn't want to go anyway, so we went back to the hotel, probably to watch *Midsomer Murders*. And afterwards some of the cast told us how we'd had a lucky escape, having avoided a restaurant that had bowls on the sides of the tables to wash your cutlery in before you used it, and the guy had bought everybody fried pigeon heads as a starter.

We couldn't wait to get out of Macau. I really wanted to get home to England, back to our life, back to the album. We looked so ill when we got back, Sarah's mum got us a hotel room in Maida Vale just to recover for a couple of days, and we went to the doctor because Sarah was convinced she had bird flu. He said, 'Were you around any farm animals in China?' She said, 'No but I have the bird flu!' She was very insistent, she was convinced she had it, along with half of Britain.

We moved into a rented two-bedroom farmhouse cottage in Woodstock in Oxfordshire, stayed there for a couple of years, and it was a lovely little place apart from the squirrels living in the walls. You could hear them scratching in the night, which was a tad disconcerting. I bought a car, which racked up the miles because I spent those two years driving myself all over the country doing little gigs everywhere. And straight after every one I'd drive back to Oxford so I could wake up in the morning with Sarah.

The Classic FM album went to Number 2 in the classical charts, but Neil wanted us to sign with someone else for the next one and made some more phone calls, flung out the line for people to bite. We went with EMI; I think they were looking for another Russell Watson or Katherine Jenkins, which wasn't where I wanted to go, but it was exciting. They were really enthusiastic and promised us the Earth, so we signed a five-album deal. The first one they wanted, *Onward*, was a collection of sacred arias, because Andrea Bocelli had done one which had sold 5 million copies, and that was the sort of material that pretty much guaranteed a spot on *Songs of Praise*. It was a bit of a curveball for me. I was concerned about being pigeon-holed with the religious set, and I'd been banging on about the Neapolitan album I wanted to do, but they said I could do that next. So I came up with a list of great oratorio choices, less religious suggestions, from Handel's *Messiah*, Haydn's *Creation*, Verdi's *Requiem*, Mendelssohn's *Elijah*, Mozart's *Requiem*, fantastic tenor arias. All in Latin, it would have been quite credible for that classical market. They screwed up that list and threw it in the bin. They said, 'This is what we want you to do.' 'Be Still My Soul'. 'Amazing Grace'. 'The Lord Is My Shepherd', which at the time was the theme tune to *The Vicar of Dibley*. Opera for motorway service stations. Just next to the Jim Davidson comedy tapes.

We did open the album with 'A Living Prayer' though, the Alison Krauss song, beautiful song, and credit to EMI for that. I really like Union Station, her bluegrass band. I'd like to pull that song out of the bag again and re-record it because, again, we did the whole thing in something like 12 hours, even less time than the Classic FM album. We recorded it in the Liverpool Philharmonic Hall, and on the way there got caught in traffic on the M42 for hours, which was particularly unfortunate for Sarah as she desperately needed to relieve herself. We pulled over on the hard shoulder and she jumped out, climbed over a fence, legged it through some farmer's field and down the bank to some bushes, way away. All these cars were honking their horns, it was brilliant. She's a hero. And we recorded some extra bits, including the choir, in Abbey Road a few days later, which made my day. I was actually recording one of my own albums there, and I thought this was a great new start, an amazing opportunity to build my career, on a classic label who were promising us so much. I was really excited that this was all happening for me in Abbey Road. I kissed the stairs. Neil just looked around and said, 'It could do with a lick of paint.'

The album got me some attention but it hardly took off. And it was an odd, shaky promo period. We were told I'd get on *Songs of Praise* if I sang in the BBC Manchester canteen, which I duly did. So humiliating, singing my heart out in there while all these TV people just sat around eating their lunch. Singing these spiritual songs while they scoffed down their pie and mash. Pathetic really. And then EMI sent me on tour as support for the Fron Male Voice Choir, because they'd sold 300,000 copies of their last album, but their manager was unbelievable. He wanted me to go on stage every night and perform at 7:10pm, before the doors opened. Before the doors opened. I'll say it again. Before the doors opened. I don't know if he felt threatened, I don't know what he was thinking. We managed to reach a compromise, I went on at 7:30, but just for 15 minutes. All just utterly bizarre. I vowed there and then that anybody who ever came to support me would be looked after and treated the same as I would want to be. On my last tour, Laura Wright had two spots throughout my show and she joined me at the end, finished the show with me every night. We all deserve a chance, there's room for us all.

It was just me and a pianist on that Fron tour, but it was nice to do that, to strip it back. Some of the music, like 'A Living Prayer', really made sense like that. On the last few gigs of the *Bring Him Home* tour I did one song, 'Rank Strangers', a cappella and I did John Prine's 'Angel from Montgomery' with just three cellists. Things like that will always be a part of my shows I hope, just to have a moment without all the glitz and glamour, without the lights, without the band. Get to the heart of things.

Onward was nominated for Best Album at the Classical Brits in May, that was when I bumped into Sting and his lute. After the award show that evening, Universal gave Neil and me tickets to their after-show party, which we would have loved to have gone to. That's kind of unheard of, for an artist on one label to be invited to another label's party. We didn't go, because EMI's A&R girl said, '*Please* don't go to the party. I'll be heartbroken if you go.' The EMI party, in a hotel in Kensington, consisted of a glass of wine and a leaky ceiling because somebody above had left a bathtub running, so there were towels and buckets all over the place. Universal probably had buckets of champagne at their bash; we had buckets of bath water. Drip drip drip.

We followed up *Onward* just a few months later with the Neapolitan album I wanted to do, *La Passione*, although it turned out to be very different to the album I'd had in my head. Because it means a lot to me, that music. We were encouraged to listen to it at college – it's really good training for the voice. It's easier to sing than the arias, but also it develops the softer side of the voice, the *passaggio* that tenors and singers try to develop, you really have to work on it. The Neapolitan stuff really brings it on, brings it forward. It's just like, if you're a guitarist, sitting and doing your scales. It's bloody good training because it's a workout, it's not going to damage your voice, it's healthy and fresh, it's muscle-building and stamina-building. And it's fun to do. The ice cream van in Fleetwood used to play 'O Sole Mio' when I was a kid, there's a magical quality to those songs.

Through travelling in Europe, I used to always see street musicians playing them. Strasbourg, Paris, Venice, all the buskers played that music so naturally. The summer after Dad died, before I went off to the National Opera Studio, we went on holiday to Venice, me, Mum, my brother Michael, one of his friends, and their girlfriend, it was the first holiday we'd had in a long time. We were walking through Piazza San Marco one afternoon and I lost them. They'd wandered off, or I had, we'd split somehow, and I was left with Michael's friend, nice girl. Round the side of the square they have buskers, and each individual band takes turns playing a set: pianist, drummer, clarinettist, flautist, violinist, accordion player, typical Neapolitan bands. And I thought an effective way to find my family would be to get up and sing with one of these bands. So I asked one of them if I could, and they were very welcoming. I reeled off a list of Neapolitan songs I knew, which of course they also knew, and we did 'O Sole Mio'. And the whole crowd in Piazza San Marco came and stood in front of this tiny stage, I was blown away. I couldn't believe I was standing in Piazza San Marco singing my heart out, and I was looking around for Mum and Michael. I got really into it, sang a couple of songs with them, and the crowd went nuts. But Mum and Michael didn't show up – we found them later. My plan to find my family with my singing had failed, but it was an amazing moment, singing those songs with that band, taking in the smell of the food from the cafés, the birds flying around, the gondolas tied to the poles, it was all so iconic.

The point is, this music's in their blood, these street performers. It's what they grew up listening to. It just comes naturally to them. It's '*per la gente*', by the people, for the people, it's been passed through the generations – they're like old folk songs. So I wanted to pay homage to that, to respect their heritage and traditions and their sound, and use street musicians on the album. And I thought it would also have been a great selling point, a good press hook, to say that we used buskers. I didn't want to use a conductor or arranger. I wanted to get authentic artists and performers, musicians who were born with that music in them. And I wanted to mix it up a little as well, have a real broad spectrum on the album, Neapolitan songs, French songs, some Django Reinhardt maybe. But again, EMI said no to a lot of the things I wanted to do. They said no to street musicians, they said we needed big strings, that I was a classical artist, and they brought in a 60-piece orchestra. Which is great if that's what you're going for, but it wasn't the point of that album. I wanted an accordion on there, I thought that would be something at least. 'You don't have an accordion in Italian folk music,' they said. They weren't having it. They just seemed so narrow-minded. We ended up with an arranger who was useless, a conductor who was more useless. It was absolutely embarrassing – I was appalled. That arranger couldn't arrange a table-setting. He got himself so worked up that I didn't like the first run-through – he'd added timps and cymbals and percussion on snare drum from a keyboard, and he was playing it with his fingers. There was a cymbal every five seconds. I stripped it down and wrote paragraph after paragraph for them about every single song. And to be fair they did what I said, but it was far from perfect.

I was so pissed off and depressed about the whole project – we drove in to the studio one day and I nearly punched a car park attendant, because he was having a go at Neil. He'd only told him that he couldn't park in a certain spot, but he was a snotty jobsworth and I was so upset about everything, I was just on the edge all the time. The album wasn't what I wanted it to be, but I love that music, it's so strong and the songs win through. I'm going to do those songs properly one day. I've got a nice little group of musicians together at the moment, my own little rhythm section, I want to use them. I'd still like to pull in some street musicians as well, certainly get an authentic accordion player for a few tracks, and I want to put a beat to it all. There's a guy called Raul Malo who was on Terry Wogan's Radio 2 show with me a couple of years ago. He sang 'O Sole Mio' with his band and it had a real Cajun swing feel to it, it was great. I really want to do it. One day.

One fantastic part of that experience was our trip to Ravello, on the Amalfi coast, where Neil and I went to do some promotional material for the album, a photo shoot and a video. We got a hotel deal through Raymond Blanc, who's an old friend of Neil's and has connections with Orient-Express hotels. I sang 'Caruso' on the album, so off we went to the Hotel Caruso, stunning marble floors and pillars, heart-stopping view of the coast. There's a lot of Neapolitan music written about that area, like 'Torna a Surriento' – Sorrento's down the coast from Ravello. And Ravello's really beautiful. We went to this amazing, amazing place, the best place on Earth as far as I'm concerned, certainly for food. Mamma Agata's Hidden Treasure. Mamma Agata is a little Italian woman whose love for food matches her love for people. It's a beautiful thing. It's a self-sufficient school for teaching Italian cooking, just the best home-cooked Italian food, and I can't recommend it enough. All the produce is picked from the side of their mountain. Gennaro, Mamma Agata's son-in-law, farms the land, picks all the produce, gets the tomatoes, rears the chickens, makes his own wine that knocks your socks off. And the limoncello . . . my word, they make the most amazing limoncello.

In five minutes she taught me how to cook a proper pasta puttanesca. Pasta, capers, olives, tomatoes, garlic, basil, in a pan, throw it in. Stunning food. I was filmed in the kitchen chopping up tomatoes, crushing garlic, talking to her at the same time; she was chatting to me in Italian. Her daughter Chiara was there too – she runs the farmhouse, another diamond, a real sweetheart – they're truly beautiful people. They asked me to sing while we were all cooking, so I did 'A Vucchella', and Mamma Agata joined in with me, it was fantastic. We were cooking pasta, eating lemon chicken, sponge cake, drinking limoncello . . . red wine was swimming around my head and I was getting fat and I was thinking, 'I love this life.' I didn't want to leave. In their classes they cook during the day, then in the evening they have a big banquet on their balcony, overlooking the Mediterranean. It's just stunning. They send me Christmas baskets every year, Italian nougat, biscuits and cookies. They play my CDs now during their classes, and there's a photo of me in her cookbook – I'm really chuffed. That place is a piece of Heaven on earth. It really is a hidden treasure.

We had a great photographer there for the promo stuff, Ray Burmiston – he used to be in a punk rock band called Passion Puppets. There was one shot I really wanted to get, standing on the edge of this infinity pool. He was a little concerned, he said, 'Well we'll have to be really careful about that.' I took my shoes off and stood there on this tiny ledge, looking into the camera.

Behind me was a six inch net running along the side, the rest of it was a 1000ft drop. I can't say I wasn't nervous as hell. But I wanted it, and it's on the back of the album. That infinity view was stunning. Incredible hotel. Neil and I had adjoining rooms, with balconies overlooking the sea. One particularly stunning afternoon I was in my room and I heard an accordion. I went out to the balcony and Neil was out on his one too, soaking up the view. Our eyes met. A very romantic moment for us I must say. I looked down and on the street there were a couple of guys with accordions playing one of the songs from my album, just as I'd said in the studio. I said, 'Neil, Neil, look! See?! A squeezebox!'

Chapter Twenty-Four

BOY NEEDS A SONG

Oh, *Kismet*. The K word. That's what us poor unfortunate souls, the ones who were involved in that horror show, refer to it as sometimes because we can barely bring ourselves to utter the word. Look up kismet in the dictionary and it says fate, or destiny. Look up *Kismet* in my mind and you'll see me crumpled in a heap in a corner, possibly sobbing, or screaming.

I went straight into it from our Ravello paradise. Went to bed in Heaven and woke up in Hell. A horrendous ENO production at The Coliseum, a kooky romance set in *Arabian Nights*-era Baghdad, and probably the worst gig I've ever worked on. The director, Gary Griffin, came from Broadway, he'd done *The Color Purple*. And the Broadway way of working, similar to the West End's, is that they have everybody on call at the rehearsal, and when you're not needed you'll just sit around and twiddle your thumbs until you're summoned. Unfortunately that doesn't go down too well in the opera world – they're not used to it, I wasn't used to it. We were turning up to rehearsals at 10am and doing nothing till 4pm. Then getting used for 10 minutes and finishing. Or being used for 10 minutes, then being told that you'll be needed again later in the afternoon, and you'd wait, and nothing. That's OK in itself, a big part of rehearsing is the waiting, but not all day every day. It was happening all the time, and as we started getting close to opening night we realised that so much hadn't been done, hadn't been plotted, hadn't been rehearsed – we hadn't had full run-throughs. There were cast on the stage not knowing where they were supposed to be or what they were supposed to be doing, it was scary.

Gary Griffin fell out with the choreographer, Javier De Frutos, because he stood at the front of the stage at the men's chorus and blocked all these dance routines that Javier had set up. The poor dancers were dancing their socks off and were obscured. A lot of petty, childish nonsense kicked off between those two, it was pretty odd to watch unfold. And Javier walked out, just before we were about to open, we had to cancel a dress rehearsal. A press release went out citing good old "creative differences". You always know that means two people were about to kill each other. And someone was brought in at the last minute to finish off the work with the dance sequences. It was getting absolutely ridiculous. Even at the dress rehearsal we eventually had, major things were being changed. One of them for the better. I was supposed to walk on stage – I did at the dress rehearsal – wielding a Kalashnikov rifle, surrounded by loads of corpses on the floor. It was so misjudged, because it's a pretty whimsical period romance, but this was 2008 – Baghdad was practically being destroyed, and I think having me come out with an AK-47, surrounded by death, was Gary Griffin's nod to what was going on. I felt absolutely ridiculous – it was an awful political statement, if you can call it that, in a stupid show. That scene was dropped, mercifully. But other things were also being changed all over the place, and I finally said to him, 'Back off. You're not changing anything. I'm doing exactly what I'm doing now; you're not doing anything else with this.' I lost my rag with him. We were all so frustrated.

The design was bonkers, it was the worst thing ENO have ever done, and everybody knew it. We attempted to salvage it but it was a lost cause. The newspapers slated it, justifiably. A few of them noted that it was abominable timing, us putting on a magical Baghdad musical while the city was in turmoil, and that was after my Kalashnikov scene was dropped. It didn't help that Tony Blair left Downing Street the day of our first show. The *Guardian* wrote, 'Given Blair's partial responsibility for the Iraq débâcle, the incongruity between artistic statement and contemporary fact was inescapable. When we were told that 'Baghdad is the symbol of happiness on earth', it was impossible not to wince.' Well, yes. The *Evening Standard* said audience members were legging it during the interval, calling it 'torture', which may or may not have happened but I wouldn't have blamed them. Michael Ball, who played the lead, ripped into the show in the *Standard* actually, practically as soon as the run was over – he could barely contain himself. He told them it was shockingly awful, 'a cross between "Springtime for Hitler" and *Carry On Camel*,' which is an accurate assessment. He's a good guy, Michael, a real showman. We're a bit chalk and cheese, but he has a great heart and we're good mates. I sang with him on his BBC Proms show a few weeks after *Kismet*. He got a bit of flak from opera people for coming into that, what with him being a musical theatre person invading their world. As if *Kismet*'s the holy of holies. He got some of the best reviews for that show though, people liked him. And I have to say I never got any grief going into musical theatre, when I did *Les Misérables*, they welcomed me, they were excited about someone bringing something new to it. I just got grief from the opera lot for doing it. In fact it was Michael who recommended me to Cameron Mackintosh for Valjean, and I'm so grateful for that.

I had an accident on *Kismet* that, looking back, was a fore-shadowing of what was to come the next year with ENO and *The Pearl Fishers*, the near drowning–near blindness incident. Every night in *Kismet* I stepped through a hole in the curtain to make my exit. But because the crew had gone out drinking one afternoon for some leaving do, the stage manager accidentally gave a cue for the curtain to go up just as I was stepping through it and it whipped me up about 4ft and spun me back, I crashed down onto the platform on my back. Nobody came over to see if I was alright, nobody seemed bothered.

The one wonderful thing to come out of that whole fiasco was that I got to work with the late Richard Hickox. Richard was a conductor, very well established, a legend in the business, and working with him was wonderful – he was really nice to get to know and to hang out with, and he offered me a job at Sydney Opera House to play Albert Herring; he was musical director there. The people at Sydney Opera House wanted to use an Australian, one of their own, but Richard was fighting to use European singers where he could. Then he had a heart attack and died. I was really saddened by that, really shocked. He was the best thing about *Kismet* for me, and I'd go through it all again to have that experience with him again.

That year I was made an ambassador of The Prince's Foundation for Children & the Arts, which gives opportunities to kids that wouldn't otherwise have them, to inspire and encourage them. I was amazed. I think Prince Charles is a superb ambassador for this country – his charity work is incred-ible – so to get that accolade and to be involved with that was a big deal for me; it still is. As part of my work for them I got to sing on the ice rink at Blackpool Pleasure Beach with the choir from St Wulstan's, my old school, to around 1500 kids, which was really cool. I hope some of them were encouraged. Had a few dinners with Prince Charles too. There was one at Clarence House a week after I was made ambassador, with about 20 people. Neil was more nervous than I was, fumbling about everywhere – he's like a kid in a toy shop when he goes into places like that. I try to keep as calm as I can so I can do what I have to do, and he's just all over the place. I love it. Even the gigs we're doing now, he just gets so excited when it comes to show time. He's got such playful energy. Michael Fawcett, Prince Charles's aide, gave us a talk on how to behave. Do not offer your hand until the Prince offers his hand. The first time you meet him, call him Your Royal Highness. After that, it's Sir. I was singing and made a joke about him playing the violin after discovering the violinist was called Charlie. I inadvertently interrupted a conversation he was having with Penelope Keith for that.

I sang at Buckingham Palace for him and the Duchess of Cornwall, Camilla, that month as well, in the Throne Room. The royal gigs are always a lot of fun. In December that year I sang at the naming ceremony for Cunard's new liner, the *Queen Victoria*, in Southampton dock. Charles and Camilla were there to launch the boat. I did 'I Saw Three Ships' and 'Nessun Dorma' with a couple of other tenors. Derek Jacobi was dressed as Phileas Fogg and did a talk about Cunard's history. I've got his voice lodged in my brain now as well – had to listen to him forever when we had Gracie because he does the narration for *In the Night Garden*. 'Where are you going, Upsy Daisy? Somebody's not asleep! IgglePiggle's not asleep!' I digress.

It was a really surreal evening on that boat, we stayed in cabins overnight. We all had dinner in the ballroom then went to check out the bars and the disco. Derek Jacobi was milling about, Moira Stewart and Carol Vorderman were there. Simon Weston, I was in awe of him, really proud to meet him. John Prescott, he'd given a little speech: 'When I worked at C'nard...' That's how he pronounced it, C'nard. 'I worked at C'nard as a steward, that's how I started.' He was alright actually, not a bad stick. We hung out with him and his wife Pauline, went to the bars and the disco with them – his dancing was something else. Everybody was getting drunk. We went into the smoking room and Jimmy Savile was there in his white tracksuit and his jingle-jangle jewellery, sitting in an armchair on his own puffing on a cigar, and it was pretty cool to meet him, having grown up watching his TV show, but pretty weird when he started flirting with Sarah. He said, 'You're a pretty girl aren't you. Come and sit on my knee.' Right in front of me! I saw him at breakfast the next morning, I said, 'Nice to see you last night, Jimmy.' He just sort of scowled at me.

La Passione was released that November. Unfortunately EMI was in trouble, having lost something like £250 million the year before, and was sold to Guy Hands's private equity company Terra Firma. Lots of their big bands and artists legged it, and poor *Passione* was left a little stranded, with little promotional support from them, and not much love either. They just seemed to lose interest overnight, bigger fish to fry. Neil personally invested so much in that album, they don't even know. He had so much more passion for it than they did, so much more drive. Even before their troubles I just don't think they believed in what we were trying to do. And even with my own misgivings about the album's execution, it was still something I was desperate to promote, to get out there. I loved those songs and I wanted to sing them, to as many people as possible. It's heartbreaking when even your own record company isn't fully supporting you.

Their apathy culminated in a real low point at the end of that year, at the Festival of Remembrance. I'll rewind a few months because this is where Harvey Goldsmith enters proceedings like a soothsayer, an unwitting fairy godmother. I'm sure he'd rather I have him as a fairy godfather, but it's done now. Fairy godmother it is. Harvey Goldsmith is one of Britain's biggest music promoters, produced Live Aid, has been behind a lot of opera mega-events including *The Three Tenors* at Wembley Stadium and Pavarotti in Hyde Park. Earlier that year I performed at the Canary Wharf ice rink on his TV show *Get Your Act Together*, singing 'Nessun Dorma' for Opera Anywhere's *Arias on Ice* event. Neil had a drink with him after the recording and Harvey, ever savvy, said, 'Your boy's brilliant, but he needs a song. The boy needs a song.' Something to break me, something for people to latch on to, something I could make my own.

Back to December at the Festival of Remembrance, which I'd been booked to sing at. Tim Marshall, the producer, ran us through his idea – footage of bodies being repatriated, of coffins arriving back, while I'm singing 'Bring Him Home' from *Les Misérables*, with one of the brass bands from the forces. Nothing twigged at first. I knew the song, but was very unsure about singing musical theatre at such a high-profile event. Tim's idea was so touching though, and to be honest I was also at the point where I just wanted to sing something great, something that would have an impact, and Tim's wife chose 'Bring Him Home' after seeing it sung at George Best's funeral two years earlier, as his coffin was being walked up the aisle. The repatriation footage wasn't shown in the end – they decided it wasn't necessary, that the lyrics and the emotion would communicate the sentiment well enough without it. Also at the festival were Doug Rigby and his son, Corporal Will Rigby, whose twin brother John, serving alongside him, had died in Basra after being hit by a roadside bomb. Will had sat with him for 10 hours in the field hospital while he died, and brought the Torch of Remembrance into the Royal Albert Hall. He gave a reading before I sang, and needless to say being there with them was an incredibly moving experience. They sat behind me on stage while I performed the song, it was a very emotional moment, and 'Bring Him Home' was so apt for it. And singing it there, at an event that gifted it with so much poignancy, really hit me. It showed me how much it can affect people in so many different ways, how it can mean so much. And as Neil watched me sing it, mini-Harvey Goldsmith, in a little tutu, appeared in a puff of smoke above his left shoulder: 'Boy needs a song!' And disappeared just as instantly in another puff of smoke. And that was it. We'd found the song. Or, more to the point, the song had found us.

So this is where Neil, emotional and excitable backstage, calls Mark Collen at EMI and says, 'We're 10 minutes away at the Albert Hall, Alfie's just sung "Bring Him Home", this is it! I've recorded it, can I meet you for 10 minutes and show you the footage?' And they said they didn't have 10 minutes. That they weren't particularly interested, they didn't have the time.

Neil was practically crying. They weren't interested, they weren't listening to him. He didn't know what to do. And Neil and I were getting frustrated with each other in that period. We had some heated moments but we'd always phone each other up later. 'You alright?' It would never last long. The record industry was cracking at the seams at that point, and a lot of artists that were around at the same time were dropping their management like flies – first big blowout and they'd ditch them.

First problem, bang, blame the manager. Find another one. But me and Neil stuck through shit and gruel, we took them all on. And I'm proud of that, and proud of our relationship, because we've worked so hard at it. Neil just never stops. And he will never stop.

Chapter Twenty-Five

GOLDEN LIGHTS
ON DARK DAYS

We'd found out Sarah was pregnant at the end of my *Kismet* run. Creation amidst catastrophe. I ran around the bedroom when she got a positive on the pregnancy test, jumped up and down on the bed then got over-sensitive about it, worried that I'd hurt my pregnant wife with my exuberance. I was more sensitive about it than she was.

The first opera I did after *Kismet*, in April 2009, was Franz Lehár's *The Merry Widow*, and it was a hell of a lot of fun. I had a wonderful, wonderful time on that. ENO again, and the polar opposite to *Kismet*. John Copley's one of my favourite opera directors to work for. He'll stop a rehearsal and come out with these great stories, but he always gets the job done, and very well too. Working with John was fantastic. I loved every minute of that job and I got some nice reviews for it. I played Camille and knew some of the music already. Dad was a big fan of Richard Tauber, one of Lehár's main tenors, we used to listen to him a lot at home in Fleetwood. Every Sunday we'd sit around the dinner table and Dad would put a Richard Tauber record on, take out his bottle of Benedictine and have a small glass. So I already knew a few of the duets and the waltzes – Tauber sang a number of them. It really meant a lot to me to do that opera. Not least because Roy Hudd was in it. The little cameo roles were often played by celebrities in those days; the opera houses went through a stage of doing that to sell seats. Dawn French played in *La Fille du Régiment* at the Royal Opera House a couple of times. And Roy Hudd was great, really solid, exactly what you'd expect if you've seen him on TV, great fella, full of stories. We shared a dressing room, and the only downside of it was seeing him in his underwear, he'd just come up and talk to me in his string vest and trollies. Roy, go and get dressed man! Please!

Sarah came to see it with Neil and Jilly and decided to start having contractions in the foyer. I was told backstage. What?! No, false alarm. She waited until the next week when I was at the Classical Brits for the real thing. I was nominated for Best Male Artist and Best Album, for *Onward*, got a text from her in the interval: 'Can you come home, I think it's started.' That's Grace for you. Loves a bit of drama. Oh, you're at the Brits, Daddy? Good, I think I'll be born now. I jumped in the car with Neil, shot off to Oxford and was up all night with Sarah in hospital, poor Sarah, whose epidural was administered too late; all it gave her was one numb leg. And Gracie was born the following day, the best award I ever could have won. I realised what everything was about as soon as I saw that little girl. I thought, 'That's it. It's all for her. Everything.' Nothing compares to holding your newborn child, nothing. To have experienced the death of my father and to have held him when he died, and then to have held Gracie when she was born ... to be hit by those two extremes, physically feeling life leave, and then feeling life arrive . . . I mean what else is there? To have had those experiences, it's a blessing.

Grace was a golden light on dark days. At exactly the time that she was born, EMI decided not to pick up the option on me as an artist. They'd been bought out, they were perhaps frightened of losing their jobs, perhaps frightened to take any risks, and didn't want to spend money, obviously they didn't believe in me enough. But it was a really heavy blow, a bitter pill. And I thought that was it, that my chances of making albums were over. Getting another deal was going to be like climbing a mountain again, I was really gutted. I carried on doing the operas and the gigs, gigging and gigging and gigging, getting out there to make money – we certainly weren't seeing any from the albums. And we promoted them ourselves with those gigs we were getting, playing concerts and festivals around the UK: Kings Lynn, Henley, Chester, Swansea.

A week or so after Gracie was born, in-between my final *Merry Widow* performances, I had the pleasure of singing at the wedding of Autumn Kelly and Peter Phillips at Windsor Castle, which was like our own bizarre episode of *Curb Your Enthusiasm*. Autumn was Michael Parkinson's PA. I'd met her a year earlier at an ITV event I'd sung at, *The Music of Morse*, which he hosted. She and I had become friends and she asked me to sing at her wedding. I sat next to Kate Middleton at the reception – William was at another wedding in Kenya. She was really sweet. She asked me if I wouldn't mind swapping my lamb with hers because hers was too big. Of course I obliged – I'd never say no to more lamb. So I ate Kate Middleton's lamb. And she ate mine. Sarah had to go up to one of the courtrooms, and was sat on a beautiful antique four-poster bed with a breast pump for Gracie, the machine pumping milk, whirring, nnnrrr, nnnrrr, nnnrrr. We bumped into Prince Harry on the dance floor.

'Great singing,' he said, I think – the music was banging. I went up to Prince Philip and offered him my hand first, no, no, no, – wrong! Sorry, Sir, sorry. He said, 'Are you the singer?' Yes Sir, Alfie Boe. 'Alfie Boe, of course, of course,' and he flung his arm around me and walked me over to The Queen. 'Darling, darling, have you met Alfie, the singer?' Sarah called her Your Royal Highness instead of Your Majesty – we were getting everything wrong. She was lovely. She said, 'Wonderful singing, very nice.'

I said, 'Thank you Ma'am. Could you hear OK?'

She said, 'Yes of course I could hear you.'

I wasn't making any sort of reference to deafness – they were in the back signing the register when I was singing and I just wasn't sure if they could hear me properly.

David McVicar was directing *Der Rosenkavalier* for the ENO, which was starting a week before *Merry Widow* was finishing, and I was brought in last minute because their tenor pulled out for some reason. So I did those two operas back to back, over-lapping for a week or so. I was flying by the seat of my pants on that one because I'd had no rehearsal. My rehearsal process lasted 10 minutes. Literally. Then I was put in costume and make-up and practically thrown on stage. It's not a big role, I basically had to stand at the front of the stage, sing an aria and clear off. I then did an even smaller role, in *Elektra* at the Royal Opera House, despite having thought that I wouldn't be welcome there again. And it felt great to be there actually – I was pleased to be back on that stage and to be playing a role that wasn't that high pressured. It was a foot back in the door. It was a cool little role: I just jumped out of a trap door and screamed my lungs out for 57 seconds. It's one of the shortest roles ever written, although there's a lot of text in those 57 seconds, a lot of high notes – it's a highly emotional, fired piece of music. It's a really tricky moment to get right, timing-wise; you really have to be on the ball, and Mark Elder, who was conducting, was great to work with – he really helped me through it and encouraged me.

Then it was on to have my third stab at *La Bohème*, for Jonathan Miller at The Coliseum, and it was an odd one, all told. I'd first met him to discuss it back in August 2007, shortly after *Kismet*. I was sat in his kitchen talking about the role while he made coffee for us, then he sat opposite me, stuck his spoon in the sugar bowl, and while he was talking to me he put one spoonful of sugar after another into his coffee and just. Did. Not. Stop. 'So, Alfie, how long have you been singing?' One spoon. Two spoons. Three. 'Great. And how many performances did you do on Broadway?' Four spoons. Five. Six. 'And how was it working with Baz?' Seven. Eight. Nine. 'What was Baz's approach to *La Bohème*?' Ten, eleven, twelve. I think fourteen spoonfuls of sugar went into that cup of coffee. And he stirred it once, put his spoon down, and drank it, I was gobsmacked. How does he have teeth? I could barely answer him, I was so transfixed with what he was doing.

That production was hard work. It was exciting to do it for him, but when we got on stage we realised how difficult it would be – because the set was pushed way back up, there was a hell of a lot of space to fire the music out into. We had a young conductor who was playing the orchestra far too loud, so it was like playing to a brick wall of sound, trying to fire our sound out. People said they couldn't hear the singers. And Jonathan asked me to play Rodolfo without much sentiment and emotion. I think he wanted to try to find a new take on it, and I went with it. I tried, but I didn't really gel with it, and a lot of people complained that Rodolfo was too cold with Mimì. So when ENO revived it a couple of years later with a different director I reverted back to the way I'd played him before, more romantically. We also had a conductor that time who knew how to play the orchestra down so we could be heard. It was a much more satisfying production.

Sarah and I went to Salt Lake after Jonathan Miller's *La Bohème*. I'd been dropped by EMI, didn't know what to do about getting another record deal, was enjoying the operas but wanted to do something new somewhere else, make the jump. A few months earlier, just before *Elektra*, I went to Berlin a couple of times, sang to the Staats Opera and the Opéra National du Rhin, that came to nothing. We couldn't afford to live in England so decided to make a go of it in America again. It seemed like a great opportunity. We'd saved up enough money for a house deposit, we thought we'd get something in New York and I'd try to start an operatic career up there. Sarah wanted to be nearer her family, she'd be able to settle there with Grace, and I would travel around the States working in different opera houses. That was the plan. I thought my time in *Bohème* there and everything I'd done here would count for something. So I went to see a number of agents, and basically got slapped in the face.

A friend of mine recommended an agent, who I called, and he said, 'I'm going to book a studio, and I want you to book a pianist, and I'll come and see you sing two or three songs for me so I can get to know your voice.' So I flew to New York with Sarah and her mum and Grace. They all went off to the zoo, I met the pianist I'd booked, and went and sat in this studio. And we waited, and waited, and waited . . . 45 minutes, no sign of the guy. I called up the agency, no answer on his phone. After it had been an hour I just lost it. I found out where his office was, marched in, went up to the receptionist, asked if he was in, and she said, 'Yeah, he's in his office round there, can you tell me what your name is please?' I said, 'That doesn't matter,' and I walked round to his office. Receptionists were following me asking me who I was, and I kicked open his door. He was just sat there, and he jumped.

'Where were you? I've been waiting an hour.'

'Alfie, yeah?'

'*YES*, Alfie.'

'I'm really sorry, I got stuck on the phone.'

'You couldn't bother to call me or call the studio?'

'I'm really sorry.'

'You're sorry. You know what mate, you fucking will be.'

I turned around and walked out, got back to our hotel and kicked in an air vent. That was basically my state of mind. I was getting desperate. I couldn't understand why agents weren't giving me the time of day. I'd seen three or four with no success. I saw one in a big agency in New York. She said, 'Come in on Saturday because I'll be in the office anyway, and we'll have a chat.' So I went into the office and apologised for disturbing her weekend, said I could have met her in the week, and she said, 'No, no, no, it's fine, great to meet you.' Very glamorous lady with her fur and rings. She asked me what I wanted to do. I said I wanted to try to break into the American opera market and play some of the American houses. She said, 'I think these houses are far too big for you.' I asked if I could work up to them, or audition for any at least, just to see what work I could get. I asked her if she'd consider taking me on, and she said, 'Can I show you a list of who we represent?' And she handed me a list, pushed it across the desk to me. 'Those are the sort of people we represent.' Ian Bostridge, Tom Allen, José Cura, big names. And I looked at her, waiting for her to say something, but she didn't. She just expected me to look at that list and real-ise I wasn't worthy of being at her agency. 'I'm not worthy of being on this list among these people, I'm really sorry for embarrassing myself and being here in your presence, and now I shall leave.' I guess that's what she wanted to hear. So I left. And then she phoned up my agent and complained that I'd gone to see her on a Saturday. I was thinking, 'What makes these people tick? Why are these people like this? Why am I in this business? What's it all about? I just want to sing! I just want to sing, to work.' I was losing a lot of heart.

We decided on Salt Lake City, and bought a lovely house in a lovely neighbourhood, an infinitely bigger and better place than anything we could have afforded in England. I had some shows to do in Ireland, and Sarah put on a yard sale in Woodstock – the first yard sale Woodstock had ever seen – got rid of a lot of our junk, made about £500, which was a godsend, and we moved. It made sense. After years of being on the road, with little stability, we had Grace now and needed to settle. It was tough for Sarah, bringing up a baby in Woodstock while I was away in operas all the time – that place has a very specific demographic. The next youngest person on our street was 80. She was really missing her family, and the sort of life she could have out there. My career had ground to a halt, I wasn't getting anywhere, and was beginning to think I was wasting my time with it all. So I wanted a new life too, and it's hard to argue with that one. The house we bought was 15 minutes down the canyon from the ski resorts, it had a back garden, we could hike, we could go into the mountains at the weekends. You can see them from the house, it's unbeatable. You don't get that in Kilburn.

Chapter Twenty-Six

FRENCH CONVICTS, AMERICAN COWBOYS

Of course, as soon as we'd decided to settle in Salt Lake, everything changed. We just didn't know it yet. Just after we bought that house, Cameron Mackintosh's producer Trevor Jackson called Jilly, Neil's co-manager and wife, and asked if I'd be interested in playing Jean Valjean for *Les Misérables*' 25th Anniversary concert.

Up to that point, Neil and Jilly and I had been very careful about what jobs we were taking on. To an extent I still felt like I was breaking back into opera and classical music, and we didn't want to take on work that would endanger that. I needed the classical world to view me as a legitimate classical artist. There's no going back after crossing that line into musical theatre. In terms of my opera career, it was a huge risk to take a gamble on. And Neil sympathised with my concerns but said he thought it could really put us on the map. I gave it a couple of days and said to Sarah, 'This could really cause me problems with the opera houses, it could stop me getting work.' She said, 'But it could also do lots of other things for you. There's a chance it could shut that door, but it could open others.' She said the music in *Les Misérables* was beautiful and suggested we sit and listen to it, because I didn't know it well at all. I'd sung the one line from 'Do You Hear the People Sing' back at Lottie Dawson's when I was 14, I'd done 'Bring Him Home' at the Festival of Remembrance, that was about it. So Sarah got a CD and we sat and played it. First listen, I thought, 'I can rock this like crazy.' I could really hear myself singing it.

I was coming round to it. Not completely sold, still unsure about the risk – those old voices in my head were telling me this wasn't the sort of thing I should be singing. But I was looking for my next big project and I was feeling buzzy about it, excited about what it could bring. Cameron Mackintosh and the show's composer Claude-Michel Schönberg wanted to meet me, to hear me sing, so I went to Cameron's office in London one afternoon. He wasn't there at the initial audition, it was Trevor Jackson, Claude-Michel and Stephen Brooker, the Musical Supervisor. Now Claude-Michel was by no means sold on me. He was a bit reserved about using an opera singer to play the role at all, because he'd worked with Plácido Domingo and the experience wasn't what he'd expected. I sang the 'Prologue Soliloquy' and the 'Epilogue', which he liked, but it all hinged on 'Bring Him Home'. They're strong, powerful songs, but 'Bring Him Home' is one of the show's pinnacle moments, it's difficult to sing, so that's the one that really has to be right when you audition. As I sang it, Claude-Michel was sort of frowning at me. I finished, and he said, 'Can you do it one more time?' and he stood literally 2ft in front of me and conducted me. And as I sang, his frown turned into a smile, and by the end he had a tear in his eye. And he threw his arms around me, it was really touching. And from that day on I knew I'd made one hell of a friend. I've got so much respect for Claude-Michel. He's a great man.

Singing those songs for him at that audition felt so right. Despite my misgivings, it was the most natural thing. It was a strange experience, it felt like that music had been lying dormant in my body, waiting for me. Other than 'Bring Him Home' I hadn't done any work on it before, and I just felt it sitting there, it was like it had been released from a box. I connected to the character. And I thought, this is it. This is what I'd been waiting for. I thought, I'm gonna sing whatever I damn well want to sing now. I'm not going to try to convince people if they're not already convinced about me, I'm not going to fight any more, I'm just gonna sing bloody good music. I thought it could open the door for opportunities for other repertoire, different avenues, giving me the chance to do what I always wanted to do, to combine genres: rock, pop, jazz, blues. And I said to Neil, 'I'll do it.'

However, at that point the event was very much an unknown quantity. As enthusiastic as I was for the material and the opportunities it could give me, we assumed it would be a one-off event, a celebratory evening. We didn't know how seismic it would be. They wanted it to be at the O2, but that was very far from being confirmed. There was no glamorous fanfare about it, no real sense of what it would bring, and it was a year-and-a-half away. Neil meanwhile had been talking to a small record company in Scotland about getting me into the studio again. Let's just do it, make an album again, something personal, something we have control over, on our own terms. Neil was a fan of Linn, a high-end stereo manufacturer in Glasgow who have an accompanying record label, and they are absolute sound fascists. They record staggeringly beautiful albums, mostly classical, and had just won a Brit Award for a Mozart album with the Scottish Chamber Orchestra, wiped the floor with it. They're very cool. They were thinking of doing a Bernstein or Sondheim album with me, but having recently done *The Merry Widow*, I suggested Lehár. It's lush, romantic 1920s music and it brings back so many memories for me, of my childhood, my father and his Richard Tauber records. And they went for it.

We recorded it in the Glasgow Royal Concert Hall and although we did it for next to nothing I tried to do the material justice, and we did a great job. That album has a real sentimental feel for me – vocally and emotionally and even technically, I think everybody was emotionally connected, even the orchestra. It was a really warm experience. I was working with a great conductor, Mike Rosewell, who was one of my teachers from college. And it was a beautiful environment, I stood right in the middle of the orchestra to sing, which I loved. I'm not a massive fan of recording in vocal booths, which is usually the set-up. It's magic to be able to sing surrounded by the orchestra, you really soak up the vibes like that, you're part of the music, you feel it. And singing those songs did bring back a lot of memories for me, it was lovely, and one of my favourite albums I've done, certainly the most personal. I hold it close to my heart, I dedicated it to my dad. We didn't do it for the money – it was a tiny little deal – but that wasn't the point. We knew it probably wouldn't break the charts, and indeed it didn't sell many, but it really wasn't about that. It was actually freeing to know we wouldn't change the world with it, and to be satisfied with that. I didn't expect it to rocket me to stardom, I just knew we'd made a really good-quality album and, there and then, that was all I was concerned about. No politics, no arguments, just great music, everybody on the same page. Doesn't happen very often.

After that I didn't know what to do. I was beginning to feel I might be done with opera. ENO were providing me with a lot of work. I was doing two or three shows with them every season, but I just felt like I was chugging along, and I was having a crisis of confidence. Didn't know where to start. Should we make another little record with Linn? Try to do one ourselves? I started panicking. I didn't know what we were doing or where we were going, and I was questioning everything. I couldn't get work in Germany, I couldn't get work in America – it had got to the point where the only place I was regularly working was The Coliseum for the ENO. Why couldn't I get work anywhere else? What was I doing wrong? Was I not sounding right? Did my face not fit? I was getting really frustrated, I really felt like I was wasting my time, and I was frightened.

I went home to Salt Lake for June. Sarah's father, and my brother-in-law, and one of his friends and his dad were going off to the family log cabin in Idaho one weekend for a bit of fly-fishing, and Sarah told me to go with them, get away for a bit. I didn't really fancy it, I wanted to stay at home with her and Grace, but I'd never fly-fished before – I'd fished from shore and from a boat, but never fly-fished, so why not? My brother-in-law's friend's dad is a very good fly-fisher, and he tried to teach us. I couldn't get a grasp of it at all, I was there with the rod and the line and the flies but I just couldn't figure it out. The only thing I was catching was the hook in the back of my head, it was pathetic. And I just got so sick and tired of this hook getting stuck in my head, and my line getting tangled, and just not getting a bite, I slammed my rod down and said, 'I'm going. I'm off. I'll see you later, here's another rod for you, David.' And I stropped off, and went to Sarah's uncle's house.

Pierre's a bit of a cowboy. He sounds like one, real cool drawl. He's a good guy, we'd grown really close through hiking together, been out on treks. We just clicked. Brothers from another mother. We took epic day trips. We'd trekked in

Elephant's Perch in Idaho, caught the boat across the lake, hit the trail and hiked for hours. We once sat overlooking this Alpine lake, he'd scattered his brother's ashes around there, and it was one of the most peaceful and idyllic moments in my life sitting there with Pierre, eating smoked oysters and cheese. On the way down I was so hot I stripped down to my underwear and threw myself into this pool. He's a bit of an old rocker, big Rolling Stones fan, loves his music. He used to follow the Stones, went to a load of their gigs in the '60s and '70s and took great photos of them – he gave me an amazing photo of Keith Richards on stage, really up close, fag hanging out his mouth.

Whenever I'm up in Idaho I see Pierre. I could always rely on him for moral support, so I went to find him that day when I'd had enough of the fly-fishing. I got to his place and he said, in his cowboy drawl, 'Hey, Alf, you look stressed.' A little bit, mate. Tried to do some fly-fishing for ages and I just walked three miles to your house. He said, 'Well, take a seat in the truck.' We jumped in and he backed the truck up to the garage, took out a TV from the garage, shoved it in the back of the truck and said, 'Let's take the dogs for a walk.' I didn't know what the TV had to do with anything. The dogs jumped in the back with this TV, and we drove off into the mountains. We found a really secluded spot, took a little stroll up and back down a hill with the dogs, then he put them in the back, backed the truck up to a little mound of dirt and rested the TV on top of it. Then he backed the truck away, took out a 38mm Magnum and handed it to me. 'OK, shoot the hell out of that.' What? I'd never shot a handgun in my life. I shoved some bits of rolled up toilet paper in my ears to block the sound, aimed the gun at the TV, pulled the trigger, and shot right through the middle of the screen. And the TV *exploded*. It was great. And we shot for an hour and a half. Shot the TV, shot some cans . . . at one point one of the bullets ricocheted off a rock into a tree and snapped a branch off.

While we were shooting, a mountain biker appeared out of nowhere, right in the line of fire. Pierre said, 'OK, Alf, guns down.' We pointed them at the floor, at which point, in some sort of nervous panic, I accidentally pulled the trigger and a bullet went right between my feet. Could have shot my foot off. The mountain biker said, 'Hey how you doing. Carry on, guys, have a good day.' Like it was no thing to see two guys there stood in the wilderness shooting all hell out of a TV. And we carried on shooting. It was thrilling, but it wasn't about the empowerment of shooting a gun, it was, for me at least, about the accuracy. Yes, shooting a handgun is something else. An air-rifle or a rifle is one thing, but a handgun . . . they're designed for defence, they're not designed to go hunting with. To have a gun in your hand that's designed to defend you against others is a weird feeling. But it soon became about the accuracy, how close I could get to the centre of the target, rather than how good it felt to shoot. We went shooting another time as well, just went off into the wilderness, he pulled out the Magnum again and handed it me, stuck up a load of tin cans on some rocks and we shot them. That time we were both drinking from a bottle of bourbon, which was probably not the best idea. For an hour and a half I was a compete redneck.

Pierre's a strong figure out there, he was a social worker. We grew really close, but unfortunately he hit some hard times and ended up in hospital, in a coma. And one night I was back in England, walking back from a show one night in Blackheath, back to my friend's house where I was staying, and I said to myself, 'I know you're here, Pierre, I know you're with me, man. I can feel you here. I hope you're alright buddy. And I'm gonna turn around and I'm gonna see you.' And I turned around, and about 10ft away from me was a fox, just stood there looking straight at me, eyes locked, for ages. I turned back around, carried on walking for a few seconds, turned around again and it had gone. And every night after that, that fox came to my back door and I fed it – there are photos somewhere of me feeding it. Then I got a message from the family in America saying Pierre had come out of his coma. When he woke from it, somebody said, 'Where have you been, Pierre?'

And he said, 'I've been in London with Alf.'

Chapter Twenty-Seven

VALJEAN TO THE RESCUE

It was there in Salt Lake that summer, mulling things over amid the exploding televisions, that I considered becoming a personal trainer. It's a great life over there, and with an uncertain future, settling with my family and raising my daughter among the mountains seemed like the way forward. Having thought about becoming a chef a few years earlier, I was now pretty hooked on the idea of getting people fit. I was in good shape myself, eating healthily and working out a lot in the gym because I had to get my kit off for Verdi's *La Traviata*, which I'd be performing for Welsh National Opera that October. That was a first, and I was nervous about it. I wanted to look right, to look good. And working out was making me feel good, it gave me a release, something to focus on when I was away from my family. I threw myself into it, started discovering more about the body and muscles and nutrition and health. I started taking protein powders and energy boosters and muscle enhancers, just to look right on stage when I took my clothes off, and I got a little obsessed, was working out twice a day, two or three hours each time. I was really pushing myself. I got big. I look at photos of myself back then and my goodness had I bulked up. There wasn't that much definition, but I put on a lot of weight, a lot of muscle. I went from 11½ to 14 stone. It even hurt to bend down, I'm a bit slack with my stretches.

As a result I was also getting very aggressive, which was worrying. Anger was boiling up inside me, I got short-tempered with people, I was looking for trouble. If someone was being a dick in the street I'd home in on him and have a confrontation. It really wasn't me, or at least it brought out the worst in me. I didn't like it at all. I guess it was a combination of the endorphins party in my brain, and also the frustration pent up inside me in terms of my career, the fear of the unknown. Despite being unclear about what the Les Mis concert would be – it looked like the O2 was falling through at one point, one minute it was going to be at the Albert Hall, the next it looked like it might be cancelled altogether – I was banking on it being the thing, and I was well aware that I'd done that before, banked on TV programmes, on concerts, festivals, videos, albums that I thought could have set things alight for me, and I'd so often been disappointed. I really didn't want this to be another one of those. And even though I'd said yes to it, these jobs are never cut and dry until they officially offer you a deal – I'd learnt that much. I hate to dwell on that doubt, but there's always an element of that, for me at least. Diminished expectations.

I was enjoying doing the concerts, the Kings Lynn sort of gigs, anything from 100 to 500 people, not even sold out. I loved them actually. They were a lifeline in a sense – they kept me busy, kept me working, kept me performing – Heulwen Keyte, my UK agent, was booking everything for me, kept things happening, she's great. But those gigs can wear you down, that endless cycle. Driving, driving, driving, four times a week, hundreds of miles to different venues, and then half the time I'd turn up and there'd be no microphone, or no dressing room. Eating my dinner in the back of the car. My rider request was minimal, tea-making facilities, a towel, some fruit and some crisps, but often I'd be lucky to get a bottle of water and a towel. I never knew what the venues would be like, what the audiences would be like, or if there'd even be an audience at all. And I'd walk on stage and bust myself silly every night, sing my heart out, drive home, repeat a day or two later. I didn't want that to be my life for the next 30 years. So I really was pursuing the personal training. I was trying to get my head round it, to convince myself that singing wasn't everything, as much as I wanted it to be. Sarah was trying to find a good balance with my mindset, encouraging me to do it if I wanted to do it, to take classes and get certified, but equally encouraging me not to give up on the singing. She was happy, she was teaching kids drama, but she was upset for me, watching my career crisis escalate as I downed more protein shakes. I bought loads of books, went to see a friend who was a personal trainer and ran a gym in Salt Lake City. He told me more about it and said he'd offer me a job when I qualified. I'd start working for him straight away. Training pensioners, no less. I'd built myself into this big muscle mass and I'd be training pensioners.

I was really convinced that this was what I should be doing – it scares me now. It was all a bit scattershot though. I pursued it more and looked into becoming a trainer for the Salt Lake Police Department. I was still working out and I'd started cutting down the protein powders. I was feeling fit, healthy, strong, and I thought it made sense. Because I'd become so tired and depressed about living on my own and being away from my wife and my little girl, that touring opera life, it wasn't working for me. Even if good work started to come in from everywhere, that wasn't what I wanted to be doing, not like that. Grace was a year old, and I felt like I was missing out on so much. Sarah wasn't coming to England because we didn't have a life here, a place of our own. She wanted to have roots, and the support of her family and friends to help her with Grace, while I was working in England. That's why I was looking for opera work in America, that's why I wanted to be a personal trainer over there, that's why I applied to the police department. I wanted to be with my family. And if it came to it I would have done it. Deep down though, I knew I didn't want to throw it all away. I still had that flame flickering inside, that little voice telling me that something would happen. I couldn't ignore it. And the closer I came to *Les Mis* the louder it got. The more and more we talked about the concert and found out what their plans were, there were more and more reasons for optimism.

I toured the UK with *La Traviata* for three or four months. That was a really good opera, David McVicar directing again, my fifth production with him. I really enjoyed the show, enjoyed singing with the Welsh National Opera, great cast, great bunch of people. And I didn't end up having to go completely nude every night, thankfully. I did in the dress rehearsal. The first scene was me getting out of bed and walking across the stage with my backside on show, picking up my trousers from a chair, turning around, giving the audience the full-frontal and putting my pants on. But it was such a moment, such a distraction, and I think a few of the older folk were a bit upset about it all, so David canned it. In the end I'd swing my legs over the side of the bed, grab my trousers and pull them on, all people saw was a quick flash of my backside really. But I was certainly glad to be in shape, and I still like to keep fit, although I don't go to the gym as much as I'd like to, and I don't take any of the protein stuff. I still get regular emails from Salt Lake Police Dept, telling me they're hiring. I should unsubscribe really – it's not healthy.

In September I came to London to watch *Les Misérables* for the first time at the Queen's Theatre. I went to see it a few times, and was really impressed with it; the more I saw Valjean, played by Jonny Williams at the time, the more I connected with it, with him. I thought, 'I can do this. I know this role. That's me.' I could see myself up there doing it. I thought, 'This is my role. This is the one,' and we formally accepted the offer. We still didn't know where it was going to be, how big it would be, but I was thrilled. And I went into *Káťa Kabanová* for the ENO, gave it everything I had, and it was incredible. Kudrjáš is an awesome character to play. Fiery guy, bit of a fighter. He's a teacher, philosopher, bit bohemian, he's the show's narrator in a way. And I got good acclaim for that, probably the best reviews I've had for any opera I've done, which was a real boost. I was starting to feel my confidence building again. We were finally given the date for the *Les Misérables* performance, half a year or so down the line, confirmed for the O2, which was unbelievable news. Everything suddenly seemed fantastic. I felt the best I'd felt in years. And then . . . then *The Pearl Fishers* happened. The drowning, the blindness, the pneumonia. Just when you thought it was safe to go back in the water.

You do one job that's an absolute thrill and joy, for an opera company that you really respect, then you do another job for the same company that completely floors you. Completely floors you. I lost so much respect for the people that run that place when all that happened, because of the way I was treated. Neil found out that the legal maximum amount of time you're supposed to spend in a chlorinated tank is three hours, and you have to shower every 10 or 15 minutes. I'd been in there for nearly seven hours and I'd showered once. Nobody had said otherwise. Neil kicked up a proper fuss with the ENO and tried to find out who was at fault. They deflected it onto the underwater production company, didn't apologise. Nobody took the blame. I don't know if they gave a damn about me or not but I was certainly left feeling as though they wouldn't have cared if my heart had exploded on that plane because of the compressed air I'd been inhaling. Or if I'd never be able to see my kid again because I'd gone permanently blind. The director said, 'If I'd only known, we would have done it in an hour.' They got me a counsellor, at least. They wanted me to get better so I could get back into the show. She wasn't really a counsellor, she was a performance psychologist, she gave me a lot of encouragement to get back on stage. And she did help me a hell of a lot, built my confidence up again. That was around the time Pierre was in hospital. I was pretty screwed up and it was helpful to talk to her, I got back on stage and did the last five shows. I think I did 8 out of 13, did the last few, then I went back to Salt Lake for the summer to learn *Les Misérables* – I really took the role on board. I was due to go into the show in the West End for two weeks prior to the O2, at the Queen's Theatre, so I really thrashed it out over August, spent the whole month learning the show, read up about the characters, watched DVDs, listened to other recordings ... I knew the music, I knew my role back to front.

That summer was really hard. Sarah had been in a play, she was happy, and she didn't really want to come back to England. She wanted to stay in America with Grace, to get her own career back on track. She hadn't really expressed doing that before; after all the years of running around with me she was taking a stand to make things work for the family. She was finally settled, things were going well for her and she just didn't want to leave home. I said, 'What if things happen with *Les Mis* and I need to be back in England?' And she said, 'I don't know. I don't know what's going to happen.'

She couldn't have been more supportive of me, she always has been, but she was so tired of waiting for the big thing that would turn our lives around. I was desperate for it too, we were both doing the best we could to make it all work. But just hearing her say that, that was a sucker punch. I thought my marriage was over. My insecurities and doubts were coming back to haunt me and I felt stranded, so insecure about everything. Things were looking up for me, and things were looking up for her, but on different continents, and she was there with Grace. And I thought, that's it, I'm going to be on my own again. I was really heartbroken, really frightened to leave this time. Flying out of Salt Lake City and leaving those mountains was really tough. I was so nervous on that plane, I remember it vividly. Because as irrational as it seems now, I didn't know if I might get an envelope from Sarah through the letterbox. Or if I'd see my daughter again. I was scared, really scared. More than she knew. If I'd expressed this to her at the time I'd have known how supportive she was, of course she was. But that flight was the worst.

On the first day of rehearsals in London in September I did a sing-through, and Adrian Sarple, the associate director, explained the show to me in great detail, really in-depth – he really helped me immerse myself in the character. I got to know everything about this Jean Valjean, to understand him. And they pushed me, boy did they push me. That first week of rehearsals, I was throwing everything I had into it, and then they'd ask for more. I didn't know how I could go further. I was drained at the end of each day, going back and crashing in my hotel room, then dragging myself out of bed to read the text and soak it up even more. I was jet-lagged, sat on the floor in my room looking at this score, absorbing every single word, and what every single word meant to me. In rehearsals I'd analyse every single movement I was doing, and I was trying to naturalise everything, to make everything feel spontaneous, instinctive. And the more I did that, the more they asked for. Push more, drive it more, be angrier, stronger, more aggressive ... I felt like my brain was about to explode. They were pushing me much more than I'd ever been pushed in operas, much more. In opera, unless you're working with an exceptional director or you're really pushing your*self*, the focus is all on the music and singing. Nothing can jeopardise that. Anything that threatens to do so is scrapped, which is why a lot of conductors and directors in opera tend to argue. Because the director wants one thing and the conductor will say, 'Well you can't do that because it will jeopardise him singing this top C.' In musical theatre, it's nothing like that. You throw *everything* into it, from every angle, you give your guts, your blood, your sweat, your tears. The whole damn lot. You expose yourself to that piece of music and those characters. And they still want more. When I was doing my 'Prologue' each night in the West End, people said I was so angry, wolf-like. There were times where I'd be drooling.

For the first week of those rehearsals I was also performing the role every night at the Queen's Theatre, and Valjean really became part of me. He's a passionate guy, an angry guy, he hates injustice, and I just got him. I felt his frustration. And every single day I was taking another step towards reaching the mark for where I wanted to take that show – it was great. I never got tired of singing the music. People were saying, 'Take it down, you don't have to sing it out so much.' You need to save your voice for the performances. But I couldn't help it, it felt natural, it was in my blood, I was thoroughly enjoying it and I loved working with the cast, they were awesome. And then we started rehearsals for the O2. That was when things really started to fire up. Things with Sarah were levelling out, she was really happy for me because things were working out with *Les Mis* and she could see how much I was enjoying myself. I was so optimistic and she was so encouraging – she said I was the man I was when she'd first met me in San Francisco. And I had the overwhelming satisfaction that I'd left the opera world, left that *Pearl Fishers* nightmare behind to do a job that I was truly loving, to play a character I really wanted to inhabit. And I was being given so much more respect! Just as a human being, let alone for the work. It was such a relief, it really was.

The size of the O2 arena, the space we were performing in hadn't quite dawned on me – obviously I knew how big it was and how many people were coming, but being there and seeing it on the night was an incredible thrill. Then Matt Lucas, who was playing Thénardier, told me to look at the TV monitor. You go through stages in the hours before you're due to perform, at least I do. I get into the venue, size it up, look at all the seats in the room and imagine people's faces in them. You become part of the room in a way – I do it every time, get a sense of the surroundings, what I'm going to have to deal with. But it wasn't until I was in my dressing room, less than half an hour before the show, that it really hit me. Matt came in with a video guy, for the documentary he was making, and said, 'Have you seen the TV?' I hadn't. He said, 'Don't look around yet,' because he wanted the camera to catch my expression. Then I looked up at this monitor and my heart almost stopped. I couldn't believe the amount of people coming into the O2. Absolutely gobsmacked. I couldn't even fathom that a place like that existed, I couldn't believe that all those people would be seeing me sing that role of Jean Valjean. It was great! Because it's the audience that bring the excitement into a room, not the performer. And it wasn't fear, it was excitement, real adrenaline-rushing excitement. A little bit of anxiety, but that's a good thing. That full-house at the O2 gave me so much confidence. The excitement of seeing all those people come into the place, getting into their seats, already soaking up the atmosphere and getting into the spirit of it . . . ah, amazing. In the minutes before the show the adrenaline was pumping so hard, I was absolutely focused. Matt, Nick Jonas, who played Marius, and Sam Barks, who was Éponine, came into my dressing-room and we all stood in a circle and put our arms round each other. And walking out for the first time and seeing that crowd was something else, a real fiery moment. And once I started I was so into my performance, the audience response barely registered, I didn't quite hear it. Totally lost in what I was doing.

I knew that 'Bring Him Home' would be my moment, the golden key. I knew that was it. 'Boy needs a song!' It's incredible, how that song came to me again, after our false alarm with the Festival of Remembrance. We knew that was the one, but it disappeared, and we didn't think of it again until Cameron Mackintosh knocked on the door. And it is such a spiritual song, it's so special. When Claude-Michel Schönberg and Alain Boublil wrote it they must have been excited. They must have known they had something special. And it was written less than three weeks before the show opened in London in 1985. Claude-Michel wrote the music in rehearsals, inspired by Colm Wilkinson's falsetto, and Herbert Kretzmer was really stumped with the lyrics, he didn't know what words he could fit to these three syllable lines. Then John Caird, the co-director, said the melody sounded like a prayer, and Herbert wrote it overnight. It is a prayer, it's actually called 'The Prayer', it's not officially called 'Bring Him Home', and I treat it as such every time I sing it. I pray. That's what makes it work.

And just before I sang it at the O2 that night, I prayed for real. I'd made my entrance onto the barricade, sent Javert off, fired the gun and walked around to the back of the stage. This was the moment I'd been waiting for. From the day I heard it was going to be at the O2, I'd thought, 'How can I stand on that stage in front of nineteen thousand people and sing 'Bring Him Home'? How can I do it?' And the whole period of time after that had culminated in that moment. That was what I was gearing up for. And what did I do? I switched off. I didn't focus on it. I got out of sight behind a little barricade, sipped a bit of water and dropped to my knees. And I prayed, I literally prayed, prayed like crazy. 'Please give me the strength to get through this song. Give me the help to do this song justice.' And then I asked Dad for help. 'Give us a hand, Dad.' I always used to say that when he was alive. 'Gis a hand, Dad.' And he always would. He always would.

So if you watch that on the DVD, when everybody's singing 'Drink with Me', I'm behind the barricade on my knees. Focusing. I had my eyes shut. And I felt this completely overwhelming warmth. A real connection, a protection. Like I'd been put in a bubble. The same bubble I was in when I took that walk with Mum on the beach in Fleetwood just before Dad died. It was really, really weird to have that same feeling again there at the O2, because I felt like Dad was with me. I know that sounds melodramatic, I know this sounds like some imaginative thing I've concocted, but this was genuinely how I felt. I felt lighter, stronger, and braver. And then instinctively I just stood up and turned onto the stage. I didn't see anybody, and I walked up to that microphone and started singing, in an almost meditative state. I just focused out – it was like someone else was singing. I'd never experienced that before. And I can get in that state now. It doesn't take away the nerves, or the edge, you still have that jittery energy, but you're in control. And at the end of the song, I didn't hear applause. I didn't hear it. I didn't hear anything. I stood there looking out, and this enormous room with 19,000 people in it felt small. It felt like everybody there in the distance, everybody around, everybody at the top, it felt like they were all there next to me. Like everybody was with me on stage, and we were praying together. I felt like I'd brought the entire audience with me into my little bubble, and they were all miniature, and I was singing to them.

It was very strange for me to watch that weeks later on the DVD, to see myself in that state. I've never liked watching or hearing myself sing, but on that DVD I can feel the emotion. At the time, I didn't hear them applaud or cheer, I didn't even clock them being on their feet. For a good 30 seconds. And then all of a sudden – it was like somebody was turning up the volume on the radio, this huge noise faded up. I looked around and saw 19,000 people on their feet. And then it died down, and I was really touched, it was really sweet, and then it started up again, another wave. It was so overwhelming. And it was the first time in the show I properly came out of character, I acknowledged the applause, because I'd sort of woken from my trance and realised what was happening. And it settled, and I felt this all-consuming, warming joy. I knew that I'd reached my goal. This was the beginning, the start, we'd done something. We've done it. That little voice inside of me that was always there telling me something would happen? Now it was saying, 'Well done, Alf.'

Chapter Twenty-Eight

RUFFLING FEATHERS

I walked down the stairs after the song, and everybody was stood at the bottom applauding, the crew, the staff, the cast. Matt came running up to me and threw his arms around me and said, 'Tonight, a star is born.' For a split-second, I thought, 'Who?' and I looked around to see who he was talking about. But then Nick Jonas came up and said, 'That was something special. Your career's made.' And it all dawned on me. What a feeling.

Sarah and her father and Gracie had come to London to see the show. Sarah was in the audience, David was at the hotel we were staying in, babysitting Gracie. And at the end of that performance I came off stage, walked down the corridor to my dressing room, and in the hallway were all these people and celebs, and all I saw through the throng was my daughter. David had brought her with him to surprise me. I saw her and just cried. That was when the emotion hit me. I'd been holding it all in to get me through the thing, channelling it into the character.

But the minute I saw my little girl it just exploded. It was out, and I was Alf again. My little girl!

The day after that I just collapsed. My body finally got some rest and I got sick, got every bug under the sun. Back to reality. Meanwhile Neil was pounding on the door of Universal Classics and Jazz, now Decca. Mark Wilkinson and Dickon Stainer, the same two guys I'd sung for when I was trying to get a deal in 2003. Neil is relentless. He's the Terminator, he absolutely will not stop. 'Fellas, I have something for you.' After having had Neil bang on their door for years, they didn't jump for joy when he told them he wanted to talk about Alfie Boe again, but he'd managed to get a couple of minutes of the 'Bring Him Home' footage, showed it to them on his laptop, and they offered us a deal. And I felt absolutely out of this world, because they were the company I'd wanted to be with since day one.

We went straight into the album. It made sense to go down the musical theatre route in the wake of the O2, although I think we kept it at the classical, classier end of the spectrum. The pressure to make that album was intense. Decca hired James Morgan and his wife Juliette to produce it, and from that point to the CDs being pressed in the factory was three weeks. We had a couple of days to record it. Flew out to Copenhagen, had a great recording session. I think I recorded all the vocals in nine hours. Then did lots of promo, loads of TV, did *The Royal Variety Performance*, I met Ray Davies. N-Dubz were there. Poor Dappy, walking around backstage with his shades on, as cool as he could, baseball cap at a jaunty angle. I was feeling slightly ridiculous, walking around in my Valjean convict rags, but then Dappy said, 'Hey, how you doin'?' then turned around and walked straight into a wall. That was great. And then my album went to Number 9. Top 10 album, in the proper charts! I'd only ever had albums in the classical charts before. Harvey Goldsmith knew what he was talking about. 'Boy needs a song!'

I was still performing in operas, did *Roméo et Juliette* for the Royal Opera House, a couple for the ENO in January, the *La Bohème* revival and then a revival of Jonathan Miller's *The Mikado*, which I got told off for because of the way I was approaching my character, Nanki-Poo. It was cool to be doing Gilbert and Sullivan again and I was experimenting a bit, I was inspired by Stan Laurel and was pushing him in that direction, he's a clown. But they wanted him more romantic, they basically asked me to play him exactly the same way that any other number of people have played him before. We're supposed to bring something to these roles, to interpret them, but they weren't giving me any freedom to play around. I said, 'Why did you hire me then? Why didn't you just hire the guy who played it last time?' John Berry from the ENO phoned Neil, had a big shouty moan about me. But I got good reviews for what I did. I don't know if people were maybe resentful of my O2 success. Some did start whinging about me. *Desert Island Discs* seemed to provoke people, but that wasn't the intention – that conversation was all spontaneous, I didn't go into that studio with a hit list. When you do that show, they play the music as you hear it, so you're sitting in there listening to the songs you've chosen, which, certainly in my case, meant a lot to me and transported me back to specific periods in my life. Kirsty Young creates an incredibly intimate environment. I almost completely forgot that it was a radio interview with tons of people listening. I even forgot about the people behind us, on the other side of the window in the control room. I had my back to them – it just felt like it was me and Kirsty having a quiet chat. She's a beautiful woman, very comforting, very disarming. I was nervous at first and I admitted it on air, but that soon went, and as I relaxed into it I gradually opened up more and more. I started talking about Dad, listening to the music I used to listen to with him. I wanted to talk about it, about his death, to share it. The girls in the control room were welling up, Neil was crying. I'd never been so open in an interview before, and it was the first time I'd spoken out about some of my more negative opera experiences. I just felt free to say what was on my mind as I listened to those songs. And what I said then got quoted in the press, and people had a snap at me. I don't think they'd really listened to what I said, which was that when I go to the opera I feel very uncomfortable, that it's not my world. I said, 'When I'm up there doing it, that's my world, that's what I really enjoy. But sitting there watching it, I'm bored stiff.' Which is true. I love the music, I listen to opera, but, as a performer, I'm just not a fan of sitting in the audience for five hours, I'd rather be singing it. And I didn't think anything of it until the papers pounced on it and got quotes from people. Jonathan Miller's response upset me a bit. He said: 'If Alfie Boe thinks opera is boring then it's very odd that he's in it at all. I've only worked with him once and he sings rather well but I know he comes from something other than opera. He was a car mechanic, I believe.'

There's a difference between what I said and people's reductive interpretation of what I said. To be fair, Jonathan may not have heard the interview. I imagine a journalist said, 'Alfie Boe said he finds opera boring, what do you say to that?' But the car mechanic thing, come on. And he said it like he barely knew who I was. I'd actually been in two of his operas, *La Bohème* in 2009, and *The Mikado* revival, only a few months before *Desert Island Discs*. There was a bit of a political scrum going on with the latter; as the production's original director 25 years earlier he was involved but was being kept at arm's length to an extent, and I was always saying, 'What would Jonathan want?' when creative decisions had to be made. So I found his comments a little hurtful, and a little arrogant, certainly facetious. 'He was a car mechanic, I believe.' Yes. I was. And I played the lead in your opera a couple of years ago, I believe.

The papers also dug up some other character from Opera Holland Park who said I was talking drivel and should be renamed Alfie Boellocks. I quite like that name. Maybe that's what I should title my next album. I was enjoying all that stuff anyway, it entertains me when their feathers get ruffled. It doesn't take much. I just like to be honest now, God knows I kept my mouth shut for long enough. And I'm going to get criticised regardless. Three weeks after the O2 concert I was slammed for it, when I played Tybalt in *Roméo et Juliette* at the Royal Opera House. At the end of the first performance, I stepped out to take my curtain call and got a bigger response than the guy who was playing Romeo, because a fair amount of *Les Mis* fans had come to see me, I guess. I wasn't doing anything different, I wasn't courting it. A lady reviewing it for the *Opera Today* website said that 'adulation' could be my undoing, and that that kind of audience isn't into opera, just chasing celebrity. The nub of what she was insinuating was that some people enjoyed my performance in one thing, so they'd come to see me perform in another thing. And that's bad? That I'd introduced people to opera, brought people with me? No thanks, close the doors. No room at the inn for you casuals. Says it all really.

The casting director had a problem with me too, he shook everybody's hand on the last performance, then when it was my turn, at the end of the line, he shunned me, turned around and walked away. I can't say for sure why he did that, but I imagine it was related to my history with the place, my premature exit from the Vilar programme before going off to Broadway in 2002. Or maybe it was that audience I'd brought with me. I don't know, but he'd obviously had his nose pushed out of joint somehow.

I'd had such a lovely success with *Les Misérables*, and I was on a high. Then going into the Opera House and getting that review about the audience, and having the casting director blank me, I thought, why are they like this? *Les Misérables* had filled me with so much joy and reinstated my love for what I do, and I came back to an opera gig and got that. It really opened my eyes to the narrow-mindedness of the industry. And *Les Misérables* meant so much to me, Valjean means so much to me. He really resonates with people, some a little too much. The O2 concert plays on TV worldwide, and after *Mikado*, I'd gone to perform a few concerts in Idaho, and had an odd experience in Rexburg. I came off the stage in the interval and there was a woman in my dressing room. She said, 'You are Valjean.' She then gave me memorial cards from her daughter's funeral, and a CD with the music that had been played at the funeral, cards they'd had at her wedding. Photos of her. Cards from her own wedding. Then these two girls who'd organised the concert appeared and got her out the room, they were embarrassed, they didn't know how she'd got in. Colm Wilkinson, the original Valjean from 1985, had told me how much the character in the show touched people, and I was starting to experience some of that up close. One lady said to me, 'When I die, I hope God looks like you.' I said, 'I don't think he'd be too happy to hear that!' But it freaked me out a bit. Some people talk about Valjean as if he was a real person, someone said to me, 'Maybe your father is in Heaven now having a cup of tea with Jean Valjean.' I said, 'No . . . no.'

But Valjean does get to people, and going back into *Les Misérables* to play him for that five-month run at the Queen's Theatre was fantastic. I wondered if it would be as exciting and as fun as it was when I'd done it initially at the Queen's and the O2 in October, but it was so much better. Five weeks of rehearsals flew by. I loved being in that theatre again, getting used to the revolving stage again, putting on my old costume. One night, with two weeks of rehearsals to go before I was due back on, Simon Bowman was ill, Jonny Williams, the understudy, was ill, and Cameron asked if I'd be willing to go on that night, because he had Russell Crowe in watching it as preparation for the movie – they'd cast him as Javert. So I did it, I hadn't even rehearsed Act Two, hadn't played it since the O2, but it all came back. Shoved on at the last minute, really threw myself into it, and loved it. Cameron of course came up to me afterwards with a big pile of notes about what I'd done wrong. Constructive notes though – Cameron's a very clever man, he doesn't do it frivolously, he knows what it's about. And it works. It upsets you and it stresses you out, but you put it back into the role – you can transform that anger into whatever you're doing on stage, and it bloody well works. Yeah I've wanted to thump Cameron half a dozen times and say, 'Man, what are you DOING to me!' But it comes across in the show I think, and I love him to pieces. He, Claude-Michel Schönberg, Alain Boublil, Herb Kretzmer, Trevor Nunn, John Caird – they've all given me the opportunity to change my life, and my respect for them will always be high. I can't thank them enough. I mean that from the bottom of my heart. They're a great bunch of people. That show will always remain in my heart, will always be a part of my life. It's in my soul. It really is. Cameron laid into me a bit after my first night at The Queen's, because we'd just found out that they'd decided to go with Hugh Jackman instead of me for the movie, and Cameron was upset about it. And yeah, I was disappointed too, but you can't have it all. I had a two-hour audition with Tom Hooper, the director, and I really enjoyed it, I learnt a lot, how to play it down, subtler, smaller, for the cameras as opposed to people at the back of a theatre. And I did the 25th Anniversary concert, I did it at the *Royal Variety Performance,* I did five months in the West End. Hugh Jackman's a great performer, a great singer and a great actor, and he'll do it justice, it's his turn. Jean Valjean does not just belong to me. There have been many Valjeans before me and there will be many more. But I have a very nice little piece of him.

Chapter Twenty-Nine

MY LITTLE WORLD

I really pushed it on my last night of *Les Misérables*. I punched the stage, bust my hand, I broke as many props as I possibly could. I didn't plan it, I just got so caught up in the performance. Smashed some goblets, bent a candlestick. I didn't want people to look upon that stage and see me. I wanted it to be like the clock had been turned back 200 years and they were seeing Jean Valjean. I ripped my shirt open in the scene where I reveal myself as Valjean and it wasn't for effect, I felt it, deep down. If I could have ripped my chest open I would have done, that was what it was about. I took a few liberties. Especially for 'Bring Him Home'; instead of sitting with Marius I stood at the front of the stage and sung it out to the audience. It was really emotional, leaving that role. I was tired, I was ready to call it a day and have a break, but I really felt it that night. And ripping the shirt, and ripping up the paper with my prisoner number on it – that was, subconsciously, like tearing off the role in a way, ripping it off.

Playing in the West End is such an honour, it's a great world, and these musical theatre singers, they're the hardest working people in the business. Seriously. As my time was coming to an end at *Les Mis*, they were doing nine shows a week for three weeks including rehearsals for the guy who was taking my place. And that's as well as all the other things they've got going on outside the show. *And* they go out drinking afterwards. They're young and they can handle it, I can't. I've got so much respect for them, because it's so damn hard. They're great people. And I made a fantastic friend in Matt, who made me and Sarah and Grace so welcome in his house for a few months, he's so supportive, and so creative. We did The Kitchen Sessions there, me and him singing for YouTube. The first one, where I did 'Nessun Dorma', was fantastically spontaneous, we had a lot of fun.

I went back to Prague to make the *Alfie* album. In a break before recording 'When I Fall in Love' I got an email from Sarah – a photograph of her pregnancy test, positive. I called her, I was in tears, and then had to sing. I think you can hear the emotion in my voice. I think I sound serene, blissfully serene on that song, because I was. I did it in one take. And I sang 'In My Daughter's Eyes' for Grace.

We recorded 'Song to the Siren' with Robert Plant in London. That was one of those moments in time for me that I can't quite fathom, I still can't get over it. That man means so much to me and Sarah. It's so fitting that he should be on this album, the album named after our son – I said before how he's basically soundtracked our relationship, how we listened to Led Zep when we first met, had our first dance at the wedding to 'Rain Song', how we met him together last year. There was no grand plan, it wasn't as if I weighed all that up and said, 'OK, we have to have Robert Plant on this album. Somebody sort it out.' You can't calculate that stuff. Leave it to the universe. We met him randomly. I wasn't even going to go out that night, I wanted to stay in, get a takeout and watch TV. But some friends from America were in town, Sarah dragged me out and we ended up in the Soho Hotel for a drink to meet them. And while we were there this tall guy walked in, long blond hair, leather jacket, girl on his arm . . . my God, it's Robert Plant. It was like the fog machine had just been fired up for his entrance into the bar. Whoooosshhhh. 'Get all the fog going, Robert's coming!' Backlit, choir of angels circling him. He went over to the bar and practically lit it up. I thought, I am not leaving this bar until I've spoken to Robert Plant. I said, 'I'm going up to talk to him,' and Sarah went, 'What?!' And I went up to the bar with £20 in my hand, pretending I was waiting to get served, and said, 'Hi, man, nice to meet you, I'm a big fan of your music. Love your new *Band Of Joy* album. We happen to be on the same record label actually.' Really? 'Yeah, I've recently signed to Decca. I'm making my second album for them.' We started chatting and his girlfriend Sophia knew who I was, she knew *Les Mis*, which helped. And what I thought might be a two-minute conversation turned into an hour conversation about music.

I got his number, and when I eventually called him it was like talking to an old mate. I'm so in awe of these rockers, these iconic rock legends, and they're just blokes that used to play bar-rooms. I asked him if he wanted to record Tim Buckley's 'Song to the Siren' with me; the first time I'd heard it was the version Robert recorded on his *Dreamland* album. He asked me for a demo of my arrangement, so James Morgan and I got one together for him, and he called me a few days later when I was poking around in a drum shop. Didn't recognise the number, just heard someone say, 'Alfie! Robert here,' I didn't have a clue who it was. What can I do for you, mate? He said, 'I'm in the

States at the moment, I'm on tour with The Band of Joy . . .' I fell against the cymbals, apologised, asked him how he was. 'Yeah, I'm cool man, I'm just about to go out and get a bowl of porridge.' I thought, Robert Plant eats porridge!

The more he sang in the studio, the more his voice opened up. The thing I really admire about Robert is his consistency as an artist. He's from the rock world but has done a number of different styles over the years and adapted them for himself without ever compromising the way he sings. He's never changed his voice for the sake of a genre, and that's my philosophy. I come from the classical world, but I don't change the sound of my voice if I sing blues or rock, it will always be the voice that I use when I sing Puccini or Verdi. Although I do tend to channel people when I sing with them, I soak up their energy a bit. When I do 'Song to the Siren' on tour I feel like Robert's there duetting with me.

The *Bring Him Home* tour, my first official tour as a solo artist, brought me full-circle in many ways. Playing in the Blackpool Opera House was eerie. Going through the stage door into the back of the venue that afternoon gave me the jitters, knowing that I was there to perform on the stage I used to set up, going up to inhabit that dressing room I used to sit outside while The Everly Brothers and Duane Eddy were in there . . . an odd feeling of displacement. I've brushed that stage so many times. That was probably the one I was most nervous for, it was a homecoming gig of sorts, some of my family were in to see me, there was a different sort of pressure with that gig. I was very uncomfortable at first. I didn't know if the audience would accept me. Yes they'd all paid to come and see me, but that doesn't count for much until you're out there and it's going well. My old boss Duncan was still there, same job, same office. I said hi to him beforehand, and he was still as miserable as ever.

An odd awkwardness there. So much has happened in the 20 years since I worked for him in that place. I mentioned him on stage, told the crowd I used to work there, I joked I was gonna smash his face in. One of his staff heard and called him out of his office to listen, apparently he wasn't too impressed. My driver Jim was hanging around backstage – he said Duncan looked like his nuts had been nailed to the floor. He has a way with words, Jim. Preston was similar, playing in the Charter Theatre, where I did *West Side Story* when I was 19. That was electric, again – my family were there, I was really happy that night. A couple of songs in I mentioned that I'd performed that show there when I was 19, and a handful of people in the second row hollered – it was some of the guys who'd performed with me in that production. I was over the moon, really touched. In Bristol, a little girl who'd been in *La Bohème* for the ENO with me a couple of years earlier was there, she ran up to the stage at the end when we were doing 'Jacob's Ladder', got up for a dance. That tour was full of moments like that – it was incredibly affecting. I ended the set every night on the drums, just how I started 25 years ago. Most of all, we had fun. I wanted everybody involved to have fun, no matter if they were sweeping the stage at the end of the night or wrapping up cables or pushing flight cases onto the trucks or cooking the food. Sarah and Grace unfortunately weren't able to come on the tour because of the baby, because of Alfie, who was due in the halfway break, smack in the middle, New Year's Day. So the team became my family, they looked after me so much, and I sometimes wonder if I deserve it.

I delivered Alfie in hospital in Salt Lake. The doctor was really cool, Dr Yamashiro, Hawaiian guy. He said, 'How much do you wanna be involved?' I said I wanted to be a support for Sarah and hold her arm, that sort of thing. And he said, 'You're gonna deliver this baby today, Alfie.' What? 'You're gonna deliver it. We'll cap and gown you. You're gonna do it. My hands will be right by yours, I'll guide you, I'll tell you exactly what to do, but you're gonna do it.' I didn't know what to expect. And the moment came when Sarah was ready, she needed to push, and she said to me, 'Are you OK? You look like you're gonna faint.' The midwife said, 'If you're gonna faint, faint away from the table.' I sat next to Dr Yamashiro on the bed and saw the top of the baby's head. A few pushes, he was getting closer and closer. He said, 'We need to do it in stages so we can check the umbilical cord isn't wrapped around his neck.' So I had my hand on top of Alfie's head, and Sarah gave one big push and his head came out and I held it. And I could feel the force. Dr Yamashiro checked the cord and said, 'Now put one hand underneath his head, and one hand on top of his head.' Either side of his head. He said, 'Now one big push, Sarah.' And his arms came out. He said, 'Now grab hold of his shoulders and pull him out.' Then one more push and he was out. And I had my son in my arms. I can't describe how incredible that felt, to actually deliver my son into the world. What a treat. It was lovely. I laid him on Sarah's chest and cut the umbilical cord. He was screaming, definitely voicing his opinion. To have delivered my son and brought him into the world, and to be the first one to hold him – not a doctor, not a nurse, not a midwife – me, I was the first one to hold my son. It was like I'd said goodbye to my father and hello to my son. And they're both called Alf. It's magical for me, that. That's my little world.

We knew he'd be called Alfred, but we were trying to think of a middle name. We were thinking Aaron, Gabriel . . . and over Christmas, I thought, 'I've said I'm naming my son after my dad. And if Dad's full name was Alfred Robert . . . then that's what I'll call my son.' Alfred Robert. I'm crying as I write this.

Alfred Robert. My dad, my son. I was Skyping with him while I was on tour in February this year, a month after he was born, and he looked so much like Dad. Sarah picked him up and put him in front of the camera and I looked and I saw my dad. Even the little hair combed down flat on his head, his wide eyes . . . I really saw my dad, and it was wonderful to know that he lives on. That album's named after both of them. When we christened him in Fleetwood in March, we toasted them both with some port that Dad had produced himself. We'd found a gallon of it when Dad died, enough for four bottles, one for each of his sons. I saved mine, and it was very emotional for me to share that with my family for the christening of my son. It was very special to bring a new Alfred Robert into the house that the last Alfred Robert died in. That time a few months before Dad died when he said I'd see him again, I thought I realised what he meant when I started recognising him more in myself. But he's in my kids too, so much. Gracie's got his spirit, she's such a comic like he was, always larking about and pulling faces. So I do, I see him all the time. And the love I have for my father, for my family, and for my boy and my girl and my wife fills any concert hall, more than the music.

ACKNOWLEDGEMENTS

First, I'd like to thank Sarah, my wonderful wife, for giving me so much help and support during the writing of this book. Thanks hugely to Alex Godfrey for the months and months that went into these pages, for helping to tell my story. My gratitude to Rory Scarfe, Carly Cook and the editorial team at Simon & Schuster, and my literary agent Felicity Blunt, who were all so excited about this book, from the day we met and first talked about it through to now; it's finally in your hands. For my dad and my mum – thanks Mum, you always encouraged me to pursue my dreams. Dad was always there for me – I miss you Dad. Thanks also to all my brothers, sisters and family.

Please allow me a moment to thank so many wonderful people that have been so important in my life. My close friends from home, John Ginley, Bob Mc'Creath, Michael Parkinson (not the presenter) Michael Gawne, Mike Rolands, Frank Salter, the people of Fleetwood and the player from the Cod Army. Friends in the business I'd like to thank: Robert Plant, Matt Lucas, Derren Brown, Melanie C, Tom Fletcher,

Michael Ball, Michael Parkinson (this time the presenter), John Owen Edwards, Darren Henley, Simon Bates, Baz Luhrmann, David McVicar, James Morgan, Juliette Pochin, and all of you I've forgotten to mention, I do love you all. Everyone at Decca Records, Dickon Stainer, Mark Wilkinson, Tom Lewis, Emma Newman, Alex Cowan, Kieran Thurgood, Alex Johnson, Becky Allen, Jude Dexter-Smith, Molly Ladbrook-Hutt, Caroline Crick, Chloe Gillard, Sarah Bates, Emma Hurst, Nancy Coburn, Laura Monks, Karyn Hughes, Jackie Joseph, Dee Ryan, Liz Trafford-Owen, James Tornianen, Hass Choudhury, Paul Horner, Sarah Hutchinson, Marc Robinson and David Heath. My agents: Neil Warnock, Heulwen Keyte and Juliet Liddel at The Agency Group in London and Andrea Johnson in New York. Simon Moran and all at SJM, the promoters of my UK tours. My touring team, Helen Fitzgerald, Uncle Geoff Clennell, Chris 'Freddie' Andrews, the orchestra and crew (Paul Hatt & Tristram Mallet for sound, Sam Sutcliffe for lights, Mick Thornton for catering, Joe Neale for trucking and all the riggers and local crew). Sir Cameron Mackintosh, Trevor Jackson & co., and Claude-Michel Schönberg, Alain Boublil, Herbie Kretzmer – I can't thank you enough. Helen Parker and her awesome team at NBC/Universal Pictures. Kirsty Young, whose *Desert Island Discs* caused so many people to want me to tell this story. Radio, TV & press friends who have supported me for so long. PBS for inviting me to join their illustrious family. Sarah Adams and Jodie Dunleavy, who battled against my old record company and every mistake imaginable. Tracey Bell for powering the fansite all these years. All in Glasgow at Linn Records. The team of supporters at Classic FM. Photographers I've had the good fortune to work with, especially Ray Burmiston and Paul Marc Mitchell. Shure microphones,

Nicola Lange at Lufthansa and the crew at Firebrand Live. My team: Vick Shuttleworth; Nigel Jones; Mellissa Bradbury, assistant to my managers at Brilliant!; and my Brilliant! managers, Jilly and Neil Ferris.

Finally, to you, my fans across the world – love to you all.

Alfie x

INDEX